MW01631228

Altamonte Springs City Commission meeting in commission chambers at City Hall, January 24, 1995. From left to right: City Manager Phillip D. Penland; Commissioner Pat Fernandez; Commissioner Robert Lerner; Mayor J. Dudley Bates; Commissioner Russ Hauck, and Commissioner Eddie Rose.

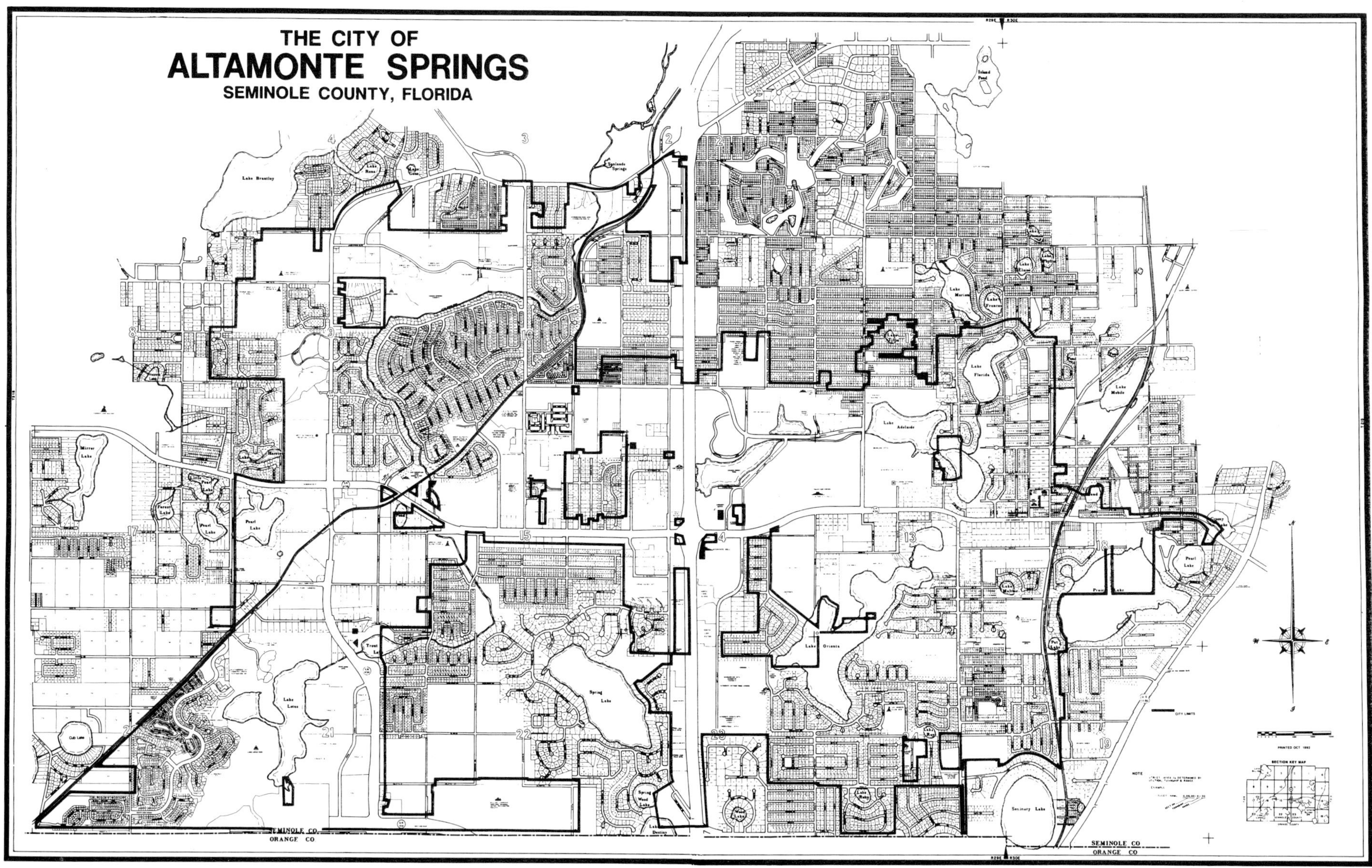

A map of The City of Altamonte Springs. The city limits are shown by the black line around the outer part of the city. Those areas within the city limits that are unincorporated are outlined in black.

A History of Altamonte Springs, Florida

A History of Altamonte Springs, Florida

Jerrell H. Shofner

City of Altamonte Springs
281 N. Maitland Avenue
Altamonte Springs, Florida 32701

In association with Tabby House
Charlotte Harbor, Florida 33980

Manufactured in the United States of America
Library of Congress Catalog Card Number: 95–13254
ISBN: 0-9645863-0-4
Cover design: Pearl and Associates, Pompano Beach, Florida
Page design: Abigail M. Grotke

Library of Congress Cataloging-in-Publication Data

Shofner, Jerrell H., 1929–
A history of Altamonte Springs, Florida / Jerrell Shofner.
p. cm.
Includes bibliographic references and index.
ISBN 0-9645863-0-4 (alk. paper)
1. Altamonte Springs (Fla.)--History. I. Title
F319.A4S48 1995
975.9'23--dc20 95-13254
CIP

Published by
City of Altamonte Springs
281 N. Maitland Avenue
Altamonte Springs, Florida 32701

In association with Tabby House
Charlotte Harbor, Florida 33980

For Bill Goddard

Jim,
I hope you enjoy reading this as much as I did researching it!
Bill Goddard

Contents

Acknowledgments

During the research and writing of this book, I have incurred obligations to numerous residents and officials of the City of Altamonte Springs. Included among them are all of those named in the first section of the bibliography, but there are many others. I would like to thank each and all of them. I am especially indebted to B. D. McIntosh, Jr. for spending many hours relating his recollections of a lifetime spent in this community.

William F. "Bill" Goddard, to whom this book is dedicated, has provided extensive research assistance, especially in the land records. I wish to acknowledge my appreciation for that, as well as for his continuing advice, encouragement, and friendship during this lengthy undertaking.

Special thanks are offered to David Coles of the Florida State Archives, Tallahassee; Elizabeth Alexander of the P. K. Yonge Library of Florida History at the University of Florida, Gainesville; Frank Mendola of the Orange County Museum, Orlando; Gertrude LaFramboise of the Rollins College archives; and Rene Bennett and Donna Rhein of the Winter Park Public Library for their assistance. I was also aided by the staffs of the National Archives; the Library of Congress; the manuscript division of the George Washington University Library, Washington, D.C.; the Boston Public Library, Boston, Massachusetts, and the Orange County Public Library.

Cheryl Walters of the interlibrary loan department of the University of Central Florida made available to me many sources from distant libraries which would otherwise have been unavailable.

Richard A. Miller, director of the Altamonte Springs City Library, has generously managed the collection and identification of the many photographs which appear on the following pages. Thanks also to Richard M. Wyman for his excellent drawings of several of the old homes of the town.

I would also like to acknowledge my indebtedness to Shelly Nooft of Leisure Services, Stanley Phipps of the Police Department, and Stanley

Human of the Fire Department for assitance in selecting and identifying many of the photographs in Chapter Twelve. Thanks also to Virginia Bates Wyman, Dorothy Fuller, and Heidi Haines for sharing their extensive photograph collections with me, and to James B. Cara for use of his extensive postcard collection.

I am obliged to Patti Dillon of the University of Central Florida History Department for her extensive research in the *Sanford Herald* and for proofreading the finished manuscript.

I wish especially to acknowledge my obligations and my thanks to my longtime secretary and friend, Carole Gonzalez, for the assistance and encouragement to which I have become accustomed but have never taken for granted.

One

The Land and Its Early Inhabitants

The land was first inhabited by prehistoric animals including mastodons, saber-toothed tigers, and spectacled bears. . . Hoosier Springs [later] became a favorite watering place for central Florida residents and visitors.

Aerial view of the chain of lakes which the Bostonian founders of Altamonte Springs found so appealing. From the north those shown here are Lake Marion, Lake Florida, Lake Adelaide, and Lake Orienta. The photograph was taken by L. Tolar Bryan in 1950.

The Florida peninsula that we know assumed its present shape some 30,000 years ago, after millions of years of being shaped and reshaped as sea water rose and fell during the Ice Age. When the polar ice cap grew, the sea level dropped and the peninsula's land area expanded so that it was at times about twice as large as it is now. When the ice melted, the water rose and covered part of the exposed land surface. That part of Central Florida which includes Altamonte Springs was once an island separated from the mainland by a trough which ran northeasterly from the Gulf of Mexico to the Atlantic Ocean. Geologists have identified several terraces between the central ridge of the peninsula and the present shoreline caused by varying water levels during the Ice Age. Those changing water levels shaped the physical features of the peninsula which—together with its balmy climate—made Central Florida so attractive to the Bostonians who launched Altamonte Springs as a "Florida Boston town" in the 1880s.

The long periods of submersion left marine deposits which formed a thick layer of limestone under most of the peninsula. That porous rock formation, sometimes hundreds of feet deep, is known as the Floridan aquifer, through which percolates the billions of gallons of water comprising the state's primary water supply. But that limestone is also water soluble and it sometimes gives way. The resulting sinkholes form the numerous surface lakes which have done so much to enhance the beauty of Altamonte Springs and its surrounding area. Lakes Orienta and Adelaide were prime reasons for the original location of the Altamonte Hotel which, in turn, became the focal point of the community.

The land was first inhabited by prehistoric animals, including the now extinct mastodons, saber-toothed tigers, and spectacled bears. Although the dates of these and other forms of animal life are speculative, they seem to have been driven into the peninsula by the advancing sheets of ice during the Ice Age. That they were here, however, is beyond doubt. Fossilized remains of some of them have been retrieved by underwater archaeologists from nearby Rock Springs. These remains have been dated from the Miocene Era, about seventeen million years ago.[1]

The same chain of lakes viewed from east to west. Lake Marion and Lake Florida are not visible on the right, but there is a better view of the entire length of Lake Orienta. State Road 436 winds between lakes Adelaide and Orienta. The Altamonte Hotel was just south of S.R. 436 where it bends. Prairie Lake is visible at bottom of picture.

Some anthropologists believe that the large animals were still around when the first humans arrived. Others think that they were already extinct. There is also disagreement about the date when the early human inhabitants arrived. New discoveries are constantly changing the earlier estimate that humans first entered the peninsula about 10,000 years ago. Whatever may ultimately be decided, the best evidence presently available suggests that humans first came to the Central Florida area about 7,500 years ago. Depending heavily on fish and shellfish from both the sea and inland rivers and lakes, they built villages along the shorelines and left mounds from which records of their existence have been extracted.

One such village dating back to that time was located and excavated near Lake Apopka in the early 1970s. There are other unexcavated mounds in what is now Wekiva Springs State Park. The reclamation of several dugout canoes from the Lake Apopka mucklands suggest that there was some trade between villages. Indians may have plied the waters of the Wekiva River several thousand years ago. These early inhabitants did not practice agriculture, but they continued to supplement their marine diets by hunting and gathering nuts. While there are no known village sites in the present limits of Altamonte Springs, it is likely that hunters ranged over the area.[2]

The layering of the artifacts taken from the Lake Apopka site indicate that it was inhabited until about A. D. 100 and then abandoned. Other groups lived in the area from time to time, but it was uninhabited for several centuries after about A. D. 400.

Hoosier Springs, shown here in its pristine state, subsequently became a favorite watering place for Central Florida residents and visitors. It was eventually developed as Sanlando Tropical Park.

The natives who met the Spaniards upon their arrival in the sixteenth century were not descended from those earlier inhabitants.[3] At that time there were several loosely identified groups living throughout the peninsula, some of whom practiced agriculture while others did not. All depended at least partially upon hunting, gathering, and fishing for their livelihoods. The occupants of the Central Florida area were the Timucua, a comparatively large group which had migrated into Florida from the northeast and occupied the St. Johns valley from the mouth of that river southward. Central Florida was at the extreme southern limit of their land. The Timucuans were agriculturists, cultivating fields of corn, squash, and other crops. Like the people who had preceded them, however, the Timucuans seem to have preferred the shorelines of waterways and the larger lakes for their village sites. A Timucuan tribe known as the Acuera occupied the Ocklawaha valley and camped as far south as Lake Apopka. During his fateful 1539 expedition, Hernando de Soto purchased corn from an Acuera village, the descriptions of which suggest that it was located near the big lake. The Acuera were mentioned in historical literature as late as 1604, after which they disappeared from the records.[4]

Another Timucuan village headed by Chief Mayaca claimed the territory along the St. Johns from the south end of Lake George to the Orlando area. When Pedro Menendez set out to establish his mission system in the 1560s, he traveled up the river to Mayaca's village, intending to leave Catholic missionaries to instruct and possibly to convert the heathen natives. Chief Mayaca was at first receptive to Menendez but then launched an attack on the Spanish expeditionary force. Menendez withdrew from the region and left Mayaca without the benefits of religious instruction. There were subsequent encounters between the Spanish governors and the Mayacas, however. In 1699, the Iroros, a subordinate tribe of the Mayacas, living near present-day Sanford, were provoked into a revolt by the harsh policies of Governor Laureano de Torres y Ayala. After two years of controversy, the Iroros abandoned their village and fled northward. A new governor sent a column of troops to bring the fleeing natives back. The Spanish soldiers succeeded in returning the Iroros, but such policy did not do much for Spanish relations with the natives.

During the two centuries of Spanish exploration and occupation of Florida, the Timucuans and their neighbors succumbed to European diseases to which they had no immunity, territorial wars between Spain and England in which they were often used as soldiers, and the repressive policies of the Spanish governors. The peninsula was practically depopulated by the time the English acquired Florida in the 1760s.

When the English arrived, bands of Muscogean and Hitchiti-speaking Indians were already migrating into the vacant peninsula from areas to the north. After Florida was retroceded to Spain in 1784, they were joined by the Red Stick Creeks who survived Andrew Jackson's victory at the Battle of Horseshoe Bend in 1814. These disparate groups became the Seminoles. Having migrated into Spanish territory to escape the advancing waves of white American settlers, they were dismayed when Florida was ceded by Spain to the United States in the early 1820s. Further advances of white farmers and planters into the rich lands of northern Florida brought about measures to move the Seminoles southward into the peninsula. That in turn led to the Second Seminole War which was the catalyst for the settlement of Orange County.

Two

The Seminole War and the Origins of Orange County

Most of the new settlers were from southern states, where plantation agriculture was familiar to them.

A number of Seminole chiefs reluctantly signed the 1823 Treaty of Moultrie Creek by which most of them and their tribesmen were obliged to vacate the red hills of northern Florida and relocate to a four-million acre reservation in the central peninsula that included part of Orange County. Although some of the Indians moved to the reservation, few of them were pleased with the land they found there. Some remained on the reservation, but others returned to their old habitats in northern Florida where confrontations with white settlers increased rapidly. While the United States slowly developed an Indian policy which would require removal of the Florida Indians to a western reservation, white Floridians urged early action amid considerable strife. By 1835 several chiefs had agreed to take their bands westward to Oklahoma territory, but a majority of them followed a group of younger and more militant leaders who decided to fight rather than leave what they by that time considered their home. Fighting broke out in late 1835 and lasted for nearly seven years. During those years every general in the United States army became involved in the Florida War, the nation spent some $20 million, the Florida economy was brought to a virtual standstill, and the Seminoles persistently eluded their pursuers.

Although there was little actual fighting there, the war came to the area which was soon to become Orange County. In the first place, two prominent Seminole chiefs had villages in the area. King Philip lived with his band on Lake Tohopekaliga while his son, Coacoochee (Wildcat), was chief of a village of about two hundred souls on Lake Apopka. Both abandoned their homes and moved about the peninsula in response to movements of the United States Army and neither ever returned. But both figured largely in the fighting of the war. Coacoochee became one of the most formidable and most respected of the Indian leaders. With his warriors he fought in every major engagement from the massacre of Major Francis Dade's column near Fort Brooke to the Battle of Lake Okeechobee. It was he upon whom Colonel William Worth prevailed in 1842 to go out and bring in for relocation the few straggling bands still remaining in Florida.

That there was little fighting in the Orange County area did not mean that it was neglected. United States soldiers at various times occupied Fort Mellon on Lake Monroe's southern shore, Fort Reid a short distance from there, Fort Maitland at the sight of the city of that name, Fort Gatlin near the site at which Orlando originated, and several others scattered to the east along the St. Johns valley. The military road which was laid out between Fort Mellon and Fort Maitland ran near the site of the future Snowville from which Altamonte Springs evolved. The old military road became a postal route after the Civil War.

Colonel William Worth was authorized to declare an end to the war in 1842 at which time all but about one hundred or so warriors and their families had been expatriated to the West. Those remaining were deep in the Everglades where military officials believed they would be nearly impossible to capture. This unusual end to the conflict was accompanied by legislation which brought the first permanent settlers to the area south of Lake Monroe. The Armed Occupation Act was intended to settle Central Florida with citizen-soldiers who would farm the land in normal times and defend it from the Indians when necessary. Individuals could obtain title to 160-acre tracts upon which they would make permanent improvements and live. A number of them did.

By 1855 when Orange County was divided so that it lay south of Lake Monroe and the area to the north became Volusia County, there were several small settlements in existence. Daniel Stewart had founded Mellonville at the site of the old fort by that name.

L. H. Clay was farming at Clay Springs (subsequently known as Wekiva Springs). Orange County masons were meeting at Robert Barnhardt's mill on the upper Wekiva River, but they were planning a more centrally located lodge. When the Masonic Lodge was completed at 453 E. Main in 1859, the surrounding community continued to be known simply as "the Lodge" until it was renamed Apopka. Near Fort Gatlin, a post office known as Jernigan was established in the early 1840s. From that site, Orlando evolved over the next several years. William S. Delk was operating a sawmill on his small plantation at Rock Springs.

Most of the new settlers were from southern states where plantation agriculture was familiar to them. They were soon engaged in converting pine forests into fields for cotton, corn, and sugar cane crops which they and their families had always grown. Most of them had hogs and cattle which ranged untended in the sparsely settled countryside. The open range cattle industry was becoming an important part of the locale as well as the state economy by 1860. Whether Orange County might have become a place where plantation agriculture and cattle grazing coexisted was never to be known. Sectional disputes, especially over slavery, were developing beyond the state of peaceful negotiation at the same time the

Orange community was still in its infancy. The Civil War and its turbulent aftermath would alter the course of development of Orange County at the same time it accelerated its rate of growth.

Somewhat isolated from the increasingly volatile debate over slavery, Orange Countians were more concerned with their own affairs than national issues until states began leaving the Union after Abraham Lincoln's election as president. Even when Florida voted to secede, Orange County's lone convention delegate was one of only seven to vote against the secession ordinance. Once the state had acted, however, most local residents supported their state when it joined the Confederacy. A large proportion of the county's able-bodied male population went to war while those who remained at home suffered the privations of food and supply shortages, interruptions of the mail, separation from family members, and the like. Most took their problems in stride. Women cultivated the fields and a few families went to the coast to make salt from sea water. There were no military engagements in the county, but reports of Union military activity along the St. Johns River kept everyone alert to the possibility of invasion.

The Reconstruction years following the war were turbulent and traumatic for the southern states, but they had the paradoxical effect of stimulating immigration into Central Florida in at least two ways. In the first place, the United States Congress was interested in finding a place where some of the millions of emancipated slaves could be located on their own land. The vast unpopulated area of peninsular Florida naturally came to its attention. Lt. Col. George F. Thompson, an agent of the newly created Freedmen's Bureau, was instructed to investigate the region and report his findings. During late 1865 and early 1866 he led a party through central and southern Florida and reported its balmy climate during the winter months, vast expanses of land uninhabited except for a few cattlemen who grazed their herds over miles and miles of open range, and its potential for agricultural development. No colonization program for freedmen materialized, but Thompson's report was the first of many over the next few years which were widely distributed by the northern press. Many northerners, such as the Bostonians who founded Altamonte Springs, were impressed by information about a place where the climate was mild in December and January.

In the second place, many white southerners found post-war conditions in the old plantation areas extremely distasteful. Wishing to escape the military occupation, Negro enfranchisement, and disorder which followed congressional legislation in 1867, some of them packed their belongings and left their old homes. Since the St. Johns River offered the best available transportation into sparsely populated Central Florida, a number of them went to Jacksonville and embarked on steamers which took them to Enterprise or Mellonville on Lake Monroe. From there they walked or rode wagons over sandy trails to their new homes.

Immigration from either north or south was at first only a trickle, but by the early 1870s both Orlando and Sanford were experiencing some growth. It was not long before new communities were springing up between them.

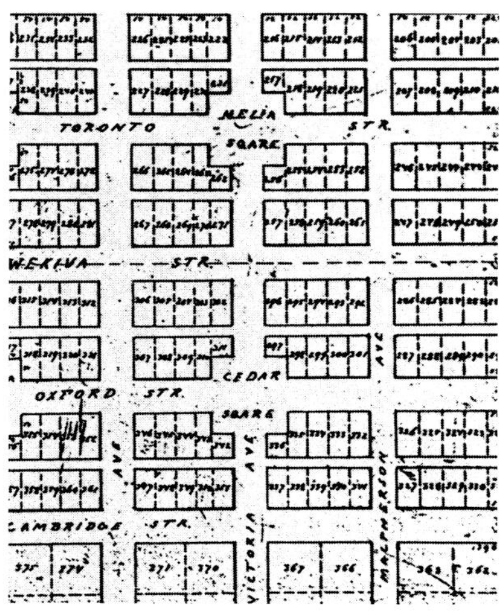

Three

Getting There: Post Roads, Railroads, and Waterways

The railroad gave impetus to the first Florida land boom which was focused on the central part of the peninsula.

While the St. Johns River provided an avenue into Central Florida for both disenchanted southerners and northerners eager for winter homes in a mild climate, prospective settlers were left to their own resources beyond the river landings.

Inadequate transportation was not a problem for Dr. Washington Kilmer. The New York-born medical doctor was working for the *Cincinnati Commercial* when he read about the warm climate and the availability of land where he might restore his declining health. He set out on foot and walked all the way from Cincinnati to Orange County. Arriving in 1872, he was one of the first to settle at Altamont and is credited for naming the place. Kilmer acquired land which presently lies between Interstate-4 and the Rolling Hills Country Club and began setting out trees for one of the area's first orange groves. He was joined by a few others and a post office was opened in 1874 with Delia S. Katline as the first postmistress. It was located just east of the Little Wekiva River not far from the place where present-day S.R. 434 crosses it.

The loosely defined community of Altamont at that time included a few households as far west as Lake Brantley. The community also extended northeastward toward Palm Springs and southeastward beyond Dr. Kilmer's place. Mail was received weekly from Mellonville. William H. Gleason was the mail contractor for a route from Mellonville through Altamont, Clay Springs, and Apopka to Eustis and back. The mail was carried by a man on horseback over a twisting sandy road.[5]

Few were as resourceful as Dr. Kilmer, but E. W. Henck came up the St. Johns River to Sanford in 1873 and walked southward on a surveying trip of about thirty miles because there were no horses or wagons for hire. An engineer from Boston where he had helped lay out the suburb of Longwood, Henck settled on land about nine miles south of Sanford and named it after the Boston suburb. He was joined shortly by Peter A. Demens, a Russian immigrant who had allegedly escaped his native Russia after involvement in an abortive political coup. Part dreamer, part huckster, and part hard-working lumberman, Demens operated a sawmill

Early roads were mere trails. The one shown here had been cleared so that vehicle axles would clear the stumps, but there was nothing done to improve the surface. With the advent of automobiles at the turn of the century, "good roads" associations began advocating improved roads. Considerable progress was made by the second decade of the twentieth century.

at Longwood where he cut vast quantities of longleaf pine timber, some of which came from land which is now the Rolling Hills Golf Course and the suburb of Knollwood. He also opened the first novelty works south of Jacksonville and hired J. B. Clouser as his foreman. Clouser had arrived in 1875 and, while working for Demens, built the Longwood Hotel.[6]

Mail was delivered over a sandy post road which followed the old military trail laid out during the Seminole War. From Sanford the road wound through largely unsettled terrain to Longwood, Snowville, and Maitland—where a post office had been established in 1872—to Orlando. The mail carrier traveled by horseback until Joseph Bumby obtained the contract in 1875. Launching his "Bumby Express," a wagon which required a full day for the round trip, Bumby handled the mail, passengers, and small amounts of freight between Sanford and Orlando for several years. But an increasing number of settlers and visitors created a demand for better transportation.

The years following the Civil War were an era of railroad building in the nation. Floridians had long advocated railways through the peninsula to make it more accessible for development, but the turmoil of Reconstruction had prevented their construction.

There were people in Central Florida, however, who had access to private resources outside the state. E. W. Henck, with his Boston connections, was such a person. Joined by C. C. Haskell, a member of the family which published the *Boston Herald* and who had recently become interested in Maitland, Henck made plans for what soon became the South Florida Railroad.

Henck became president of the company, E. T. Crafts was secretary, and Haskell served as treasurer. They raised $400,000 through a bond issue subscribed almost entirely in Boston and launched construction in late 1879.[7] Henry S. Sanford, interested in developing his holdings south

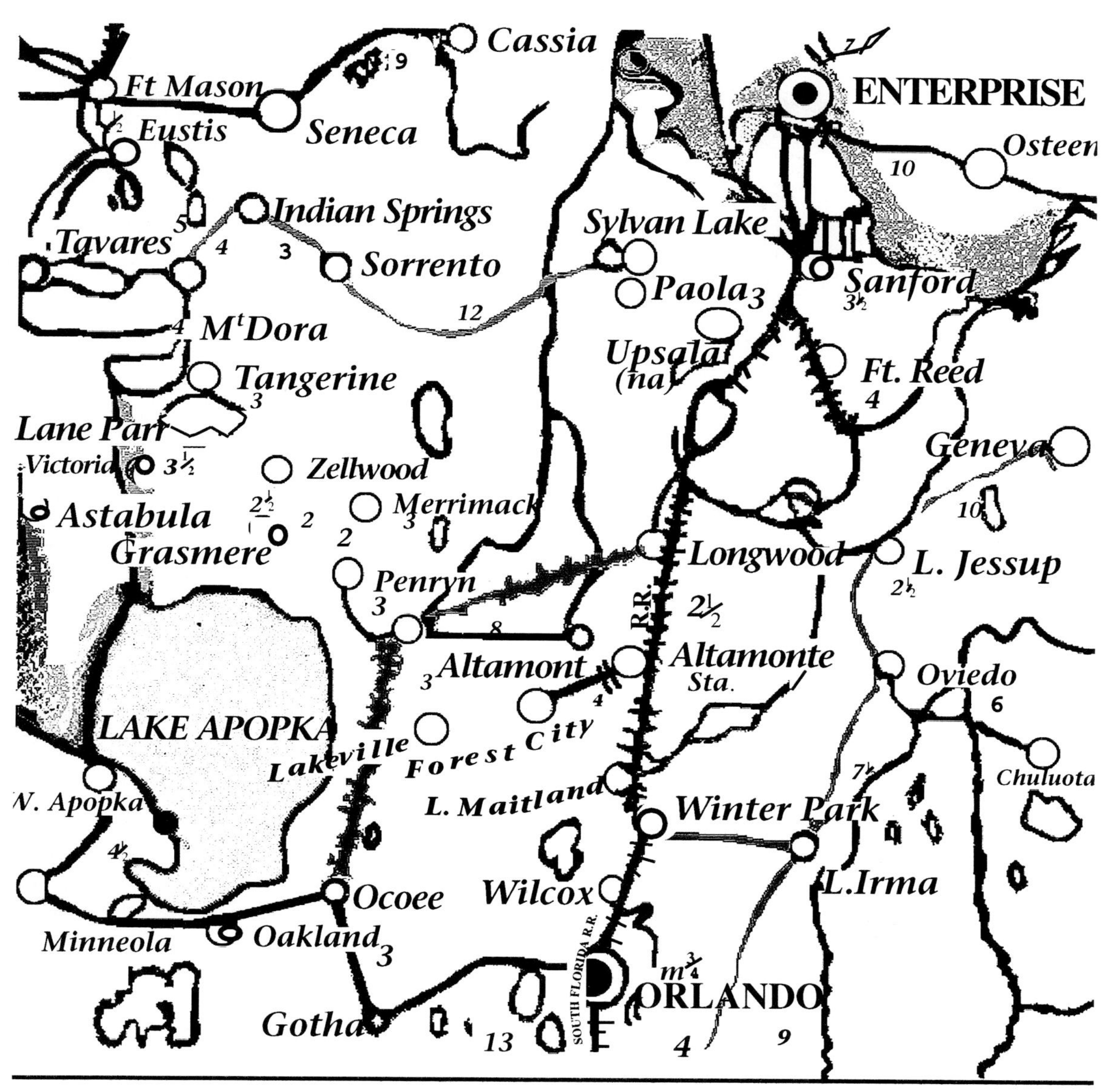

An Excerpt from

POSTAL ROUTE MAP

of THE STATE of

FLORIDA
WITH ADJACENT PARTS OF
GEORGIA AND ALABAMA

1884

This 1884 postal route map shows the recently completed South Florida Railroad and its impact on the postal delivery system. At this time Forest City was served from Altamonte Station, but Altamont still received its mail via a post road.

of Lake Monroe and promoting the small town which bore his name, also backed the enterprise. It was he who induced ex-President Ulysses Grant to turn the first shovel of earth at a ceremony which signalled the beginning of construction.[8]

With a single engine—*The Seminole*—pulling a single flat car loaded with supplies from Sanford to the steadily advancing railhead, the company opened a line to Maitland and Orlando in the fall of 1880 and to Kissimmee in 1882. The South Florida Telegraph Company completed a line along the right-of-way early that same year, connecting Central Florida with the rest of the nation by telegraph.[9]

The first schedule of the South Florida Railroad was published in November 1882, listing Snow's Station as one of the flag stops. According to the schedule, trains left Orlando at 7:00 A.M. and reached Snow's Station at 7:48, stopping only if the flag was out. It left Sanford about 4:00 P.M., reaching Snow's Station at 4:52 on its return to Orlando.[10]

At the time of its completion, the South Florida Railroad was the only railway south of Jacksonville. Immigrants and tourists left Jacksonville on any of several steamer lines then plying the St. Johns River and changed to the railroad which gave them access to an extensive area of desirable countryside. The railroad gave impetus to the first Florida land boom which was focused on the central part of the peninsula. People were already coming to the area to make their homes or to spend the winters, but the railroad made the area much more accessible.

If the decade of the 1880s was Florida's first boom, it was also the start of the railroad age. Several other lines would be built across the Altamont area during the 1880s, but major trunk lines were also under way. Henry Bradley Plant began extending his Jacksonville, Tampa and Key West line southward as the South Florida Railroad was being completed. He purchased that line and incorporated it into his road which reached Tampa in 1884. The Plant line, a part of the Plant Investment Company, served Altamonte Springs and surrounding communities until 1902 when it became part of the Atlantic Coast Line Railroad. The Jacksonville-to-Tampa branch of that national line carried passengers to and from Altamonte Springs after 1902.[11]

The Florida Midland Railway was conceived by John Butterick, another Bostonian, and financed by his Massachusetts acquaintances. Originally chartered to build from Lake Jesup to Leesburg, the firm was incorporated by S. M. Brewster, Carlos Cushing, A. Munson, and C. Munson, all of whom gave Florida addresses, and Edward Page, Charles W. Morris, and Cyrus Carpenter, all of Boston.[12] Some of those shown as Floridians were actually winter residents whose permanent home also was Boston. Under the general supervision of John Dorr, construction began in

1883, with a gang of Italians working the grade west of Longwood, and another group of blacks working eastward. The railroad underwent major changes when John Dorr suddenly died in 1885. Charles Morris, then president of the company, arrived from Boston in 1886 and implemented major changes. Probably because the Tavares, Orlando, and Atlantic Railroad was then making progress from the area around Leesburg, the company discontinued plans to build in that direction. Instead, the road was to be built to Ocoee. It was opened from Longwood to Apopka in 1886 and reached Ocoee in January 1887. Its first two stations west of Longwood were Altamont and Lake Brantley.[13]

The Florida Midland endured several reorganizations after reaching Ocoee, but was extended to Kissimmee by 1892. Residents of Altamont and Lake Brantley used its services for travel and recreational outings for several years, but the line was never profitable. In receivership from the time it was completed in 1892, it was purchased by the Plant Investment Company in 1896 and became part of the Atlantic Coast Line Railroad in 1902, along with the rest of the Plant system.[14]

The Orange Belt Railway was built by Peter A. Demens. After cutting out his timber, Demens decided to build a narrow gauge line using his old logging road as its nucleus. With extremely limited capital, he launched his enterprise in 1885 and had completed grading nearly to Ocoee by July 1886. The Orange Belt, which crossed the Florida Midland near Palm Springs and passed through Piedmont (near the intersection of present-day U. S. 441 and Piedmont-Wekiva Road), Lakeville and Clarcona on its way to Oakland, eventually reached the Pinellas peninsula. By that time, Demens had lost control of the road and was on his way to California. Like the South Florida and Florida Midland lines, the Orange Belt was absorbed by the Plant system and became part of the Atlantic Coast Line Railroad in 1902.[15]

Railroad-building fever accelerated as more and more communities sprang up. Some roads were launched with too little concern for the large capital investment necessary and without regard for the competition of competing lines. One such enterprise grew out of a provision of Henry Plant's charter which authorized a branch of his main line "from some point between Sanford and Maitland to Apopka City." That was the catalyst for the Apopka and Atlantic Railroad which was to be built westward from Mayo, one of the flag stops on the South Florida Railroad about a mile and a half south of Snow's Station. The project was launched before either the Midland or the Orange Belt, but it was delayed for about three years because of several right-of-way disputes. With the legal questions settled, work began on the road in 1885. Sixty men were then at work grading, and rails and rolling stock were on the

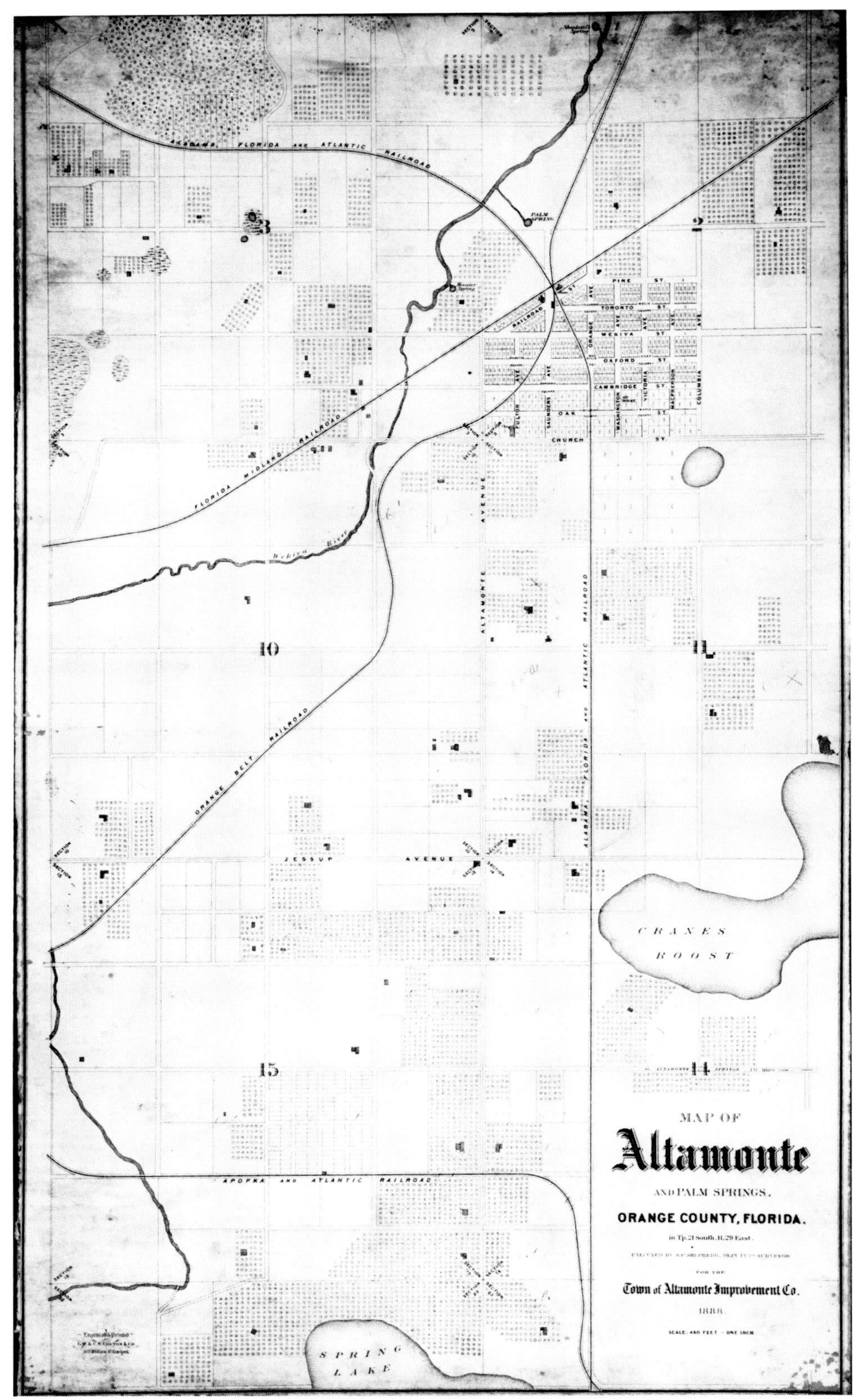

Published by the Town of Altamonte Improvement Company in 1888, this map was intended to promote development of the older Altamont (near what is now the intersection of I-4 and S.R. 434). It shows all of the railroads which then existed and one which did not. The Alabama, Florida and Atlantic Railroad was never built.

View of the Wekiva River as it looked in 1885. The shallow, winding stream ultimately defied all efforts to make it a commercial route between the Central Florida communities and the St. Johns River.

way. According to the *Orlando Sentinel*, the line was expected to be operating from Mayo to Clay Springs by late 1886. That did not happen. The line *was* operating in 1888, but only between Mayo and Forest City, a distance of about five miles. By that time both the Midland and the Orange Belt were already serving Apopka and there was too little traffic for competing lines to operate profitably.[16]

A much more ambitious enterprise was the Alabama, Florida and Atlantic which was planned to run 633 miles from Montgomery, Alabama to Turtle Harbor, Florida, via Clay Springs, Altamont, Altamonte Springs, and Orlando. Having acquired the rights to the Sanford, Indian Springs and Ocala Railway Company in 1885, the new firm used them as a basis for its larger line. Grading began at Eustis in 1887 on a section from that town to Orlando. By October the right-of-way was cut through and grading had progressed far enough that a commissary department was set up at Altamont. About the same time the Alabama, Florida and Atlantic acquired the little Apopka and Atlantic which was almost ready to begin service between Mayo and Forest City. That was as far as the enterprise ever went.

Only about twenty-five miles of crossties were laid on the grade between Eustis and Clay Springs. The Alabama, Florida and Atlantic never reached Altamonte Springs, much less Montgomery, Alabama or the Atlantic Coast. Inclusion of the line on a map published by the Altamonte Improvement Company in 1888 was a part of the optimistic boosterism of the booming 1880s.[17]

Although railroads were crisscrossing Central Florida rapidly in the 1880s, water transportation was still popular. The St. Johns continued as a major highway into peninsular Florida and many people thought the Wekiva was a suitable tributary to that river. In the 1870s, William Mills and Matthew Stewart of Apopka had formed the Wekiva Steamboat Company to clear the stream of brush and other obstacles and open a channel from Clay Springs to the St. Johns. Although it was a larger undertaking than they had anticipated, small steamers were enabled to ply the stream by 1875. Captain E. R. Laws announced plans in 1877 to make two trips each week between Sanford and Clay Springs on his *Mayflower*, a 70-foot sidewheeler which drew only fourteen inches of water. That enterprise apparently did not succeed and a new venture soon followed. Captain Thomas Lund was then navigating the upper St. Johns from Sanford to Titusville in vessels of extremely light draft and thought he could do the same on the Wekiva. With Mills and Stewart, he launched yet another effort to open the stream to regularly scheduled transportation. They were again unsuccessful, but barges were carrying freight on the river in the mid-1880s. Optimism was high again in 1886 when Will L. Church arrived at Altamont with a boat which he planned to place in regular service on the Clay Springs Run and the Wekiva. He had reached Altamont by way of the river "after the various mishaps consequent on the first navigation of a narrow, tortuous and shallow stream." Church was apparently unable to overcome those "various mishaps" because nothing was heard of him after that first announcement.[18]

An even more ambitious idea came in 1882 with the incorporation of the Altamonte Land, Hotel and Navigation Company. Among its several planned enterprises was one anticipating a canal from Lake Adelaide to the Little Wekiva River to provide transportation from its proposed Altamonte Hotel. Considering the topography of the land between Lake Adelaide and the river, the lack of depth of that stream in comparison with the main body of water, and the inability of qualified riverboat operators to navigate the larger stream, the intentions of the Altamonte Company with regard to the canal may be doubted.

Nothing ever came of the proposed waterway, but the company's extensive real estate transactions and its construction and management of the Altamonte Hotel were catalysts for the community of Altamonte Springs which acquired that name in early 1887.

In the long run, it was railways rather than waterways which provided transportation into Central Florida south of Lake Monroe. Beyond that it was the South Florida Railroad—not the Florida Midland, Orange Belt, or the still-born Alabama, Florida and Atlantic—which carried the bulk of passenger traffic to and from the region. As railroads succeeded waterways as the primary means of transportation in the nation, the main trunk of the Plant line carried passengers from the upper east coast through Jacksonville and Orlando to Tampa without a change of trains. It was no accident that Altamonte Springs, with a station on that main line, became a permanent community, while some of its neighbors on the other lines fell victim to the adversities of the 1890s.

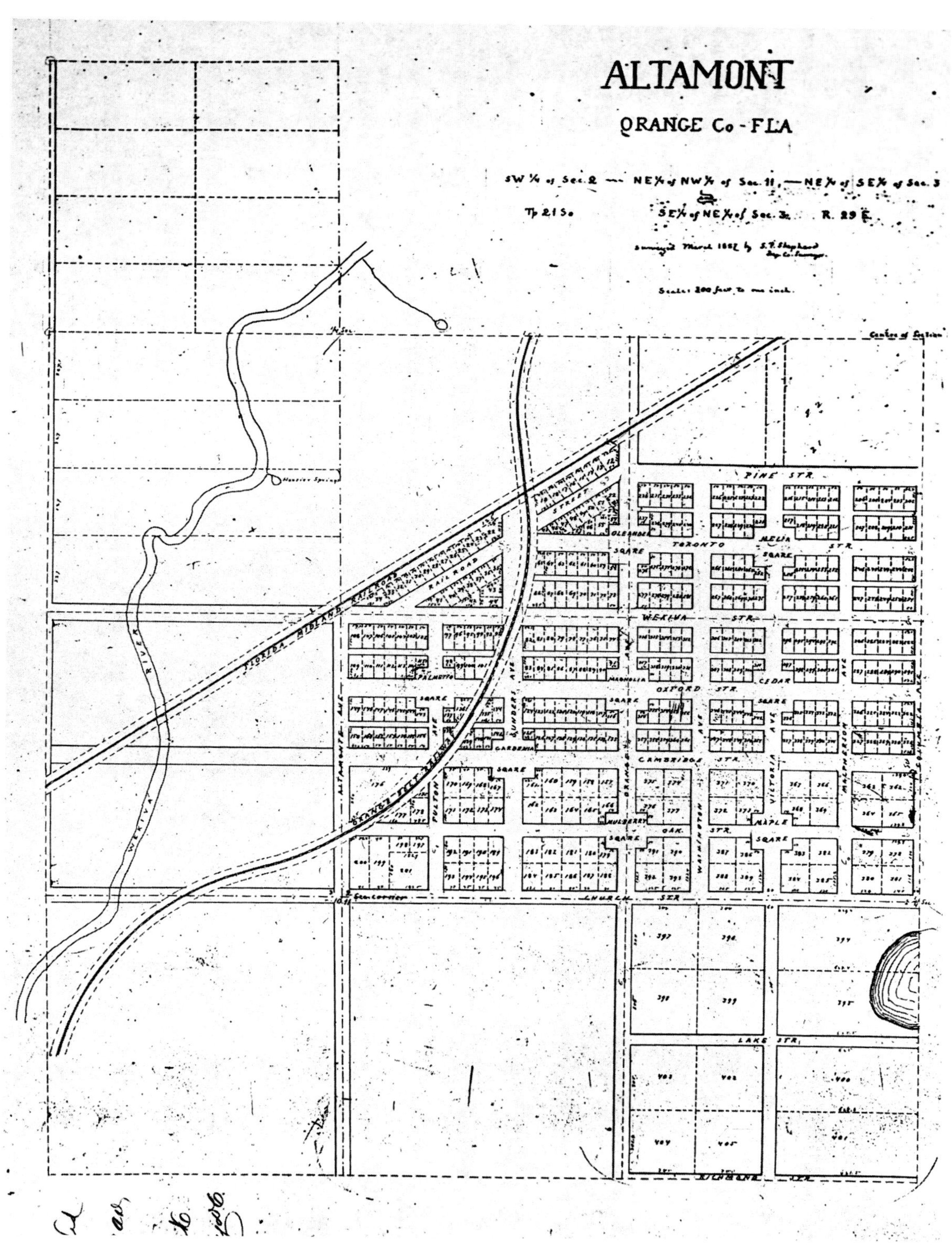

Altamonte, platted in 1887 by Byron S. Ashley and R. D. Fuller, was located just east of the Wekiva River at the intersection of the Midland and Orange Belt railroads. It did not survive the great freezes of 1894–1895.

FOUR

Altamonte Springs and Its Neighbors: 1880-1900

Snowville was reported in 1880 as a "tiny hamlet" whose winter population grew to about three hundred people, nearly all of whom were gone shortly after Easter each year. That was changed by the Altamonte Land, Hotel and Navigation Company which was chartered in late 1882.

Central Florida was a frontier experiencing a population and land boom by the early 1880s. Both Sanford and Orlando were becoming towns of consequence and Apopka, about eight miles west of the future Altamonte Springs, was not far behind them. People were taking up land at several locations in between and town building was rampant. When a few people settled near each other, one of them usually started a store and asked the United States government to open a post office. The government was generous in granting such requests if the applicants could show that as many as thirty or forty people would be served. And no one looked too closely to see whether the numbers might be exaggerated. The proposed post office sites were sometimes described as towns, sometimes as settlements, and sometimes as neighborhoods, but in all cases a name was required for the post office. Place names thus appeared all across the landscape, sometimes within a mile or two of each other. They came and went quite rapidly, but some endured. Each had its own sphere, but they often overlapped. People might get their mail at one place and attend church or send their children to school at another. There was competition between them but there was also interdependence.

Altamont and Altamonte Springs were typical of new towns in this expansive era. Although they were less than four miles apart, land developers laid out towns at both places. The two plats almost abutted. As people took up the land they affiliated with one or the other of the towns, and sometimes both. Reporters traveled across Central Florida and identified the small towns along with their inhabitants and major features. Different reporters placed the same residents in different towns. Identity was further complicated because Altamont was older, while the first railroad was built through the place that would become Altamonte Springs. The railroad drew some of Altamont's inhabitants toward the new town. George E. Wilson, for example, was Altamont's storekeeper and postmaster in 1882, but about that time he became affiliated with the Altamonte Land, Hotel and Navigation Company. The distinction is further blurred because Altamont, heavily dependent upon citrus culture, virtually disappeared after the freezes of 1894 and 1895. Despite all this, Altamont and Altamonte Springs were two separate places for a time.

Several other communities sprang up in the area and lasted for short periods. They prospered briefly and then declined for one reason or another. Some of them disappeared completely, while others later became part of Altamonte Springs. But, for a time in the late nineteenth century they had their places on the Central Florida frontier.

There were four people living at Snowville in 1870. They were joined by a few others, but it was still a tiny place without its own post office when the South Florida Railroad arrived in 1880. Daniel W. Holden became the first postmaster at Snowville, usually referred to as Snow's Station, in October of that year. He was followed in September 1883 by George E. Wilson—who oddly enough was still listed as the postmaster at Altamont at that time. William F. Rudisill assumed the office in November 1884, just one month before the name was changed to Altamonte Station. Rudisill was still postmaster in January 1887 when the name was again changed to Altamonte Springs. Much had happened there during the nearly seven years since the first post office was established at the flag stop on the South Florida Railroad.[19]

Snowville was reported in 1880 as a "tiny hamlet" whose winter population grew to about three hundred people, nearly all of whom were gone shortly after Easter each year. That was changed by the Altamonte Land, Hotel and Navigation Company which was chartered in late 1882 by a group of Boston capitalists who wanted to build a "Florida Boston Town."

Among the prime movers of the company were James H. Foss, Thomas C. Simpson, and Henry M. Cross of Newburyport, W. D. Kingsmill Marrs of Boston, and George E. Wilson of Altamont. Wilson had also come from Boston before settling in Florida. Foss, Simpson, and Kingsmill Marrs, joined by Stiles Frost, another Bostonian, visited Florida and investigated the proposed site of the development soon after the railroad was built. They reported, not too surprisingly, that the area was highly desirable and would produce nearly all the crops and fruits of the "middle, northern and southern states." The proposed hotel was to be erected in an extensive yellow pine grove near the banks of a clear water lake "affording ample facilities for boating, fishing, gunning, mid-winter open-air bathing and commanding an outlook for miles over picturesque scenery."[20]

According to the company prospectus, the future site of Altamonte Springs could be reached by steamship from either Boston or New York at rates of $31 for regular passengers and $13 for immigrants. There was also through rail service to Jacksonville at $36.50 for a trip that required only forty-five hours.

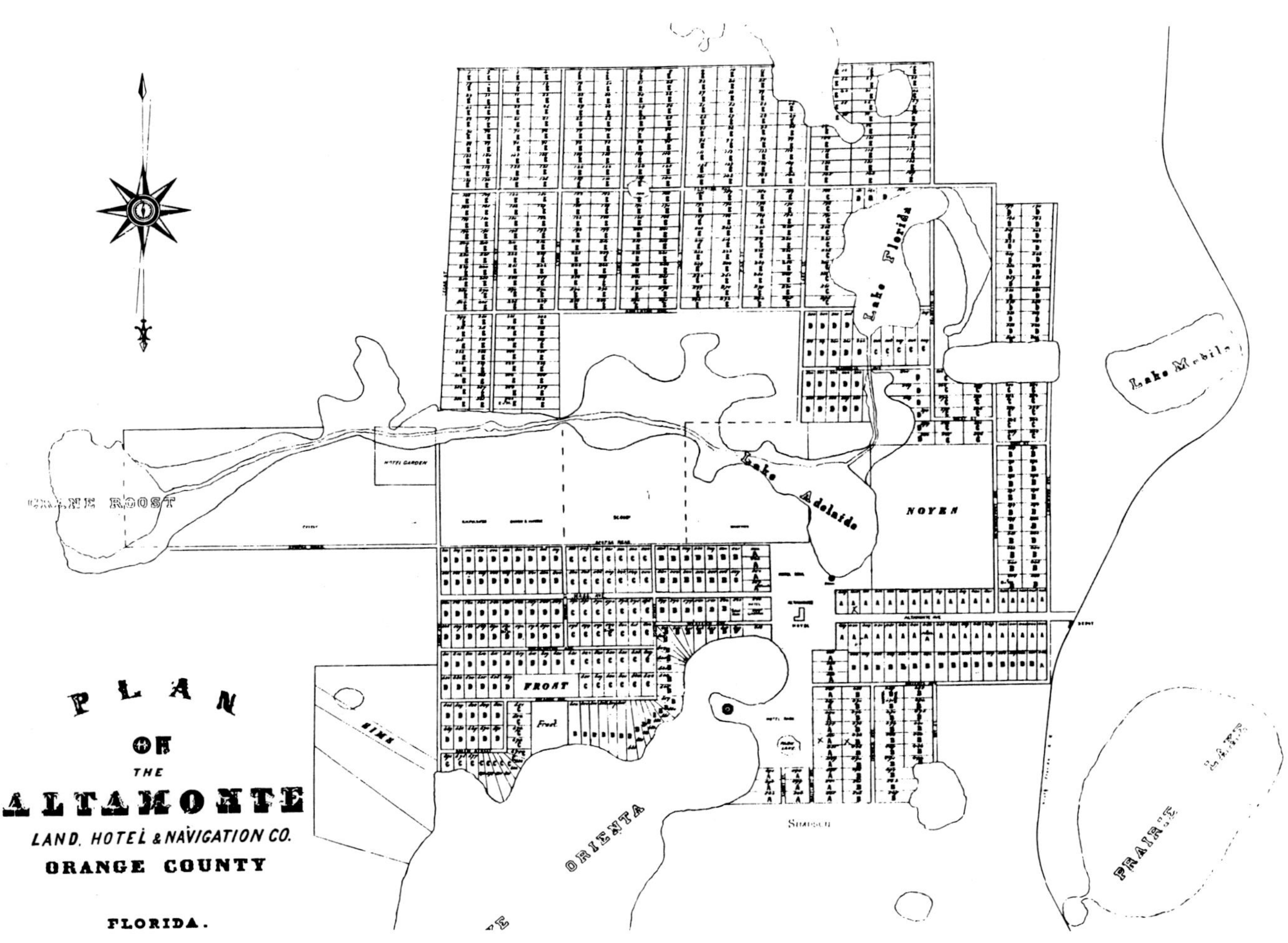

Filed with Orange County in 1892, the plan of the Altamonte Land, Hotel and Navigation Company was completed in 1882 and sales began that year. Its Altamonte Hotel was built late in 1882 and the first guests were registered in early 1883.

View of Altamonte Avenue from the hotel toward the railroad station about 1882–1883, before the tramway was built. From glass negative 104 by Stanley J. Morrow in the Florida State Archives.

Viewed from the north, this is the Altamonte Hotel as it looked in 1883, before the tramway was completed. Some of the first guests can be seen on the verandah and the adjacent grounds.

View of Altamonte Station from the north.

Altamonte Hotel tram and crowd waiting for a train at the South Florida Railroad Station about 1887. Photo from glass negative 107 by Stanley J. Morrow in Florida State Archives.

The company planned to build a "first-class town" with a hotel of the same quality. It also envisioned building a saw mill and buying steamboats for operation on the Wekiva River, the navigation of which was—according to the prospectus—the exclusive right of the company. Capitalization was $100,000 and a limited number of shares were available to the public at $100 per share. Purchasers would be entitled to "one acre of good land in the vicinity of the hotel, together with a proportionate part of the large profits which must arise. . . ." A list of original stockholders included the names of forty-eight investors, all of whose addresses were Boston or nearby towns.[21]

Officers of the company were Benjamin Hale, mayor of Newburyport, president; Dr. Arthur Kemble, Salem, vice-president; Honorable Harvey N. Shepard, Boston, clerk; Dr. F. A. Howe, Newburyport, treasurer. Foss, Simpson, Cross, Kingsmill Marrs, and George Wilson constituted the board of directors. Foss was general manager.[22]

The first hotel building was constructed by Joseph M. Lewis, who had himself come from Boston in 1881. It was completed and opened for guests in February 1883. The company celebrated the late season opening with a "grand excursion" at "greatly reduced" rates for stockholders and patrons.[23] During the summer of 1883 the hotel grounds were improved and a tramway was built from the railroad station to the hotel entrance, a distance of about half a mile.

Joseph M. Lewis had been engaged in the construction business in Boston as well as other places before settling permanently at Altamonte Springs. He built the first hotel and the George Frost house, and was involved in some way with the construction of most of the houses in Altamonte Springs between 1881 and 1910. He was also superintendent of many of the groves owned by winter residents, and in 1915 had six groves of his own in and around Altamonte Springs. He shared with Nathan H. Fogg the distinction of being one of the few permanent residents of the town, having lived there more than thirty years by 1915. (C. E. Howard, *Early Settlers of Orange County* (Orlando, 1915).

W. Wood managed the hotel during its first full season in 1883–84. With accommodations for only fifty guests at the time, it actually entertained more than eighty according to the jubilant *Orange County Reporter*. The paper explained that guests willingly tolerated the overcrowding because the Altamonte was "one of the most thoroughly equipped hotels in the South." The attractions of the place, the rural scenery and the facilities for boating and fishing could not be resisted. The editor added that the "hotel stands upon an elevated ridge between and overlooking a number of lakes. Croquet fields are on one side and a bowling alley [is] at the rear of the house. Boating is within two hundred yards on each side. A broad avenue has been cleared from the hotel to the station and a street car runs to all trains." The hotel also had a steam laundry and an engine to provide water at all times. "An immense tank above the roof" held water for use in case of fire. Rates for "full board" were $3 per day, or from $13 to $21 per week. Full season rates were also available. The enthusiastic editor might also have added that the hotel kept a steam launch on Lake Orienta for the guests.[24]

The hotel was located in a twenty-acre "Hotel Park" on the north end of Lake Orienta. The smaller Park Lake was included in the property. The hotel grounds were bordered on the east by Maitland Avenue. Western Avenue—a street running westward about where Jasmine is now—was just north of the hotel. Across Western Avenue was Lake Adelaide where a pavilion had been erected at the spring for which the town was named. A forty-acre tract adjacent to the Hotel Park was divided into lots for villas and a number of them were taken up almost immediately. The Hotel Park and the two beautiful lakes became the center of the "Florida Boston Town" which evolved in the mid-1880s. Several fine winter homes were built near the hotel grounds by 1887.

The Altamonte Land, Hotel and Navigation Company had acquired 1,200 acres of land extending more than a mile west of the railroad station. Some of its tracts were taken up by investors in the company, but sales were quite brisk for a time in the mid-1880s. One of the first purchasers was William L. Bradley of the Bradley Fertilizer Company, a Boston firm with a regional office in Augusta, Georgia. Benning C. Noyes, who was a company stockholder, acquired title to a large tract on the north side of Altamonte Avenue between Newburyport on the east and Lake Adelaide on the west.

Whether or not the company ever earned the "large profits" promised in its prospectus, it underwent numerous changes of leadership as well as ownership while still in its infancy. A new slate of officers was named in late 1883 with only Dr. Kemble remaining as vice-president. The new president was Leonard F. Cressy of Boston. Thomas Swadkens, Jr., of

Altamonte Hotel in 1887, after a 40 x 200 ft. addition was completed in 1884. Note the water tank atop the original building which was used both for a water supply and fire protection.

Guests arriving at the Altamonte Hotel on the hotel tram in the late 1880s.

Altamonte Hotel guests cruising Lake Orienta on the hotel steam launch about 1887.

The Altamonte Hotel Springhouse on Lake Adelaide in 1888.

Nathan H. Fogg was from Boston where he had worked as an electrician for the White Dry Goods Company. Arriving at Altamonte Springs in 1884, he became one of the most prolific boosters of his adopted town and the Central Florida region. A frequent correspondent of the Jacksonville *Florida Times-Union*, the *Tampa Tribune*, the *Orlando Reporter-Star*, the *Orlando Sentinel*, the *Orlando Citizen*, and the *Sanford Herald*, he reported the arrivals and departures to and from the Altamonte Hotel, the agricultural activities around Altamonte Springs, and news items of interest. He planted groves, grew tropical and semi-tropical shrubs and trees, and pecans and Japanese cane on his Oak Knoll Farm, a sixty-acre tract in what is now the southern part of the city of Altamonte Springs. C. E. Howard, *Early Settlers of Orange County* (Orlando, 1915), p. 36.

the same place became secretary. Henry L. Chase was the new treasurer. Directors were Cressy, George Frost and Charles Whittier of Boston, and Dr. J. W. Goodell of Lynn. One of the first acts of the new officers was to enlarge the hotel. A new edifice measuring forty by two hundred feet and three stories high was built during the summer of 1884. [25]

George Frost was an important addition to the Altamonte Company. Not only did he build a large home on one of the lots near the hotel, but he also acquired additional land for his Frost addition to Altamonte Springs. The new addition straddled the railroad on the north side of Altamonte Avenue and extended eastward.

Frost also assumed a prominent role in the company itself. In September 1885, the Altamonte Land, Hotel and Navigation Company sold the hotel property and all its remaining real estate to the Altamonte Company, a new firm chartered in Massachusetts. Charles Whittier, an

George Frost of Boston and a prominent official of the Altamonte Land, Hotel and Navigation Company standing in the Spring Lake "pinery" in the 1890s.

officer of the old company was president of the new firm and Henry L. Chase, also from the original company, was secretary/treasurer. According to the deed transferring the property, the sale was made to "George Frost or to the Altamonte Company. . . ."[26] Frost had apparently replaced James H. Foss as the manager of the company's interest in Florida.

Whatever the reasons for the corporate maneuvers, Altamonte Springs—still known as Altamonte Station at the time—was unaffected. The first store in town was built in 1884. Situated on a siding off the railroad it was able to handle hay, grain and other items suitable for a rural village.[27] William F. Rudisill, the postmaster, was also in charge of the railroad station and the Railway Express Agency. Joseph M. Lewis was a building contractor and Nathan H. Fogg offered his services as a machinist and engineer. Charles E. Pierce was listed as a cabinet maker and contractor.[28]

There was a graded school for whites with Miss Prentiss in charge. School was held in a building on a lot just west of the hotel property which had been donated by the company. A school for blacks was conducted at Spring Lake beginning in 1886 and a second one was added east of the railroad in 1888. There were both Methodist and Baptist church congregations. Rev. Lucien Drury was the Baptist minister and the Rev. Mr. Taylor officiated for the Methodists. Church services were held in the school building.[29]

An important addition to the growing list of winter residents was Henry Herman Westinghouse, the younger brother of George Westinghouse of Pittsburgh. The younger Westinghouse purchased eleven villa lots west of the hotel property and another seven lots on the east along Maitland Avenue about 1885. It is likely that he was acquainted with Altamonte Springs through George Frost who was affiliated with the Westinghouse Company. Whatever the case, he soon contracted with Nathaniel Bradlee, one of the leading architects of Boston, to build several "cottages" on some of his lots[30].

These so-called "cottages" were actually large, three-story structures with twelve- to-fifteen rooms each. Representing some of the best of the Victorian architecture of the day, they were designed by Bradlee and built according to his supervision. Joseph Lewis and Charles Pierce both participated in the construction. Situated on the east side of Maitland Avenue, near Boston Avenue on the west side of the hotel, and north of the hotel just west of Lake Adelaide, these impressive mansions formed an imposing nucleus for the community which was one of the more sought-after winter resorts of Florida during the latter nineteenth century.

Pierce's home was a remarkable dwelling located at the corner of Boston and Western—now Jasmine—avenues. Subsequently known as the "inside-outside house," it was a prefabricated structure which Pierce had

Henry Herman Westinghouse—born at Central Bridge, New York in 1853, the youngest brother of the more famous George Westinghouse, joined the Westinghouse Air Brake Company as an ordinary foundry worker in 1872. Rising rapidly in the firm, he became general manager in 1887 and vice president in 1899. When his brother died in 1914, "H. H." succeeded him as president and chairman of the board. An inventor in his own right, the younger Westinghouse, patented the Westinghouse single-acting steam engine in 1883 and organized the Westinghouse Machine Company of which he was president for many years. In his senior years, he was also chairman of the board of the Canadian Westinghouse Company, Ltd., a director of Westinghouse Electric and Manufacturing Company, director of Westinghouse Brake and Saxby Signal Company, Ltd., London, and president and director of La Compagnie des Preins Westinghouse, Paris. He was also a director of Westinghouse Brake Company of Australasia, Ltd., Sidney.

H. H. and his family spent many winters in Altamonte Springs from the 1880s to the 1920s. A strong supporter of Rollins College, he was made a trustee of that school in 1928, and received an honorary degree of Doctor of Science there in 1929. At a memorial service for him at Rollins in February 1934, it was revealed that he had contributed stocks valued at $108,000 to its endowment fund as well as several other gifts for various school projects. (From the historical files of the Westinghouse Electric Corporation, 11 Stanwix Street, Pittsburgh, Pennsylvania.)

brought from Boston in the late 1870s. It acquired its name when Pierce assembled the parts so that the smooth sides of the walls were on the inside and the supporting framing on the outside. Pierce used the lower floor for his cabinet shop and lived on the upper floor.

Other houses—such as Joseph Lewis' home—were added from time to time and a number of smaller dwellings were scattered about on both sides of Altamonte Avenue between the railroad station and the hotel, but the Bradlee-built "cottages" and the hotel were the center of the "Florida Boston Town."

Henry Herman Westinghouse as he looked in the 1880s when he was building the "cottages" in Altamonte Springs. He and his family spent many winters in Florida, but his more famous brother, George, did not. The Westinghouse Company historian commented wryly that this was "probably because Thomas Edison did."

The Bradlee-McIntyre House. Probably the best known of the "cottages" built by H. H. Westinghouse, it stood near Massachusetts Avenue and Park Place until it was relocated to the Longwood Historic District in 1973. From a photo by H. A. Abercromby in the Orange County Historical Museum.

The residence of August Richardson of Boston as it appeared in the late 1880s. It was the twin of the Bradlee-McIntyre House with the facade reversed.

Known as the Orr House, this "cottage" was built on Park Place in the late nineteenth century. It stood at 130 Park Place until it was destroyed by fire in 1983.

Drawing of the Orr House by Richard M. Wyman from photographs.

Known as the Bundy House, this structure at 115 N. Maitland Avenue was built about 1892 and is one of the oldest residences still standing in Altamonte Springs. Photograph was taken in 1991 by History Associates of St. Augustine.

The "inside-outside" house which Captain C. E. Pierce brought from Boston, Massachusetts in the late 1870s and reassembled on Boston Avenue where it stood until 1973.

Martha and Nellie Ginkham at Shepherd Springs in 1888.

By 1886, the new and enlarged hotel—with seventy-three rooms—was under the management of Frank A. Cofran, who was proprietor of a hotel in the White Mountains during the summer. He was assisted at the desk by George Hays. Visitors arriving at the station were met by a horse-drawn coach which ran over a narrow gauge tramway to the hotel about half a mile away. One observer wrote that a panorama of villas, groves and truck gardens were visible along the way. The hotel was a large square building with broad verandahs opening on a brightly flowered plaza. It was in a beautiful setting with Lake Orienta on its southwest side and Lake Adelaide a short distance to the north. A lighted wooden pavilion stood on the border of Lake Adelaide. Another effusive visitor declared the Altamonte Hotel "a sweet place to be tired and hungry in . . . . Elevators, electric bells, all the smooth ingenuity . . . is adopted here.[31]

In announcing the 1886–1887 season, Cofran was slightly boastful about the hotel's highly reputed dining room. According to him it was supplied with "meat from New York and Boston, fish from Tampa Bay, and vegetables from the hotel garden." Eggs and poultry were supplied by local farms, and pure spring water "flows from the ground." Some new facilities included a billiard and pool room, a barber shop, and a livery stable. The livery stable was an especially important addition since the Altamonte Company had purchased Shepherd Sulphur Springs, about three and a half miles from the hotel. The spring's water was recommended by Dr. A. M. Cushing, president of the Massachusetts Homeopathic Medical Association as a cure for "dyspepsia, rheumatic, catarrhal, pulmonary and bronchial diseases."

Guests at leisure on the Altamonte Hotel porch in the early 1890s.

Built on Park Place in the early days of Altamonte Springs, this home was known as the Julia Day House.

Mrs. Frank Cofran (wife of the manager of the Altamonte Hotel) and her dog, Pug, at Hoosier Springs in 1885.

A maturing orange grove on the western side of Lake Orienta in the mid-1880s. Another grove is discernable across the lake in the upper right corner of the photograph. From glass negative 326 by Stanley J. Morrow in the Florida State Archives.

A significant proportion of the winter residents purchased land and started citrus groves. Since the groves, especially in their early years, required care which absentee owners could not provide, they usually contracted with permanent residents to tend them. The caretaker would clear the land and plant the young trees—either seedlings or budded stock—and keep them cultivated, watered, and fertilized. He was sometimes compensated in cash but he might also receive a share of the crop once the trees began to bear. Joseph M. Lewis handled many of the groves of absentee owners at Altamonte Springs. Of course, like most of his neighbors who lived there year around, Lewis planted his own groves, too. Observers had always praised the beauty of the high, rolling pine land of the place, but the increasing acreage of orange, lemon, and lime groves soon added to its attractiveness. Some of the early grove owners were J. K. Coiner, Leonard F. Cressy, George Frost, B. C. Noyes, William L. Bradley, Anna E. Griffin, Obed Foss, and P. D. Coombs. They were joined by such permanent residents as N. H. Fogg, Lucian Drury, Thomas Simms, and Joseph M. Lewis. Fogg was one of the few who planted vegetables in the early years. Cotton was being cultivated in a field between Altamonte Springs and Longwood as late as 1880, but it was eventually edged out by the more profitable citrus.[32]

Located just west of the lake by that name, H. H. Westinghouse's Spring Lake Grove became a show place by the early 1890s. Managed by Arthur H. Fuller, it included several acres of citrus and two acres of pineapples, but its center piece was a ten-acre field of Japanese cane from which syrup was manufactured.[33]

Arthur H. Fuller's home at Spring Lake in the 1890s when he was managing H. H. Westinghouse's Spring Lake Farms.

Population figures for the 1880s were largely speculative. Not only did they increase greatly during the winter months, but permanent residents were often counted as part of more than one settlement. While all sources at that time suggest a winter population of more than three hundred for Altamonte Springs, the summer count ranged from as few as fifty to as many as two hundred fifty. The lesser figure seems to have been closer to reality.

Published in 1889, Elliott's *Florida Encyclopedia* gave the population as fifty during the summer. There were some changes in the business portion of the town by that time. Edmund P. Tebeau had succeeded W. F. Rudisill as postmaster and station agent. George Barclay, who had planted a grove in 1886, was listed as a contractor, although he may have been a winter resident. F. A. Philbrick was shown as a contractor as well. Florence Griffin was in charge of the white school. Elliott did not show a storekeeper in 1889.[34]

"Do not forget that Altamont is not Altamonte Station," the *Orange County Reporter* cautioned in 1886. "The Altamonte [Altamont] post office is three miles west of Longwood and the area encompasses Hoosier Springs."[35] Despite the frequent confusion of the two places by directories and gazetteers which were published at distant places on the basis of information gathered by travelers hurrying through the rural areas of Central Florida, the two places were separate if not always distinctly so.

Unidentified girl on a bicycle in the cane field at Westinghouse's Spring Lake farm. The gazebo on the right was near the residence of Arthur Fuller who was managing the farm in the 1890s.

A cart loaded with cane for the mill at Spring Lake.

After a brief period in 1878 when the officials in Washington attempted to close the Altamont post office, the community was soon thriving. When he visited Altamont in April 1879, J. J. Combs, editor of the *South Florida Citizen*, found along the road, "new dwellings, groves, and clearings, indicative of new life." Combs stopped at the "handsome residence" of Mrs. Lorenzo Wilson, a recent widow who was cultivating a grove of oranges, lemons, and limes. She had arrived in 1874 with her consumptive husband. A strong advocate of the recuperative qualities of Florida's climate, Combs lamented that Wilson had "come to Florida too late to help." The editor met Mr. and Mrs. Henry Wadsworth of Maine who had been boarding during the winter at Mrs. Wilson's place. They liked the area so much that they were staying on to build their own winter home which they planned to occupy the following season.[36]

In the booster fashion typical of Florida editors, Combs wrote that "judging from the number of dwellings and young groves, Altamonte is thriving and prosperous, and has enterprising people." He was enthusiastic enough to arrange for an Altamont correspondent for his Apopka paper.[37]

When George M. Barbour toured the state in 1882 he took a "two-horse rig" from Sanford and reached Altamont after a four-hour journey. He visited with George E. Wilson who, according to Barbour, had settled at Altamont in the late 1870s. Wilson was the community's only storekeeper, but also kept a large orange grove that was about to come into production. Barbour visited around the place and "saw evidence of good soil and energetic people." He noted that the "residents are generally cultured people from the north. . . ."[38]

Writing about a year after Barbour's visit, Sherman Adams, an Orlando real estate agent, described Altamont as a place with about two hundred permanent residents "besides the great rush of northern visitors." Its special attractions were "the famous Hoosier and Shepherd Springs, and charming Lake Brantley." The spring water "as a bath, or taken inwardly, is very beneficial to patients troubled with rheumatism or any blood diseases, being strongly impregnated with sulphur and other minerals." Adams saw many groves, a number of which were several years old, but he estimated that only two or three of them had been put out before 1874.[39]

Altamont was served by a daily stage line from Snow's Station in 1884. George Wilson was still postmaster with an office in his general merchandise store. Like many storekeepers at that time he also handled real estate. Mrs. Eva Collamer kept a boarding house, Peter Hoequist was a blacksmith and wheelwright, and D. C. Hill was a butcher. The Bose sawmill had been acquired by George W. Moyers and John D. Wilson who were operating it in partnership. Alonzo A. Wilson was a job printer who also sold "Florida curiosities" in his shop. J. M. Katline, who had been Altamont's second postmaster, was the justice of the peace. F. G. Baldwin, owner of a large grove, was a notary. Dr. William Heron was a physician who also had an orange grove. Dr. Washington Kilmer still owned his grove at Altamont, but he was spending much of his time in Orlando by that time. There were at least fifty-seven grove owners in the Altamont area in 1884.[40]

The steam-powered cane mill in operation at Spring Lake farms.

Dr. Washington Kilmer had taken an interest in Orange County and state affairs after his walk from Cincinnati in 1872. Appointed to the Orange County School Board in 1877, he served as its chairman until 1885. He also practiced medicine in Orlando for nearly thirty years and served as surgeon for the Seaboard Air Line Railroad after it acquired the Tavares, Orlando, and Atlantic, a line which ran from Orlando through Apopka to Tavares. Dr. Kilmer was applauded for volunteering to treat yellow fever patients in Tampa during the epidemic which raged there in 1887. C. E. Howard, *Early Settlers of Orange County* (Orlando, 1915), p. 18.

Byron S. Ashley and R. D. Fuller launched their Altamonte [Altamont] Improvement Company that year, inviting investors and settlers to buy land in Altamont, the "Queen of the Hills." According to them, there were one hundred Bostonians, one hundred Buckeyes, and one hundred Wolverines with an investment of $1 million "making Altamonte the most beautiful place in the state." Ashley and Fuller platted a new town of Altamont in 1887 at the crossing of the new Midland and Orange Belt railroads. Showing both of those roads as well as the proposed Alabama, Florida and Atlantic, their 1888 promotional map implied that Altamont was destined to be a railroad hub.[41]

The Altamonte Improvement Company's claims may have been somewhat exaggerated but the community was growing quite rapidly by the mid-1880s. E. C. Jackson succeeded George Wilson as postmaster and took over his general merchandise business when the latter moved to Altamonte Springs. Jackson had competition by 1886 when the Baker Brothers opened a second store. Ashley and Fuller also had competition in the real estate business. F. G. Baldwin had added an agency to his other interests. He had also been appointed justice of the peace, apparently succeeding J. M. Katline. Another real estate agency was A. W. Daniel and Brother. Stephen Jenkins was operating the Florida Preserving Company which dealt in fruit products, but he also had time for his own real estate business. W. D. Gunning was listed as a physician along with Dr. Kilmer, although it is unlikely that the latter was actually practicing.[42]

Although they were spread over a sizable area of countryside, Altamont had both schools and churches. An excellent example of late nineteenth century church architecture, the Lake Brantley Union Church building was started in 1882 when Mrs. Carlos Cushing, a winter resident from Boston, induced her husband to start the project. The edifice was built on land donated by George and Louise Lewton and was completed in 1885. Although the Lewtons retained title to the land, the church was managed by a trusteeship composed of Carlos Cushing and Walter H. Hunt. The Winter Park Congregational Church sent a minister to officiate at monthly services. By 1886 there were also Methodist and Presbyterian congregations at Altamont. It is likely although not certain that they held their services in the Union Chapel.[43]

There were several schools around Altamont. It was a simple matter to start a school in those years. If a group of parents could show that at least ten students would attend, the school board usually approved requests for new schools and provided a small sum—usually twenty to thirty dollars depending on the number of students attending—for a teacher's salary. The local community was required to provide the building at no cost to the county. If it was easy to start a school, it was also easy to close it or to move it around if the population changed. Altamont had a

Originally built as the Lake Brantley Union Chapel in 1884–1885, the edifice is shown here after it was removed to its present location in Altamonte Springs.

Sketch of the interior of Lake Brantley Union Chapel by J. B. Simonson in 1884.

small school during the late 1880s with Miss Ehihardt as the teacher, but it was apparently not continued past 1889. Another school was opened that year at Lake Brantley with Annie Holton as the teacher, followed by Miss P. L. Welch in 1890. The trustees for that school were George W. Lewton, G. B. Wood, and S. P. Shepherd. Because of the proliferation of small schools as Orange County grew in size, the board adopted a rule that schools could be no nearer than three miles from each other. The Lake Brantley school was accordingly consolidated with the one at Forest City at that time.[44]

Altamont residents had welcomed the arrival of the Florida Midland Railroad. News that the trestle across the Wekiva River was nearly completed in 1886 was heartily applauded by the Altamont correspondent of the *Sanford Argus*. They probably paid little heed when both Altamont and Lake Brantley were made stops on the new line. But there was genuine concern when the name of the Altamont station was changed by the railroad company to "Palm Springs." The center of the Altamont community was slipping away toward Lake Brantley on the west and Palm Springs on the east. In its application for a post office, Palm Springs was described as lying five eights of a mile east of the Altamont post office on the west side of the Orange Belt line and eighty feet south of the Florida Midland tracks. The Palm Springs location was approved although the Altamont office was continued for the time being. Frank S. Baker became the first Palm Springs postmaster in 1888. Roswell S. Fuller succeeded E. C. Jackson at Altamont about the same time, but he replaced Baker in 1891 when he moved his store to Palm Springs.

Apparently the post office had followed the railroad, and the community was moving in the same direction. The Altamonte Improvement Company's platting of a new town at the railroad crossing undoubtedly contributed to the trend.[45]

Palm Springs was soon experiencing its own difficulties with the school board's three-mile rule. When A. D. Buell and his neighbors applied for a school there, the board denied the request because Palm Springs was only two and a half miles from both Altamonte Springs and Forest City.[46]

Still another settlement was begun about two miles northeast of Palm Springs and less than a mile east of the Wekiva River. With perhaps some exaggeration, Glen Ethel claimed that a post office there would serve about two hundred people. The post office was authorized in 1887. A school followed in 1889.[47]

One other community grew out of the expansive 1880s. About a mile and a half south of Altamonte Station, at the junction of the South Florida Railroad and the Apopka and Atlantic, the community of Woodbridge, inhabited mostly by blacks, applied for a post office. The proposed site was fifty feet south of the Apopka and Atlantic tracks and just west of the South Florida flag station of Mayo. There were some eighty-five people in the village and it was estimated that one hundred fifty would be served by the post office. Jane B. Turner became the first postmistress there in early 1888. The community endured for many years and the post office remained open until 1929 when it was closed and the mail was forwarded to Maitland.[48]

Roswell S. Fuller at his "bachelor's quarters" where he lived when he first arrived at old Altamont.

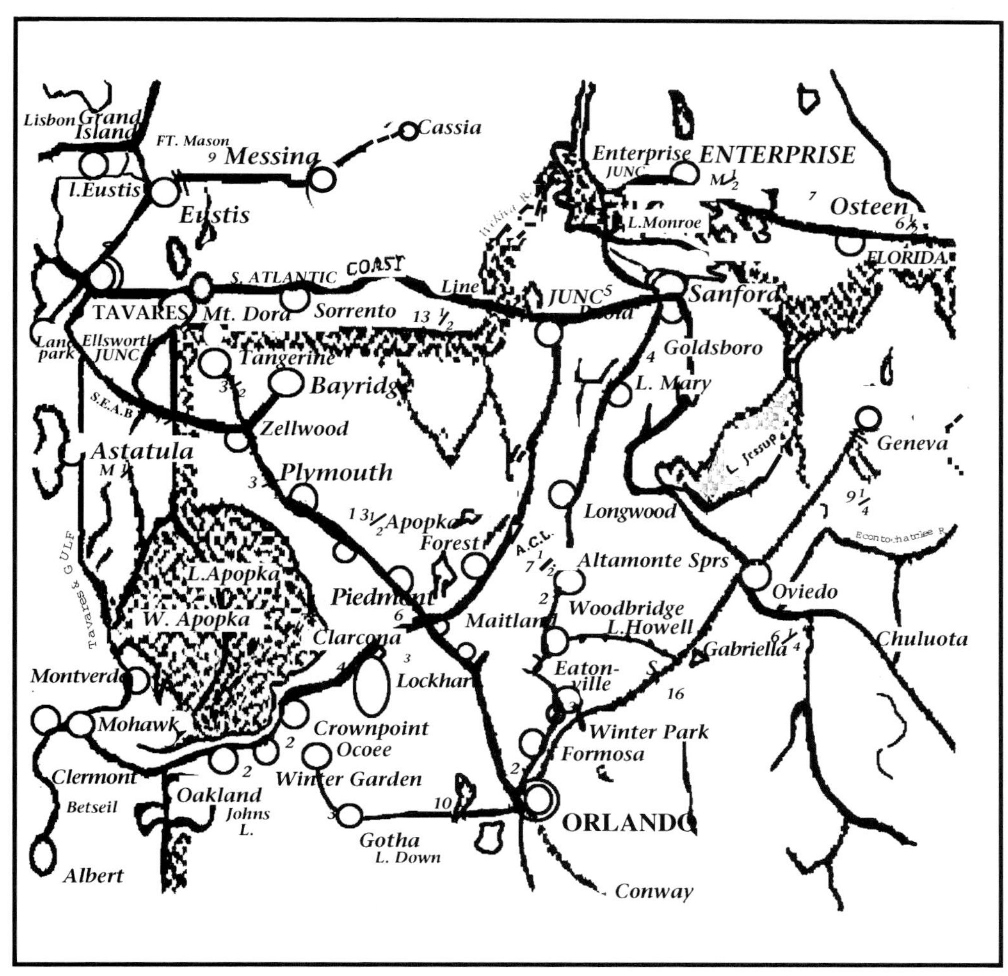

An Excerpt from

POSTAL ROUTE MAP

of THE STATE of

FLORIDA

SHOWING POST OFFICES

WITH THE INTERMEDIATE DISTANCES ON MAIL ROUTES

1 of MARCH, 1911

Excerpt from a 1911 postal route map of Florida showing the location of Woodbridge between Altamonte Springs and Maitland. When Seminole County was created in 1913, the boundary line was drawn almost exactly where Woodbridge was located. The community continued to exist until the late 1920s.

Growth of the Altamont and Altamonte Springs area did not continue long into the 1890s. The Panic of 1893 caused a severe contraction of business throughout the nation and a depression which lasted about four years. It did not stop the wealthy winter residents from coming to their Altamonte Springs homes, of course. The Bradleys, the Westinghouses, and their neighbors continued to winter in Florida. But, it did slow the pace of new buildings. The number of winter guests at the hotel seems to have diminished as well, although it certainly continued in business. It was being managed in 1895 by H. W. Priest, who was shortly succeeded by Herman L. Savage. Savage was still in charge in 1899 and Theodore Anderson of nearby Piedmont was working as an engineer, but the hotel was not being maintained in the splendor of earlier years.[49]

The Altamonte Company had itself experienced financial difficulties by the 1890s. Explaining that its capital stock had "become impaired and it is desirable that [the corporation] should go into voluntary liquidation while the same is still solvent," its directors authorized Charles Whittier—who was still president—and George W. Morse of Newton, Massachusetts, to sell all assets, satisfy all indebtedness, and wind up the company's affairs. Whittier and Morse carried out their obligations by a public auction at the firm's Boston office. Thomas Kenney of that city purchased the property for $16,000. Then, in June 1894, Kenney conveyed the property to the Altamonte Springs Company, a new firm incorporated in the state of Massachusetts. Interestingly enough, the principals of the new company were George Morse and Charles Whittier.[50]

However severely the national depression affected Central Florida, it was modest compared to the disastrous freezes of late 1894 and early 1895. The Christmas freeze, with temperatures dropping to eighteen degrees for several nights, had caused great damage to the crops and to new growth, but most of the trees survived. Then, a warm January brought renewed growth as the trees tried to overcome the earlier damage. With sap running high in the trees, the temperature again dropped to extreme lows on February 7, 1895. The rising sap in the trees froze, causing trunks literally to explode. Some observers described the resulting noises as comparable to gunfire. Many groves were completely destroyed. Three years after the back-to-back freezes, the Florida citrus crop was about 20 percent of what it had been during the 1893–94 season.

Entire communities were abandoned. Altamont and its immediate neighbors were among them. Altamont itself was already declining, but Lake Brantley, Palm Springs, and Glen Ethel soon followed. The pretty little Union Chapel at Lake Brantley was abandoned. The Lewtons deeded

Palm Springs school picnic at Clay Springs (now Wekiva Springs) in the spring of 1898. The picnic was after the great freezes and just before the Palm Springs post office was closed and the mail was forwarded to Altamonte Springs.

it to Rollins College in exchange for their daughter's tuition. Having no use for the building, the college left it unused and unnoticed until it was "discovered" by hunters—Arthur Fuller and Maxwell McIntyre—in an overgrown forest nearly a decade later. The population of Glen Ethel declined so precipitately that its school was closed and the school board waived its three-mile rule to permit combined classes at Palm Springs. That school was abandoned after only a year for "want of pupils. . . ."[51]

The Glen Ethel post office was discontinued in 1899 and the mail was sent to Palm Springs. The Palm Springs post office was in turn abandoned and its mail was forwarded to Altamonte Springs as of June 1900. Roswell S. Fuller closed his Palm Springs store at that time and relocated it to Altamonte Springs where he became postmaster.[52]

In his *Florida, Home, Farm, and Field*, the information for which was collected in 1896, Mahlon Gore, an Orlando newspaper editor, listed both Altamont and Altamonte Springs. He described both as excellent for orange culture, but there was one major difference. Altamonte Springs was one of the leading attractions of Orange County because of the accommodations available to the traveling public and winter residents at the Altamonte Hotel.[53]

Despite two more freezes in the late 1890s and a lengthy drought in the early 1900s, the citrus industry recovered, but Altamont did not. By the early twentieth century, better transportation and the need for consolidation of public services, which was already beginning by 1890—the case of the schools, for example—left residents looking toward Altamonte Springs, Forest City, and Longwood. With the Altamonte Hotel as its centerpiece, a nucleus of large winter residences owned by wealthy individuals, and its location on the major railroad serving Central Florida, Altamonte Springs was better prepared for the twentieth century than its neighbor just three miles to the west.

FIVE

Altamonte Springs in the Progressive Era: 1901-1920

With the Altamonte Hotel as its centerpiece, a nucleus of large winter residences owned by wealthy individuals, and its location on the major railroad serving Central Florida, Altamonte Springs was better prepared for the twentieth century than its neighbor just three miles to the west.

By the early twentieth century Americans were again optimistic, self-confident and eager to build a better future for themselves. Gone was the depression which had gripped the nation during much of the 1890s. The Spanish-American War, which had begun and ended in 1898, had been a popular war. The nation emerged from it as the protector of Cuban independence with overseas possessions in both the Caribbean and the western Pacific. There was sorrow over the assassination of President McKinley, but the emergence of the exuberant Theodore Roosevelt as president soon gave additional focus to the progressive spirit which spread across the United States.

Florida benefitted greatly from both the Spanish American War and the renewed national optimism. With Tampa as the port of embarkation for the Cuban Expeditionary Force and large military installations at both Jacksonville and Miami, the state received new national notice of its potential for development. With investment capital once again becoming available, both individuals and consortiums were soon buying raw land with plans for development.

Central Florida citrus groves were also recovering. Many of the older groves had been replanted and were beginning to produce once more. New acreage was being planted in oranges and grapefruit. Central Florida in general and Altamonte Springs in particular were busy.

George E. Bates and the Altamonte Hotel

Altamonte Springs had survived the devastating freezes and the national depression because of its wealthy winter residents and the Altamonte Hotel which continued to entertain guests throughout the difficult years. Both the hotel and the company which had founded it were still undergoing changes. When Charles Whittier died, the Altamonte Springs Company was liquidated and the proceeds were divided between Charles Morse and Whittier's heirs. The Altamonte Hotel, all the unsold lots belonging to the company, the eighteen-acre tract encompassing

Maitland Avenue looking south from its intersection with Altamonte Avenue about 1900.

View of Altamonte Avenue from the west. The trolley tracks are between the lines of oaks on the right. The photograph is from a postcard postmarked 1907.

View of Lake Orienta across Maitland Avenue after the road was improved and a sidewalk laid.

The Altamonte Hotel seen from the south along Maitland Avenue in 1907.

Shepherd Springs, the tract known as the "Hotel Garden," and the tramway from the station were conveyed to George E. Bates of Mont Vernon, New Hampshire, for six thousand dollars. The transaction was completed in November 1901 when Bates paid two thousand dollars in cash and gave two notes of two thousand dollars each to be secured by a mortgage on the property.[54]

Bates retained control as proprietor of the hotel after his purchase, but title to all of the property changed hands several times. Bates was apparently attempting to raise additional funds to make much-needed improvements to the hotel and grounds. In 1905 he sold everything to Dr. J. Southerland Stuart of Glens Falls, New York. Stuart already owned a winter home near Lake Orienta where he had spent several previous winters. Six months later, in March 1906, Stuart sold all the property to S. Maxwell McIntyre of New Hartford, New York. McIntyre had been wintering in Altamonte Springs for a number of years. In 1904 he purchased the fifteen-room mansion located on a three-acre tract at the corner of Massachusetts Avenue and Park Place which subsequently became known as the Bradlee-McIntyre House. By the time he purchased the hotel

Two of the "cottages" built in the late nineteenth century by the winter residents. This photograph was taken about 1910.

and accompanying property, McIntyre and his wife were leaders of the Altamonte Springs community and apparently wished to see the Altamonte Hotel succeed. In any event, neither he nor Dr. Stuart ever interfered with the proprietorship of the hotel.[55]

The McIntyres sold the property back to the Stuarts who resold it to Daniel E. Judd of Morris, Connecticut, in 1909. Within months Judd had sold it to Eli Swavely of Washington, D. C. Through these many changes of ownership, Bates ended up with a $10,000 mortgage in his favor. He then assigned the mortgage to one J. D. Dotson, presumably for cash with which to make the long-awaited improvements to the hotel property. Nathan H. Fogg, Altamonte Springs' most enthusiastic booster, proudly proclaimed in late 1909 that the "present owners of the famous Altamonte are transforming the formerly unsightly structure to a most pleasing edifice."[56]

No Room at the Inn

The refurbishing of the hotel and its grounds was a welcome enhancement of the town, but the hotel was already being filled to capacity each season. With accommodations for one hundred fifty guests, it usually opened about December lst each year and closed for the summer in April. According to the *Sanford Herald*, "the popular tourist hotel" was

View of Lake Orienta from the Altamonte Hotel grounds about 1906.

scheduled to open in December 1908 "and is already assured of a full house for the entire season." At that time the hotel was being managed by S. M. Johnson, who spent his summers as proprietor of the Shirley Hill Hotel in Shirley Hill, New Hampshire.[57]

J. K. Zerbe succeeded Johnson as the hotel's manager until the 1911–1912 season when George E. Bates and Son resumed active management. Through the *Orlando Reporter-Star* in early 1912, George and Everett Bates invited readers to "come and get the best dinner around" at the Altamonte Hotel, only nine miles north of Orlando.[58]

Proclaiming in 1915 that "Altamonte [Is] All Right," the *Orlando Sentinel* reported that the hotel was enjoying "a generous patronage," that it was filled to capacity, and that some people had been turned away to seek lodging in Winter Park or Orlando. The newspaper recommended that "rooms for next season should be arranged now." At that time, George Bates announced that he and his son would enlarge the hotel as soon as the war was over.[59]

Summer in New England

Bates continued to manage the Grand Hotel at Mont Vernon, New Hampshire, during the summers, and many of his guests followed him from Altamonte to the Grand and back again. "Bates has a large following," declared the *Sanford Herald*. The paper singled out the unusual case of Mrs. Margerita McMichael of Toronto, Canada, who had a "beautiful home in Altamonte Springs," but spent her summers at the Grand where she found the familiar company of many of her winter neighbors at her Florida home.[60]

Clearing the Title

After all the transactions involving the property of the original Altamonte Springs Company, Bates finally cleared his title to the hotel, its grounds, and the tramway sometime before 1920. That property was not included when Eli Swavely sold his remaining holdings at Altamonte Springs to J. E. Bartlett of Orlando that year.[61]

Lake Adelaide and the Altamonte Hotel's Springhouse.

The Fuller Store about 1915–1917. By this time A. H. Fuller had added a gasoline pump to accommodate an increasing number of automobiles in the town.

Fuller's Store in the early 1900s as it appeared before it was rebuilt by Arthur Fuller in 1905.

The Larger Community

While the Altamonte Hotel, surrounded by villas and fine winter residences, was the focal point of Altamonte Springs in the early twentieth century, there were important parts of the community at the eastern end of the tramway. After 1902 the Atlantic Coast Line Railroad was serving the community. During the winter season, the hotel trolley met all arriving trains at the ACL station. J. L. Baily was station agent, Western Union operator, and Southern Express Agent until about 1910. He was then succeeded by J. W. Powell who carried out the same multiple duties.[62]

Roswell S. Fuller was postmaster and storekeeper in the old store building on the railroad siding across the street from the station until 1905. He was then succeeded by Arthur H. Fuller in both positions. The younger Fuller built a new store building that same year on the same property at the corner of Longwood and Altamonte avenues. He carried general merchandise, hardware, dry goods, and drugs, offering delivery service in a horse-drawn wagon to customers in a large surrounding area. By 1913 he had installed gasoline pumps in front of his store for the benefit of an increasing number of automobile owners. Arthur H. Fuller operated the store until the early 1920s when his son, Herbert E. Fuller, took it over. The younger Fuller remained in business in the same location for many more years. The building itself was finally demolished in the late 1960s.[63]

Fuller's was not the only store in Altamonte Springs at the time. The black community of Winwood had grown to sizable proportions in the northern part of the Frost Addition. Constituting nearly 40 percent of the permanent population of Altamonte Springs, that community was served by J. W. Ford and his wife who ran a store for many years.

Fresh meat was sold by Thomas Gordon, who probably sold his product from a wagon as was customary in most small Central Florida communities at that time. Joseph M. Lewis was still a building contractor and a grove caretaker until his retirement about 1915.[64]

C. A. Dallas was a stone and brick mason who manufactured his own bricks. He did foundation work for many of the homes being built, and he was also busy building sidewalks and walkways to several homes as people began improving their houses and grounds in keeping with the progressive spirit at the time. In 1913 he was building walkways for Arthur Fuller at his handsome cottage situated on a five-acre tract not far from his store.[65]

The Altamonte Chapel

An important addition to the community came in 1908 when the Altamonte Chapel first opened for services. On a hunting trip near Lake Brantley, Arthur Fuller and Maxwell McIntyre found the long-forgotten Lake Brantley Union Chapel building in dense undergrowth. The building had been deeded by the Lewton family to Rollins College in the 1890s in exchange for their daughter's tuition. McIntyre contacted Rollins and the school happily sold the vacant building to him for six hundred dollars. It was then moved to a site facing the tramway in Altamonte Springs, and was refurbished by Fuller and Joseph Lewis.

Beginning in 1908, services were held in the chapel—during the winter months only—for many years. Visiting preachers were secured by a voluntary committee, whose task was simplified because a number of retired ministers wintered at Altamonte Springs and other nearby towns.[66]

This is Salem Avenue in front of the Fisher residence on the west side of Lake Orienta about 1917.

Schools

There were still two public schools in Altamonte, one for whites and the other for blacks. Another school for black children was located at Woodbridge. There were frequent changes of teachers at all three. Mattie McNaly taught at the white school in 1902 for a salary of thirty dollars per month. Miss Nellie O'Neil started the year at the white school in 1903, but she was removed and replaced by Miss L. R. Baker at a salary of thirty-five dollars. Mrs. E. B. Baker was then teaching at the black school for which service she was receiving twenty dollars per month. She was succeeded a little later by Allie Ward who was paid thirty dollars per month. Although it was not uncommon for whites to be paid higher salaries than blacks at that time, some of the variations were related to the numbers of children attending the different schools.[67]

The citizens of Altamonte Springs and Longwood voted in 1912 to become a special tax district which enabled the board to assess three mills in additional taxes for improvement of the schools. The board of trustees for the new district was composed of C. W. Entzminger and W. V. Dunn of Longwood and J. W. Osteen of Altamonte Springs. The same board members continued in office when the new Seminole County was created in 1913. As a practical matter, Osteen oversaw the Altamonte Springs schools while Entzminger and Dunn attended to those at Longwood. During the transitional period, Estelle Hyer taught at the Altamonte Springs white school while Kate Riley was teaching at the black school. Teachers came and went with some regularity, but there was little change in the public school system itself until the 1920s. A few local residents sent their children to schools outside the area. For example, Joseph Lewis sent his son, Joey, to Jacksonville where he boarded while school was in session. Others sometimes sent their children to the Catholic school in Orlando.[68]

The Winter Colony

The railroad station with its express agency and telegraph office were open year round as were both Fuller's and Ford's stores. The schools opened about the first of September and remained in session for six to eight months. But Altamonte Springs really came alive in late November when the winter residents began arriving, some to open their own residences and others to stay at the hotel which was usually receiving guests by December 1. The Altamonte Improvement Association is a good example of the influence of the winter residents. Organized in the winter of 1908–1909 at about the time automobiles were beginning to appear, its president was C. G. Justice, a winter resident, who owned "a palatial winter home and is extensively interested in fruit culture." The vice-president was I. McMichael, the general manager of the Great Northwest-

Tram awaiting departing guests at the Altamonte Hotel in early 1900s.

Hotel tram (known as the Dixie Flyer*) preparing to leave the hotel with guests going to the railroad station.*

Hotel tram going toward the railroad station with guests.

This group of winter visitors came up the St. Johns River by boat before boarding the train for Altamonte Springs. In the back row, second and third from the left, are Charles D. and Katherine Haines. They began visiting during the winters about 1913 before settling permanently about 1918.

The Juthe House at 724 Lake Street. Probably built by Peter Nolan about 1890 as a full-time residence. It is named for Kristian Juthe who lived there with his family for many years. It is presently the property of Tim and Bonnie Donihi.

The Caldwell House, which stood near the railroad track on the east side of Longwood Road (C.R. 427) on Altamonte Avenue (S.R. 436) for many years, was built about 1900 as a full-time residence.

ern Telephone Company of Canada, who wintered in his "Orienta View," described as "the beauty spot of Altamonte."

Organized at the same time was the Ladies Aid Society, presided over by Mrs. S. Maxwell (Annie K.) McIntyre. At about the same time that the hotel was being renovated, the two organizations were applauded for "doing a good job in improving the village."[69]

One of their projects in 1909 was "pine strawing" the road to Palm Springs, "a distance of three miles." In a story about the project, Nathan Fogg explained that Palm Springs had become quite famous "since the discovery of its medicinal qualities and the beautiful tropical scenery." People from Altamonte Springs, Longwood, and even Sanford had been having picnics there for several years. With the improvement of the road by the Altamonte Improvement Association and the Ladies Aid Society, Fogg wrote, "auto parties visit the springs daily."[70]

The local inhabitants welcomed the winter residents enthusiastically. Many watched as the hotel trolley met the incoming trains and carried the guests to the hotel. Those with their own winter homes were also welcome to ride the trolley. Quite often, they stayed at the hotel a few days until their homes were opened. Even more often, they dined in the

Orienta View. The Winter home of I. McMichael, general manager of the Great Northwestern Telephone Company of Canada. Photograph dated c. 1913.

View from the north toward Martha G. Smith's "Bide-a-wee" home near the northwestern shore of Lake Orienta. This spelling of the name was furnished by the Fuller family and is probably correct. The spelling in the text came from Nathan Fogg's letter to the Sanford Herald, *November 10, 1911.*

Martha Smith on the steps of her home talking to Lucy Patch, a well-known actress who spent many winters in Altamonte Springs. This photograph is dated 1912.

hotel dining room. Sometimes it was the other way around. Residents with their own homes frequently arrived before the hotel opened. They were often accompanied by family members or friends who stayed with them until the hotel opened. This was the case in late November 1908 when Dr. J. Southerland Stuart brought with him E. O. Marshall and his sisters, Mrs. M. J. Fabraham and Mrs. Tilson. All three were guests of the Stuarts until the hotel opened. Mrs. Fabraham apparently liked the place. She soon built her own home on Maitland Avenue overlooking Lake Orienta.[71]

Even with the winter residents, Altamonte Springs remained a small, close-knit community. Fogg was probably correct when he reported that "this beautiful little village is now in possession of tourists and winter residents . . . One big happy family and Johnson provides every need at the hotel."[72]

The Landman home on the Apopka Road just west of the Little Wekiva River about 1917. Nina Landman married Everett C. Bates, owner and longtime manager of the Altamonte Hotel.

Everett Bates at Palm Springs about 1915.

A Bates Family birthday party on the hotel grounds in 1904.

Not only was it a social event when people arrived at the station, Fogg saw to it that each new group was reported by name in the columns of the Sanford and Orlando newspapers. A typical notice was the one which appeared on November 10, 1911. Mr. and Mrs. Obed Foss of Philadelphia, who had been wintering at Altamonte Springs since the early 1880s, were accompanied by L. Johnson and family, also of Philadelphia. Mr. and Mrs. Frank Smith and Miss Ruth Graham of Lancaster, New Hampshire, were on the same train. The Smiths had also been spending their winters at Altamonte Springs in their bungalow, the "Bye-de-Wie" on a "bluff overlooking beautiful Lake Orienta." Others in this group were F. Kingsley and family from Troy, New York, and George E. Bates and family who were preparing for the opening of the hotel on December 1.[73]

The tourist season was already in full force in late January 1909 when a number of late arrivals stepped off the train. Among them were Philadelphians Daniel Lees, and the Rev. Mr. Tupper and his wife. S. Maxwell McIntyre of New Hartford, New York, and Mr. and Mrs. Thomas Sprague of Scranton, Pennsylvania, who usually spent half the year at Altamonte Springs, accompanied them. Also from Scranton came LeRoy Park. John and K. C. McCullough were from Minneapolis. Mr. and Mrs. Charles McManus and Clara M. Sperry were from Hartford, Connecticut. There was also the Honorable J. L. Briggs and his wife from Saratoga Springs, New York. J. E. Graves was from Mt. Sterling, Kentucky and Mrs. L. A. Read was the only arrival from Newton Center, Massachusetts. The "one big happy family" was also quite an eclectic one by the early twentieth century.[74]

The Altamonte Hotel was known throughout the area for its excellent dining. This view of a portion of the dining room was published by George E. Bates and Son.

View of the parlor of the Altamonte Hotel. From a brochure published by George E. Bates and Son.

George E. Bates (left) and fishing partners (hotel guests) after a successful outing on Lake Orienta about 1910–1912.

Everett C. Bates and "Preacher" Edwards with their catch from Lake Orienta about 1916.

Everett and George E. Bates brewing coffee at a hotel picnic at Shepherd Springs about 1912.

Katherine Haines (center) and friends at Palm Springs in 1918.

Katherine Haines (top) and friends posing for the camera at Palm Springs in 1918.

Another group arrived in mid-February. Among them were F. D. Larabee of Minneapolis, James Calder, Jr., of Montpelier, Vermont, Mr. and Mrs. E. A. Gillespie of Woodhaven, Rhode Island, Mr. and Mrs. J. B. Hallett of Bridgeport, Connecticut, and Mr. and Mrs. Frederick S. Ely of Granville, New Hampshire.[75]

There were also visitors from other Florida locations. People frequently motored from Orlando to dine at the hotel and some spent a few days there from time to time. Two noted guests were Mr. and Mrs. James Laughlin, III, of the Jones and Laughlin Steel Company, who themselves had a fine estate at Zellwood. The Laughlins spent several days in 1908 at the hotel as guests of Mrs. M. J. Fabraham.[76]

Lillian Wilkens from Amherst, New Hampshire, posing near the Altamonte Hotel in 1917.

George E. and Everett C. Bates and their wives in front of the Altamonte Hotel in 1920.

The Social Scene

In addition to golf on the hotel links, bowling, boating and fishing on the local lakes, horseback and carriage rides, and picnics at Palm Springs, the winter colony seems to have enjoyed a full social life. The Saturday evening hops "in the spacious hall of the hotel" were popular. There were also lectures, musicals, and card parties. Many of the socials were at the hotel, but individuals also opened their homes for parties. About fifty people attended a Wednesday evening card party held by Mrs. Franklin F. Davis where "her large parlors and beautiful grounds were lit with Japanese lanterns and other lights."[77]

A special party was celebrated in March 1909 when about fifty of his friends gathered in the home of Charles H. Brown for his eighty-ninth birthday. Well known for his development and manufacture of the "Brown steam engine," the celebrity was toasted by Frank Smith and S. Maxwell McIntyre, both of whom had known him in national business circles. Mrs. Frank Smith read a poem written for the occasion.[78]

Not all the celebrities were winter residents. At a Fourth of July celebration at Sanford in 1913, special notice was taken of Joseph M. Lewis and Nathan H. Fogg as the two oldest residents of Altamonte Springs. Both had lived there about thirty years by that time.[79]

Spotlight on Altamonte Springs

Later that fall, the *Sanford Herald* carried a special section on Altamonte Springs which featured Lewis and Fogg along with Arthur Fuller and Thomas Sprague. Along with the three full-time stalwarts of the community, Sprague was selected as representative of the winter colony. A

View of the entire length of Lake Orienta from the Altamonte Hotel porch.

prominent business figure from Scranton, Pennsylvania, Sprague was president of the Sprague and Henwood Diamond Drill Company and vice president of the People's National Bank of Scranton. By 1913 he was spending about half the year at Altamonte Springs in a home for whose comfort and beauty "neither money nor labor has been spared." His place included about ten acres, more than half of which was devoted to orange groves.[80]

A Discordant Note

Altamonte Springs was a happy place experiencing considerable growth and improvement during the progressive era and the winter season was filled with good times and gala events. But not all the news was good. Like her neighboring southern states, Florida had reached its lowest ebb in race relations in the early years of the twentieth century. It was all-too-common for mobs to abduct and lynch blacks accused of certain crimes, thus denying them the opportunity for trial. Palm Springs, the place where happy outings and picnics were enjoyed by residents of Altamonte Springs and neighboring communities, was the site of such an atrocity in 1915. A black man named Will Reed had allegedly "assaulted a white lady" at Forest City. He was apprehended by Sheriff C. M. Hand who—realizing the potential for trouble—took him to Orlando for "safe keeping." When it appeared that the Orlando jail might not be safe, Reed was again moved to Kissimmee. About fifty men from the Forest City area

Altamonte Hotel guests teeing off for a golf competition.

Looking south-southwest from hotel grounds across the northern section of Lake Orienta.

Looking across Lake Orienta toward the Altamonte Hotel. From a brochure published by Bates and Son.

View from near the Altamonte Hotel boat landing across Lake Orienta after the gazebo was built on the point.

boarded the train to Kissimmee, overpowered the jailor, and took Reed. Early the next morning the unfortunate man was found "swinging in the breeze from a live oak branch at the railroad crossing at Palm Springs."[81]

Economic Pursuits

Not only had Central Florida recovered from the destructive weather of the 1890s, but acreage had expanded considerably. Nearly everyone around Altamonte Springs had groves. Dr. P. Phillips, one of the largest growers in Central Florida, had a ninety-acre grove at the south end of Lake Orienta. Typical of the newcomers to Altamonte Springs was A. W. Mullen from Muscogee, Oklahoma. Within "a stone's throw of the Altamonte Hotel" he had built a bungalow and planted three acres in oranges. One of the replanted groves was owned by Mrs. Elizabeth M.

Beginning in the late 1890s "bicycling" became very popular throughout the United States, soon reaching Altamonte Springs. Here, Arthur Fuller is about to board his bicycle at Spring Lake.

Guests arriving at the Fuller home at Spring Lake in the early 1900s.

Arthur Fuller's residence on Altamonte Avenue just west of his store about 1913.

Joseph M. Lewis residence.

Saunders-Massey from Toronto, Canada. Her "Hoosier Springs Grove" was located near the old Altamont community. Another of the freeze-damaged groves which was in production again was the one formerly owned by Dr. William Heron and located about a mile and a half south of Palm Springs.[82]

As the commercial importance of citrus increased, local growers joined those across the state to improve marketing conditions. Some sort of organization was needed to control the destructive practice of shipping green fruit, to obtain better freight rates, and to take advantage of the benefits of volume buying and selling. The eventual solution to these needs was the Florida Citrus Exchange, "the first few faltering steps" toward which were taken in 1909. Nathan Fogg was one of the founders of the organization. Although many growers remained independent of the Exchange, it was the vehicle through which many others, both large and small, bought their supplies and marketed their fruit in subsequent years.[83]

Nathan Fogg's home at Oak Knoll Farm. Drawing by Richard M. Wyman from an obscure photograph in the Sanford Herald, *December 19, 1913.*

N. H. Fogg & Company

Nathan Fogg was not only the voice of Altamonte Springs who wrote promotional pieces for various newspapers. He was also engaged in many commercial enterprises. He and his longtime neighbor, Joseph Lewis, managed most of the groves of winter residents in the community. Both also dealt extensively in real estate. Fogg platted the Fogg Addition to Altamonte Springs along Maitland Avenue on the southern edge of the community. He also sold individual lots in other areas and dealt in acreage as well.[84]

Oak Knoll Farm

But the centerpiece of Fogg's activities was Oak Knoll Farm which he owned in partnership with his son-in-law, J. W. Osteen, who was the managing partner. A sixty-acre tract almost in the heart of Altamonte Springs, Oak Knoll was a showplace enjoyed by many of the tourists who visited the community each year. In addition to several acres of producing citrus trees, the farm boasted a large pecan grove which produced more than a ton of nuts almost annually. Fogg and Osteen also had a large herd of hogs, which they were constantly improving. They were especially proud of their Longfellows and Duroc Jerseys which had been added in 1908 and 1913.[85]

Forest Products

During the years following the 1894–95 freezes, a number of people turned to the abundant pine forests for their livelihoods. By the

Several members of the Fuller family at Spring Lake in one of the many young citrus groves which had been planted after the great freezes.

early 1900s, both turpentine farms and lumber camps were important parts of the local economy. The Warnell Lumber Company already had extensive holdings in Central Florida when in 1901 it purchased a large tract in the old Altamont area, part of which had once belonged to Dr. Washington Kilmer. It also included land which is now part of Rolling Hills and Knollwood. In 1906 Moses Overstreet bought a half interest in the Warnell Company. Over the next few years, Overstreet erected four turpentine stills, one of which was located just north of Longwood. Gum rosin which he extracted from trees in the old Altamont area was distilled into turpentine at the Longwood plant. In 1923 the Overstreet Investment Company was organized to manage his extensive interests. Turpentine operations continued for a time, but the new firm was also engaged in real estate.[86]

The Fargo Lumber Company, owned and operated by B. D. McIntosh, Sr., moved to Altamonte Springs from South Georgia in 1919. It was in operation there on and off from 1919 until the early 1950s.[87]

Automobile Roads

The Florida Good Roads Association, which was holding conventions at Orlando by the late 1890s, had made considerable progress by the early 1900s as more and more individuals purchased automobiles. Counties were taking over responsibility for major arterial roads and taking measures to coordinate their routes from one county to another. They were still searching for suitable materials with which to surface the roads,

Arthur Fuller driving a two-horse wagon near his barn in the early 1900s. The boy on the left is unidentified.

however. Pine straw, such as had been used by the Altamonte Improvement Association on the Palm Springs road, was easily available and seemed briefly to be a solution. The Orange County road department, for example, was ordered as late as 1912 to straw the road from Altamonte Springs to Apopka by way of Forest City. But pine straw decayed too rapidly to be effective. Clay was in short supply and limestone was difficult to process at the time.[88]

By 1909 there was a road of sorts running from Jacksonville to Tampa by way of Sanford and Orlando. One could travel from Sanford to Altamonte Springs along that route in about half an hour. The road wound from Sanford through Longwood to Altamonte Springs, reaching that place near the railroad station, turning westward beside the tramway on Altamonte Avenue to Maitland Avenue, then south along that road. But the entire route from Jacksonville could be tortuous. On his way from Scranton in January 1909, for example, Thomas Sprague left Jacksonville in his "elegant touring car," but lost four days mired in a swamp on the way. Sympathizing with Sprague over his ordeal, the *Sanford Herald* boasted that he was "now making daily trips over the well-kept roads of Orange County." It was true that Orange County had made progress with its roads, but it still had a long way to go.[89]

Road-building advocates began talking about a brick road as early as 1909. Discussions were still under way when Seminole County was detached from Orange in 1913. Two years later both counties voted to issue bonds for construction of brick highways. The bonds were approved by large majorities in both counties. The Altamonte Springs precinct vote was eight to two in favor. With those funds, a nine-foot brick highway was completed over the route already laid out. It was open to Orlando in January 1917. Presumably Miss Irene Fuller was then able to drive over the new road in the runabout which she had acquired in 1914.[90]

Mamie and Irene Fuller embarking on a drive to Eustis and Mount Dora. They are on Altamonte Avenue in front of the Fuller residence and Altamonte Chapel.

The next major road issue was raised when Carl Fisher announced plans for the Dixie Highway which he envisioned to run from Chicago to Miami. Nearly every community between the two cities organized Dixie Highway Associations aimed at securing a place on the route. Seminole County was just as determined as all the others, but the coastal route was eventually chosen, along with another which meandered through Apopka, Orlando, Pinecastle, and southward. Because there was such an outcry from the towns which had been left out, yet another alternate route was chosen. The *Sanford Herald* lamented that the Sanford-to-Orlando highway had to settle for a place on the "scenic route from Jacksonville to Arcadia." Despite this limitation, people in and around Altamonte Springs referred to their brick road as "the Dixie Highway" for many years.[91]

The F. G. Rush Automobile Service Company established a bus line in 1915. It first went from Orlando to Maitland, but was soon extended to Sanford, serving the communities along the way. By 1917 Seminole County towns were being served by the Orange Belt Auto Line.[92]

And Telephones, Too

B. A. Galloway's Winter Park Telephone Company extended its service to Altamonte Springs in the early 1900s. The directory for 1913

After about 1915 when the Sanford-Orlando highway and other roads were improved, promotional motorcades became quite popular. This touring car was representing the Altamonte Hotel in a motorcade in 1917.

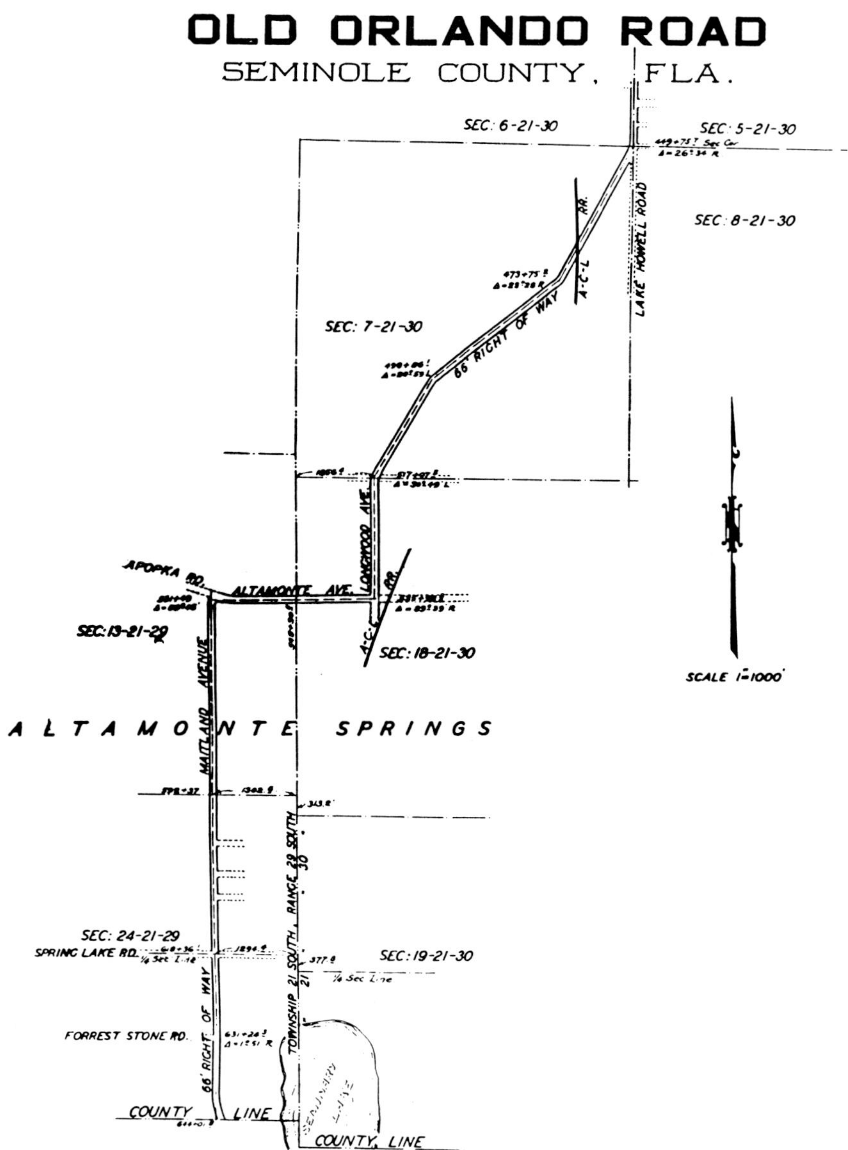

The Sanford–Orlando Road about 1915. Long known as the "Dixie Highway" this was the main route to Orlando until S.R. 3 was completed about a mile east of Altamonte Springs in the late 1920s.

showed Altamonte Springs with three numbers and six subscribers. Extension 441 served the Altamonte Hotel and the Bates residence. Extension 437 went to Fuller's Store, the Arthur Fuller home, and the office of N. H. Fogg. Mrs. F. F. Davis had her own residential line. By 1917 the system had grown to ten lines. By that time Fogg and Company had its own number, as did the Altamonte Hotel and Fuller's store. Dr. Nathan Griffin could be reached at his office and home and Dr. P. Phillips' Altamonte Grove had a telephone. Others went to the homes of A. H. Fuller, Mrs. E. M. Massey, A. A. Stone, and C. A. Dallas. There was even a pay station at Fuller's store.[93]

County Division

When State Representative Forrest Lake first called for the creation of a new county to be carved from Orange in late 1912, there seemed to be little opposition. But when it was learned that he planned to draw between Maitland and Winter Park and south of Apopka, a great hue and cry arose. A verbal duel developed between the *Sanford Herald* and the Orlando newspapers. Indignation meetings were held in all the Orange County towns from Oviedo to Apopka protesting their proposed inclusion in the new Seminole County. Nathan Fogg joined in the protest. "No county division for us," he protested. It was an outrage, he wrote, "to please a few ambitious men, who desire to hold lucrative positions in the new county." If the citizens permitted this, "they will be sorry when they are sober."[94]

Lake and the divisionists hurriedly reshaped the boundaries of their proposed new county to allay the opposition. Apopka and northwest Orange County were spared and the line was moved northward so as to leave Maitland where it was. But Fogg's protests were fruitless. The new line was drawn between Maitland and Altamonte Springs near Woodbridge. He was a good loser, though. Expressing his sorrow that Orange County was split, Fogg called on his neighbors to "get to work and make the deed a success."[95]

The First World War

With a population of only 323 according to the state census of 1915, Altamonte Springs was not a major player in the first world war, but its citizens pitched in to do their part. At a mass meeting, they resolved to plant more food crops to reduce their dependence on food shipments from outside the area. They willingly accepted efforts to conserve meat, sugar, and other scarce commodities. Perhaps most important of all they watched as several of their able-bodied sons marched off to war. William A. Samuels, George Stevens, and James M. Evans were the first to go. William T. House, Ellis Blair, Alfred Powers, James B. Foster, and Isaac H. China were first placed on a waiting list, but several of them were called later. Arthur Fuller was Altamonte Springs chairman for each of the Liberty Loan drives and his neighbors subscribed to each of them. Like their counterparts throughout the nation, however, they all cheered when the war ended in November 1918.[96]

A Seminole County Community

Altamonte Springs residents agreed with Nathan Fogg when he asked them to make the best of the new county. When a county board of trade was organized, Howard Lyman was named as the town's representative. An Altamonte Springs auxiliary to the board was organized. When voting precincts were established, Altamonte Springs was joined by Longwood and Lake Mary in precinct number 11. Inspectors changed from time to time, but in 1919 they were J. W. Osteen, H. Fuller, and F. Henkel. W. B. Ballard was clerk. The polling place—at the school house—was not too crowded. When a local election was called in 1919 to decide whether to require that hogs be prevented from roaming the streets, the electorate turned out nine to zero in favor of penning the animals.[97]

But a Dissatisfied One

The citizens of Altamonte Springs finally decided they did not like their affiliation with Seminole County. "A largely attended mass meeting" in June 1920 reminded all that they had originally opposed their inclusion in the new county. Since 1913, they had been ignored by the officials of the new county, their roads had been neglected, and they had received nothing in return for their taxes. They further pointed out that Altamonte Springs was only nine miles from Orlando, but fourteen miles from Sanford, "over much inferior roads." Having expressed their dissatisfaction, they resolved that a committee be appointed to appear before the legislature and request their return to Orange County. The committee was made up of Charles D. Haines, J. W. Osteen, A. W. Mullen, Joseph W. Lewis, A. E. Cline, George Kingsley, A. H. Fuller, A. G. Haines, Ed. N. Mitchell, C. A. Dallas, R. S. Blanchard, Howard Lyman, E. W. Mitchell, W. E. Sinclair, J. A. Collins, W. B. Ballard, Charles E. Bowers, Forest Stone, and H. J. White.[98]

Whether or not the Altamonte Springs citizens expected results from their protests is not clear. In any event, having expressed their unhappiness, they were already planning to incorporate the Town of Altamonte Springs.

SIX

The Town of Altamonte Springs, Inc.

There was considerable enthusiasm over the incorporation. . .but it was not long before disagreements surfaced. With only 441 inhabitants—a considerable proportion of whom spent only a part of the year there—the town's boundaries included a large amount of land which was used only for agricultural purposes. Some of the owners of that property were not anxious to pay taxes for municipal services which they felt they did not need.

The First World War was over by 1920 and the disillusionment over the Paris Peace Treaty had not yet set in. The eighteenth Amendment to the United States Constitution had been ratified and America was entering into the great social experiment of "prohibition." The nineteenth Amendment was ratified in the fall of 1920 just in time to permit women to vote for the first time. The progressive spirit of the first two decades of the century continued, but in a different form sometimes referred to as "business progressivism." The earlier "boards of trade" were becoming "chambers of commerce." People were increasingly more interested in improving their communities, not only for themselves, but also to attract new enterprises. Improved public services such as water works, electricity, hard-surfaced roads and streets, police and fire protection, public parks, and better schools were envisioned as desirable means to encourage growth. Since everyone would benefit from such services, it seemed logical that they be financed by public revenue. Municipal incorporation was a logical step toward those ends.

On October 11, 1920, twenty-eight "qualified voters"—including ten women—posted notices at the post office, school house, and the ACL depot declaring their desire to "form a municipal corporation to be known as Altamonte Springs, Florida." They invited all concerned citizens to meet at the school house on November 11, 1920 to carry out that purpose.[99]

On November 11, forty-two registered voters—fourteen of whom were women and at least thirteen of whom were black—met at the school house for the important occasion. H. L. Haight was named chairman of the meeting and he immediately introduced George A. DeCottes, the Sanford city attorney, who spoke about the advisability of incorporation. After some discussion, it was moved that "a municipal corporation be formed to be known as Altamonte Springs, Florida." When the question was called, the vote was thirty-eight to seven in favor of incorporation.[100]

Having decided upon incorporation, the assembly moved on to the election of a mayor, seven alderman, a town clerk, and a town marshal. Elmer T. Haines became the first mayor. The seven aldermen were:

The twenty-eight qualified voters were:

Howard C. Lyman
Lotta E. Osteen
H. L. Haight
Arthur A. Lewis
R. E. Hoffman
Elmer T. Haines
A. H. Fuller
Andrew G. Haines
W. B. Ballard
W. T. Whitehead
Herbert E. Fuller
Mary E. Whitehead
A. E. Cline
Luella Haight
C. A. Dallas
Mary A. Fuller
Joey M. Lewis
Marion T. Ballard
J. W. Osteen
Preston D. Coombs
George Kingsley
Ella W. Coombs
H. C. Tyler
Mary L. Haines
Emma Abbot Lyman
Gordon Deramus
Ruth Fuller
Emmie Deramus

The forty-two voters at the meeting were:

A. H. Fuller
J. M. Lewis, Jr.
H. E. Fuller
Mrs. Ruth Fuller
Mrs. Mary Whitehead
W. T. Whitehead
Arthur A. Lewis
E. T. Haines
A. E. Cline
R. E. Hoffman
Mrs. R. E. Hoffman
Mrs. W. B. Ballard
W. B. Ballard
Mrs. Gordon Deramus
Mrs. E. T. Haines
Mrs. H. L. Haight
H. L. Haight
Mrs. A. H. Fuller
Mrs. J. W. Osteen
Mrs. Mary Haines
A. G. Haines
H. C. Lyman
Mrs. Emma Lyman
*John Colson
Lester Mason
*Henry Simmons
*Effie Simmons
*W. L. Medlock
*A. B. Ford
*Levi Price
*W. L. Hayman
*W. L. Pearsall
*J. B. Tanner
*P. Edwards
*Ida Hayman
James Wilson
*W. E. Merritt
*Isaac Jimerson
______ Morris
Henry Mason
Eugene Orr
Fannie Orr

The asterisk denotes the black voters.

J. W. Osteen, R. E. Hoffman, H. L. Haight, A. H. Fuller, George Kingsley, W. B. Ballard, and A. G. Haines. A. E. Cline was elected clerk. The first town marshal was H. E. Fuller who served until 1922 when he was succeeded by Shade Carter. The new officials were sworn in and the Town of Altamonte Springs was in operation, awaiting only the approval of its charter by the state legislature.[101]

Charter Provisions

In the spring of 1921, the legislature enacted the charter as a routine matter. The document continued all officials in office and provided for elections in October, 1921 and every two years thereafter. The powers and duties of the municipality and its officials were then spelled out in thirty-one sections. The new town was required to preserve the peace and maintain order within its boundaries, and could establish a police force toward that end. The council—known as the board of aldermen, with the concurrence of the mayor, was empowered to pass and enforce ordinances aimed at preservation of the peace, health, safety, and welfare of the town and its inhabitants. There was accompanying authority for the mayor and council to provide a system of municipal taxes.

The charter spelled out the town's authority to "regulate or prohibit" the keeping of cattle, horses, swine, sheep, goats, dogs and other animals. Animals "running at large within the [town] limits," could be impounded without notice to the owners and sold for the costs incurred in their capture and retention.[102]

It was the duty of the town's officials to establish qualifications for voters, consistent with the election laws of the state. All persons who were qualified to vote were also eligible to hold office.

The mayor was not only to exercise the powers and duties "usually incident to that office," but he was also to preside over a mayor's court. In the latter capacity, he could require the marshal to bring before him those persons who violated any of the ordinances of the town. It was his duty to try the alleged offenders, decide guilt or innocence, and enforce penalties.

The town council was the legislative body with power to enact ordinances necessary to promote the peace, health, safety and general welfare of the town, to provide "for the working of convicted persons on the streets," and to regulate the compensation of all town officers and employees. It could levy taxes on all real and personal property, impose street taxes, and provide for the working of the streets. It was also empowered to require licenses on all occupations and businesses which were subject to state or county license fees. Taxes could not be levied at a rate higher than twenty mills on the dollar of the assessed value of the property. The mayor had five days to act upon each ordinance, after which it

The Community House was donated by Mayor and Mrs. B. L. Maltbie and was maintained over the years by the Ladies Auxiliary, the Women's Club, the Civic Club, and the Garden Club. This photograph was taken in 1955 after the Garden Club had just completed a renovation of both building and grounds.

became law without his signature. If he vetoed a measure, it could be passed over his objection by a majority of the council.[103]

The marshal was also the tax collector. As marshal, it was his duty to execute the laws of the town, arresting violators, and bringing them before the mayor for trial. As collector, he was responsible for collecting all taxes and license fees and for turning over all money collected to the treasurer. The position of marshal and collector was at first elective, but it was made appointive by the mayor and council in 1925.[104]

The town clerk attended all council meetings and kept records. He had additional duties as assessor and treasurer. He was to make annual assessments of property within the town limits, to compile an assessment roll, and certify it to the marshal and collector. He was then to receive all money collected, record it, and pay it out upon order of the council.[105]

Part-Time Residents, Full-Time Citizens

One of the council's first actions was to prescribe the qualifications for voting. Those qualifications conformed to the general laws of the state, with one important addition. While most of the forty-two voters who had attended the incorporation meeting were permanent residents of Altamonte Springs, the 1920 census reflected a population of 441. Some of them were the winter residents, a large number of whom had been active in community affairs for years. They were also among the largest property owners of the town. It was therefore logical—if not perhaps essential—that the council extended the right to vote in all elections to anyone who owned property and spent at least four months of the year there. And, of course, they were consequently eligible to hold office.[106]

The Community House

A town needs a home for its government and one of the winter residents soon provided one. Birdsie L. Maltbie, owner and chief operating officer of the Maltbie Chemical Company of East Orange, New Jersey, had been wintering in Altamonte Springs since about 1913. He had taken an active interest in local affairs since the town was incorporated. He had been, for example, a prime mover in efforts to obtain electricity for the town. He was certainly one of those whom the council had in mind when it provided that part-time residents could vote and hold office. Maltbie served several terms as mayor before eventually becoming a permanent resident of the town after his retirement in the early 1930s. He built a fine residence which still stands on Lake Avenue, bought and developed Maltbie Shores, and, because of the economic collapse of the late 1920s, became the town's major creditor.

Shortly after his election as mayor, Maltbie and his wife donated to the town a fully furnished Community House. Located on lots l, 2, and 3 in block D, of the Betts addition—almost directly across the street from the hotel—the edifice became the town hall as well as the meeting place for the chamber of commerce and most other civic organizations for many years. It was dedicated at a lavish ceremony in 1925 which featured speeches by Senator M. O. Overstreet and other dignitaries who seized the opportunity to praise the recently incorporated town for the progress it was making. The Community House and its grounds were maintained by various women's organizations, beginning with the Ladies Auxiliary to the Chamber of Commerce, in cooperation with the town council.[107]

Paying the Bills

There was considerable enthusiasm over the incorporation of the Town of Altamonte Springs, but it was not long before disagreements surfaced. With only 441 inhabitants—a considerable proportion of whom spent only a part of the year there—the town's boundaries included a large amount of land which was used only for agricultural purposes. Some of the owners of that property were not anxious to pay taxes for municipal services which they felt they did not need. Using the assessment rolls compiled by Town Clerk A. E. Cline, the council adopted a budget in early 1922 and assessed property for the requisite amount. The mayor returned the ordinance without his signature, saying that he had "received petitions from a large number of Altamonte Springs citizens opposing the measure." The board amended its figures in a new ordinance which was signed into law in September by Acting Mayor W. T. Whitehead. The townsmen who had objected to the original measure were apparently satisfied with the adjustments, but the owners of the agricultural land—especially Dr. P. Phillips and Charles D. Haines—continued their opposition to municipal taxes.[108]

Electric Service

An important ordinance was enacted in November 1921 granting a thirty-year franchise to the Altamonte Springs Electric Company. Copartners H. L. Haight, B. L. Maltbie, and T. A. Briggs were authorized to install and operate an electric light plant to serve the town. Whether or not the company ever produced electric power is not clear, but its charter was soon acquired by the Florida Public Service Company. That firm was installing transmission lines from its Orlando plant to furnish electricity for Altamonte Springs and other Seminole County towns by 1923. Power was made available to subscribers for lighting and other purposes, but it was not the full service to which residents are now accustomed. With limited capacity and a primary concern for lighting, the firm only provided electricity at night. Many local residents consequently installed above-ground water tanks which they filled during the evening hours for use the next day.[109]

Despite its limitations in the early years, electric service was a welcome addition. The council at first authorized street lights upon

The Dixie Flyer *approaching the railroad station while the tramway was still in use.*

request. A light was placed in front of the Community House shortly after its dedication in 1924 and a second one was added early the next year. At the request of those who resided nearby, a light was erected on the corner of Market Street near Will Merritt's residence about the same time. There was also a street light in the triangle at the intersection of Altamonte and Massachusetts avenues. In May 1925, nineteen additional lights were placed on Altamonte Avenue between Fuller's store and the hotel and along the street running south from that point.[110]

The White Way

The street lighting program soon became more comprehensive. As electricity became available and chambers of commerce became better organized throughout the region, it had become a matter of community pride to construct "White Ways." A town whose main street was lighted by a White Way was a progressive one. Altamonte Springs soon joined the movement. In early 1926, the town council authorized a White Way to run southward along Longwood Avenue, westward from Longwood Avenue on Altamonte Avenue to its intersection with Maitland Avenue, and then southward along that street. Foundations for the additional poles were completed in the summer of 1926, and 250-candlepower lights were turned on in the fall.[111]

In keeping with the promotional spirit of the 1920s, this sign was erected near Fuller's Store, calling attention to the Altamonte Hotel about a half mile away. Arthur Fuller is standing by the sign.

Farewell to the *Dixie Flyer*

The modern age was bringing other changes. The *Winter Park Herald* reported in 1923 that "the *Dixie Flyer*, Altamonte's famous horse drawn narrow gauge railway has been replaced. . . . No more will the rollicking car speed up and down the bumpy track occasionally running up on the heels of the horse stimulating it to dangerous antics." The paper continued that the new cement sidewalk from the station to the hotel "is a wonderful improvement to the appearance of the town." The "very beautiful avenue of trees" was retained, making the walkway, not only a utility, but also an attractive asset.[112]

Roads and Streets

As automobile traffic increased, so did the need for better roadways. The State Road Department could sometimes be relied upon to repair the main Sanford-to-Orlando road, still referred to as the "Dixie Highway," but streets were the concern of the town. In 1926, Marshal C. M. Hogg was given additional duty as road foreman. In that capacity he was to be paid eighty dollars per month for a five-and-a-half-day work week. From clay pits such as the one in the new Sanlando development near Tropic Hill Street, he and his successors put clay on a number of streets and repaired problem areas as needed, but street work was also

A view of Altamonte Avenue eastward from the hotel about 1923 just after the tramway tracks had been removed.

The Atlantic Coast Line Station in the mid-1920s. Note the automobile parked where the tram had formerly been housed.

The Altamonte Hotel as it looked from across Maitland Avenue in the 1920s.

The trains did not always run on time. This scene is the result of a wreck on the ACL Railroad in 1925 near Woodbridge, almost midway between Altamonte Springs and Maitland.

done by developers of new additions as well as by contract with individuals. In 1925, Weldon Johnson of Orlando contracted to cover Massachusetts Avenue with six inches of clay, sixteen feet wide, for thirty-eight cents per lineal foot. Pennsylvania Avenue was clayed a little later and the property owners were assessed the costs. Repairs to the Moccasin Bridge at Cranes Roost were made by contract. Orienta Avenue was hard-surfaced with money loaned to the town by B. L. Maltbie. Alderman George Bates was authorized to buy twenty-five bushels of oats to be sown along the new sidewalk between the station and his hotel.[113]

In early 1926, the council renamed several streets. Longwood Avenue, from its intersection with Altamonte Avenue northward was to be known as North Altamonte Avenue. Maitland Avenue, from its intersection with Altamonte Avenue southward was called South Altamonte Avenue. Orienta Avenue from its eastern end was to be extended northward to the intersection with Altamonte Avenue. The reasons for these changes are obscure, but the town certainly had its share of Altamonte avenues after 1926. Signs were placed at the hotel corner informing motorists that the road led northward to Sanford and Jacksonville, and southward to Orlando and Tampa. Town limit signs were erected about the same time.[114]

State Road Number Three

While the town was marking the Dixie Highway for the benefit of travelers, it was also supporting another project which eventually rerouted traffic away from it. The state road department and Seminole

This engine was apparently brought in by a crew attempting to clear wreckage from the track.

A view of Maitland Avenue southward from Magnolia in the 1920s.

County officials began planning in 1924 for S.R. 3 (now U.S. 17–92) which was to provide a shorter route between Sanford and Orlando. The county voted overwhelmingly for a bond issue to finance the project. The vote in Altamonte Springs was thirty to three in favor of the bonds. When negotiations over right-of-way and routing were completed, the new road was laid out about a mile east of both Altamonte Springs and Longwood. There was little adverse reaction in Altamonte Springs to the new road at the time, although Charles Haines spoke to the council about the advisability of connecting Altamonte Avenue with the new state highway. By the time S.R. 3 was completed and opened for traffic in 1928, convict labor was being used to open the desired connection. It might have worked out had it not been for the depression which struck shortly after the extension was completed. But, during the adversities of the 1930s, the connector fell

Katherine Haines in her touring car heading south on Maitland Avenue in the 1920s. Note the brick surface of the nine-foot road.

into disuse and Altamonte was left without direct access to the main highway between Sanford and Orlando.[115]

Building Permits

As the pace of new construction increased in the mid-1920s, the council acted to assure orderly growth. An ordinance of April 1925 provided that no dwelling costing less than $2,500 would be permitted on property abutting Altamonte Avenue within the corporate limits. An exception was made for property east of Market Street and south of Williams Street where dwellings costing at least five hundred dollars would be permitted. No garages costing less than two hundred dollars could be constructed.

Commercial construction was limited to Altamonte Avenue, beginning at Forest Avenue and running eastward and then northward "on the brick road" to East Street (now Merritt Street). At the suggestion of Ray Trovillion of Winter Park, who was then building in the business district, it was decided to make the commercial area a fire-proof zone. Consequently, all buildings to be used for business purposes were to be constructed of brick, tile, concrete, or "other equivalent," and any building "so constructed shall cost not less than $1,500." Stores, shops, and business buildings of the same value were also permitted on South Altamonte Avenue from a point just north of Ballard Street to the southern town limits.[116]

The new construction at Sanlando Springs and at the Sanlando Golf and County Club brought increased attention to the area. This road was constructed from Longwood to Sanlando Springs in 1926. Its route was similar to that of S.R. 434.

There were other restrictions. The land lying "east of Altamonte Avenue (now Longwood Avenue) and north of Williams Street" was to be designated as the "colored section" and no building permits were to be issued for residences of "colored people" outside of that district. The remaining portion of the Town of Altamonte Springs was designated as the "white section," and no building permits were to be issued to whites outside that section.[117]

To see that these regulations were enforced, George Babcock was appointed building inspector.[118]

A Cow in the Pound

Animals could be kept penned in the town limits at the discretion of the council. For example, Benjamin F. Haines was permitted to keep "mules, ducks, cows, and chickens" on his property and A. E. Cline was allowed to keep chickens. But no animals were allowed to run at large on the streets. An elaborate procedure was put in place for the apprehension and disposition of such animals. All horses, mules, cattle, swine, sheep or goats found running at large were to be impounded by the marshal. For larger animals, such as horses, mules, asses, and cattle, the cost of impounding was one dollar per head. If the marshal required assistance, there was an additional cost of twenty-fve cents per head. Keeping the animals cost fifty cents per head. The act of "making sale" was twenty-five cents per head. Penalties and costs for smaller animals, such as sheep and goats, was one-half that assessed for the larger ones. Finally, the cost for writing and serving notices was twenty-five cents. Animals were treated just as any other prisoner. The marshal reported routinely in late 1926 that he was holding "a prisoner in jail for driving while drunk, and a cow in the pound to be sold at auction."[119]

Traffic Control

Street improvements and increasing automobile traffic brought new problems. A tragedy occurred when seven-year-old Elliott Cox was struck by a car as he stepped off a school bus in March 1925. The driver was first arrested and then released when it was decided that the accident was unavoidable. But it was clear that rules of the road were becoming necessary. In an effort to stop speeding on the town streets, the council purchased a hand semaphore for the marshal's use on a measured half mile course. Alderman George Babcock donated a stop watch and the council asked the marshal to "try his hand at stopping the speeding in the town." There is no record of the success of this effort, but four months later Joseph Brinkley was hired as a temporary deputy marshal. He was paid four dollars per day to patrol the streets on a motorcycle.[120]

Prohibition

Enactment of the Volstead Act which prohibited the sale of alcoholic beverages in the nation, created a new enterprise for those willing to violate the law and a continuing headache for law enforcement officials at all levels. Seminole County Sheriff C. M. Hand and Deputy B. C. Wilcox were applauded in late 1924 when they seized a 750-gallon copper still near Lake Brantley. They were obliged to leave their car and wade through a waist-deep swamp to reach the still which was "cleverly concealed beneath a large cypress tree." The still was destroyed along with fifteen barrels of mash, but unfortunately no one was apprehended. Nearly two years later, deputies Wilcox and C. C. Stephens returned to the same area and found another still with a 2,000-gallon capacity. No arrests were made at this one either.[121]

The town marshals were also busy battling illicit liquor. Marshal Hogg destroyed a still in town in early 1927. In late 1928, his successor, J. C. Howell, found and destroyed one near Prairie Lake and another just north of town. When a tenant in a rental house in the Stewart addition was caught selling liquor, he was let off with a fine when he agreed to leave town.[122]

Murder in the First Degree

Alcohol was at least partially responsible for a much more serious affair involving Marshal Hogg. There were differing versions of what happened, but apparently the marshal drove up behind a car which was stopped on the highway because of a flat tire. An argument ensued and the marshal shot and killed Joe Cone—claiming self-defense. When it was all over John Gillespie, an occupant of the car, was charged with assault on the marshal. He and Robert and Gilbert Cone, brothers of the slain man, were all charged with "being drunk on the highway." At an inquest, Judge J. G. Sharon apparently did not believe the marshal's self-defense claim. Hogg was bound over to the grand jury on a first degree murder charge and his bond was set at $10,000.[123]

Health and Welfare

Health and welfare services were quite informal in the 1920s, but they were not ignored. When D. B. Kiegan reported a case of typhoid fever in a house near the Altamonte Garage, the council acted quickly. Alderman Frank P. Waterhouse was given full authority to handle the case and the affected members of the K. Wooten family—a man and his children—were taken to the Sanford Hospital for treatment. During their recovery, D. B. Kiegan—a neighbor—ministered to their needs while the town council paid for medicine and supplies. When it received the hospital bill of $520.93, the Seminole County Welfare Board asked the Altamonte Springs town council to pay half of it. The council agreed and a warrant for $260.46 was sent to the hospital.[124]

In early 1929, when a severe depression was beginning to grip the state and the nation, W. H. Layman, a Winwood resident, appeared before the council to report on the destitute condition of "Uncle Price." This was apparently Levi Price, one of the black citizens who had participated in incorporating the town. In this case, the aldermen each contributed to a fund for "Uncle Price's" benefit.[125]

Fire Fighting

Perhaps the best thing the town did to fight fires was to require buildings in the commercial district to be constructed of brick, concrete or equivalent, but the council did not stop there. In 1929 it voted to enter into a long term lease with George Bates for a garage to house fire equipment and Melvin Tyler was paid fifty dollars to remodel it. The council then paid $135 for a chemical engine. A siren, motorized equipment, ladders and lanterns were also purchased. Alderman B. O. Smith was put in charge of the fire equipment.[126]

Fire fighting featured cooperation among neighboring communities. It was quite common for nearby fire departments to rush to the aid of their neighbors when fires occurred. This kind of mutual assistance was demonstrated by a disastrous fire in late 1929. Mrs. Elmer T. Haines was shocked to see a fire next door in the home of Joseph Lewis, Sr., in which his widow still lived. She called the Winter Park and Maitland fire departments, both of which sent equipment to assist the new Altamonte Springs department. Despite their combined efforts, both the house and Mrs. Lewis were lost in the fire. The community was saddened by the death of a resident who had spent nearly forty years there, but it was also grateful for the assistance from Winter Park and Maitland. The mayor sent letters of thanks, and the local fire department treated the visiting firemen to a supper at Mary Stuart's Tea Room to demonstrate their appreciation.[127]

An Incipient Park Program

Altamonte Springs had been praised for more than forty years for its natural beauty and its recreational opportunities. It was a logical step for the newly incorporated town to build a park. When B. D. McIntosh of the Fargo Lumber Company offered to sell the town eight lots in the Frost addition for a park, the council set to work to complete the purchase. With its annual budget amounting to about $11,000 in the mid-1920s, however, the council was hard-pressed to find the $4,000 purchase price. B. L. Maltbie, the incumbent mayor, agreed to lend the necessary funds and the deal was concluded. Unfortunately, the financial stringencies of the latter 1920s prevented completion of the park, but the town never abandoned its desire for a park program. Its present recreational system is a tribute to that early vision.[128]

A Growing Town in the Booming 1920s

The 1920s were a period of great optimism, grand development plans, and expectations of great financial rewards. While the Town of Altamonte Springs was developing the institutions which made it a viable and lasting community, the chamber of commerce was actively promoting growth and development. The story of that growth, the social activities surrounding it, and its ultimate collapse is the subject of the following chapter.

SEVEN

Economic and Social Affairs in the 1920s

The inflationary boom which swept Florida in the 1920s was approaching its zenith by 1925. While it never affected Altamonte Springs to the extent it did the communities along the southeast coast, there was a distinct acceleration of development.

The *Sanford Herald* declared in 1921 that "Altamonte Springs has taken a spurt in the past year and having been incorporated has taken on a new life . . ." According to the paper, the newly incorporated town had long been the favorite wintering place for some of the nation's most prominent business leaders, but they had attempted to keep it to themselves. The town's new leadership was about to change that and make its "many advantages known to the outside world. . . ."[129]

The *Herald's* assertions were not exaggerated. There was a new emphasis on growth among the town's leaders. A local chamber of commerce was organized and supported by a large number of residents, including nearly all of those who had participated in incorporating the town. Howard Lyman, who had recently settled there with his famous wife, Emma Abbot Lyman, represented Altamonte Springs with the Seminole County Chamber. He saw that his adopted town was included in the promotional literature of that organization. There were other new residents determined to make the place better known. B. L. Maltbie, already introduced in the previous chapter, was "one of Altamonte's latest developers." But no one had a greater impact on the town in the 1920s than Charles D. Haines.[130]

Having first come to Altamonte Springs in 1913, the Honorable Charles D. Haines, a former New York congressman, began growing asparagus plumosis ferns shortly after World War I. According to an effusive story in the *Sanford Herald*, Haines was soon "developing on a gigantic scale his idea of catering to the esthetic sense of the nation . . . by growing ferns." By the early 1920s he was shipping ferns to all parts of the United States via the Atlantic Coast Line Railroad. His Royal Fern Corporation was chartered in 1922 with an authorized capital of $450,000. Haines was the majority stockholder with three hundred shares, but George Kingsley, the secretary/treasurer, was also a substantial investor with 145 shares. Vice President James A. Cotting of Winter Park owned five shares. Ed W. Mitchell was general manager.[131]

Charles D. Haines as he looked about 1920, after making Altamonte Springs his permanent home.

Charles D. Haines had served a single term in the 53rd Congress during a highly successful career in the railroad construction business. Starting as a telegrapher at age sixteen, he had worked his way upward quite rapidly. By the time he came to Altamonte Springs he had built and managed eighteen steam railroads and sixteen street railways in fifteen states and Canada. Coming to Florida for his health, he was captivated by the place and soon purchased an estate at Altamonte Springs on the west side of Lake Orienta. During the following years he entertained a number of national dignitaries with whom he had become acquainted during his long business and political career. One of his most famous visitors was William Jennings Bryan who was living in Miami during the early 1920s. The three-time presidential candidate for the Democratic Party had served as President Wilson's first secretary of state. A strong pacifist by inclination, Bryan had resigned from that position in 1916 rather than sign a threatening note to Germany about its predatory submarine policy during World War I. Bryan's close friendship and his pacifist views may have influenced Haines in developing his ideas about the National Newspapermen's Home which he attempted to bring to Altamonte Springs. *Winter Park Herald*, February 3, 1923; *Sanford Herald*, March 21, 1925.

With thirty-three acres in production at the time of its incorporation, the firm expanded until it was cultivating sixty-five acres by 1925. Since much of the acreage was slatted to protect the tender plants, one overly enthusiastic reporter called it the largest industry in the world under one roof. The fernery had thirty miles of irrigation pipe, a precooling plant, and its own electric light and water system. There was a complete company town adjacent to the fernery. It had forty homes for employees, a commissary, a church, a school, a park, and a moving picture theater. According to the *Herald*, the enterprise represented an investment of $500,000 by the mid-1920s. Other estimates were somewhat lower, but the Royal Fernery was nevertheless a large enterprise in the town which had long been known mostly for its hotel and resort facilities.[132]

Other Ferneries

The Royal Fernery was the catalyst which made Altamonte Springs a center for fern growing for many years. Other companies quickly followed. The Peerless Fern Company was incorporated in 1923 by S. Lee

Orange Drive in the early 1920s. C. D. Haines is standing in the roadway.

The Jasmine. Built as a theater to entertain guests of C. D. Haines, it was remodeled as a residence in the 1930s. It still stands at 447 Orange Drive.

An inside view of The Jasmine about 1923.

Phillips, Albert A. Folsom and James A. Cotting. Capitalized at $200,000, it was authorized to engage in a general nursery business. According to the Altamonte Springs tax rolls, Peerless had forty-eight acres in 1927, although only part of that was in production. Charles D. Haines was apparently a silent partner in this firm. When Ed Mitchell left his employ to manage his own Associated Ferneries, the elder Haines named his stepson, Benjamin F., as "acting general manager" of both the Peerless and Royal companies.[133]

The Standard Fern Company was located on a forty-acre tract near Lake Concord at what later became Fern Park. Incorporated by Benjamin F. Haines, Carrie B. Haines, Michael M. Dyer, and Fred Dyer, it was capitalized at $20,000. Haines and Michael M. Dyer were the major stockholders with ninety-nine shares each. Carrie Haines and Fred Dyer owned one share each. The Orienta Fern Company, a smaller company capitalized at $5,000, was also incorporated in 1923. The stockholders were Benjamin

Back at the dock, the group poses for pictures. Standing at extreme left is James (Al) Cotting. Seated at left on upper deck is Grace Kingsley with Major Raymond standing behind her. Ella Bly is standing (fourth from left). Next to her is Benjamin F. Haines. Katherine and C. D. Haines are seated near the wheel house. Webber Haines is atop the wheel house. Howard Lyman is standing at window below with Gordon Barnett and William Lewis Bly in the doorway. The man at the lower right is Ed Walker. It was good that the photographs were taken, because the Kathryn *sank at the dock in 1925 and is still resting on the lake bottom.*

The Kathryn *under way on Lake Orienta. The vessel was built in Jacksonville, shipped to Altamonte Springs, and assembled on the lake in the early 1920s.*

F. Haines and his wife Carrie, with Andrew G. Haines and his wife, Mary L. The Altamonte Fern Company was incorporated by George C. Hall, B. L. Maltbie, and Albert E. Cline. It was capitalized at $15,000 with each of the principals owning five hundred shares. There were also several unincorporated ferneries, one of which was owned by W. B. Ballard.[134]

The Jasmine Theater

Charles Haines originally built The Jasmine Theater—with a seating capacity of one hundred twenty—for the pleasure of his family and friends. He enjoyed entertaining both local residents and visitors with dramatic performances, variety shows, and moving pictures. Both local talent—of which Altamonte Springs had perhaps more than its share—and performers brought in for special occasions, performed on the Jasmine Theater stage to the delight of the former congressman's guests. But, the theater also had a role in promoting the town in the early 1920s.

Shortly after the chamber of commerce was organized, Haines set aside special days to entertain residents of neighboring towns. On one such occasion, he invited the children and "grown up folks" of Longwood to a performance at The Jasmine and a ride on Lake Orienta aboard the Yacht *Kathryn*. The vessel was a 50-foot double-decker which Haines had had built at Jacksonville. In early 1923, he set aside a week to entertain the residents of Orlando, Winter Park, Apopka, and Sanford. Tuesday was Winter Park night. Despite a torrential downpour, between thirty and forty cars made the journey. Mrs. Howard (Emma Abbot) Lyman—who

This assembly was in 1923 on the occasion of William Jennings Bryan's visit to Altamonte Springs. Oddly enough, Bryan is not present in this photograph. Those who can be identified are (3) Howard Lyman, (4) Benjamin F. Haines, (6) Webber Haines, (8-9) Katherine and C. D. Haines, (10-11) Ella Bly and Grace Kingsley.

A large crowd assembled in front of The Jasmine after an address by William Jennings Bryan in 1923. Katherine and C. D. Haines are on the sidewalk in front. The man in back in front of the door is believed to be Bryan.

A dinner party given by C. D. Haines at The Jasmine.

A group assembled at the entrance to a recreational area near C. D. Haines' home in 1923. Howard Lyman is on the left. C. D. and Katherine Haines are standing by the posts on opposite sides of the walk. Webber Haines is on the right in the nautical attire.

was becoming known as Central Florida's "premier extemporaneous entertainer"—pleased the audience with two selections before the first reel of the movie.

Mr. Bird, "a pleasing tenor from Des Moines," sang and played the piano between the reels. There were also songs and recitations by "colored boys and girls" who were employed on the Haines estate.[135]

The National Newspaper Men's Home

Perhaps Haines' grandest plan for Altamonte Springs was associated with his dream of promoting world peace. In early 1925 he announced that the International Press Association, headed by ex-Governor Frank Lowden of Illinois as president and Adolph Ochs of the *New York Times* as vice-president, had agreed to locate their home for retired newsmen—to be named Press City—at Altamonte Springs. He was donating to the association the Jasmine Theater, a club house, sixty-five acres of land, and $50,000 in cash.[136]

Successful completion of the agreement would certainly have been beneficial to the town, but Haines had a higher motive. In a speech delivered at Palm Beach in early 1926, he explained his belief that "a unified press could establish and maintain peace." He reasoned that it had taken public opinion to start the recently concluded world war and therefore peace could be maintained by reversing such sentiments. A Press City, featuring a retirement home for newsmen from around the world, would be a major step in that direction, he thought.[137]

All seemed to be going well. In February 1926, a national newspapermen's convention was held in Orlando where the plans for Press City were announced. J. E. Triplett of the Florida Press Association was chosen to manage the home. The state association held its meeting at the Altamonte Springs Community House in April of that year. Mayor Maltbie extended a warm welcome. Frank Haithcox gave a fish fry at Sanlando Springs. There was a dinner and dance at the Altamonte Hotel to complete the festivities.[138]

The bad news came in the fall. The land given by Congressman Haines was only part of what the press association needed and it had planned to add additional acreage adjacent to it.

Unfortunately, publicity surrounding the proposed Press City had set off something of a land rush and all of the desired property had been purchased by parties apparently unwilling to part with it. An obviously disappointed Haines graciously declared that "My gifts are gifts" while agreeing that the retirement home would have to be located elsewhere.[139]

Spanish-American War Veterans

Shortly after the Florida Press Association convened at Altamonte Springs, the Spanish American War veterans of Florida met at Orlando where they elected Walter B. Ballard as their state commander. The surprised but pleased Ballard invited the entire group to a party at his "beau-

The house on the left was the home of George Kingsley and was built about 1892. The house on the right is that of Charles D. Haines. The water tower in back was part of the Round Lake Water Works, built and operated by Haines to provide water for his fernery and groves. The water was pumped from the lake by an engine located near present-day Hattaway Drive and stored in the raised tank.

View of Lake Orienta from the rear of C. D. Haines' house.

The walkway from the Kingsley and Haines houses to Lake Orienta.

Katherine Haines seated in front of the C. D. Haines home. The house was a prefabricated structure purchased from Sears, Roebuck & Co. and assembled on this site in 1917. The driveway is now the site of the Lakepoint Apartments.

Katherine Haines gathering oranges from the family grove west of Lake Orienta.

Benjamin F. Haines' house facing Lake Orienta, built in the 1920s.

B. F. Haines' driveway.

This view down B. F. Haines' driveway looks away from his house toward The Jasmine at the other end. Haines orange grove is on the left and a grapefruit grove owned by Central Fruit is on the right.

tiful home overlooking Lake Orienta." The two hundred guests enjoyed lunch, followed by a motorcade to Sanlando Springs where they were invited to swim in the recently completed pool.[140]

Citrus

While the ferneries were becoming important to the community's economy, they had by no means replaced citrus. According to the *Sanford Herald*, "Altamonte Springs has in its territory hundreds of acres of orange and grapefruit groves in [a] high state of cultivation." And more groves were being planted. Chester C. Fosgate had recently added several tracts. He had groves within the town limits with a 1927 assessed value of $23,000 and a large grapefruit grove west of town in what is now the Spring Oaks section. Other local growers were pleased when Fosgate relocated his packing house from Orlando to Forest City in 1926. Most of them marketed their fruit through his facility for many years. Fosgate sold fruit under the Ace High, Fidelity, and Criterion brands.[141]

The Florida Boom

The inflationary boom which swept Florida in the 1920s was approaching its zenith by 1925. While it never affected Altamonte Springs to the extent it did the communities along the southeast coast, there was a distinct acceleration of development. Winwood Park in the old Frost addition, Maltbie Shores and South Altamonte Heights were among the smaller developments opened in the 1920s. Ipswich Street was closed at Highland and the Olmstead and Miller addition was approved in that area in 1925. It was subject to the building restrictions ranging from $2,500 for lots fronting the Dixie Highway and $1,500 on the rear lots. Just north of that addition, Lakeview Heights had been platted in 1916 by Hale, Henkel, and Rigdon. Replatted two years later as the R. L. Betts addition, it was acquired by B. L. Maltbie's Altamonte Development Company to develop as Pinecrest. Mayor Maltbie's own spacious bungalow was one of several homes built in that area during the 1920s. W. O. Cluff and Thomas Kenney were active builders in Pinecrest.[142]

The Altamonte Development Company was permitted to build "a neat office building" at the corner of South Altamonte Avenue and Mag-

The entrance to Sanlando, the Suburb Beautiful, at Hermits Trail and Altamonte Avenue in 1925.

B. L. Maltbie organized a development company in the 1920s to develop Pinecrest in what was originally the R. L. Betts addition. This is the home—still standing at 655 Lake Drive—which he built for himself in that addition in the late 1920s. 1991 photograph by Historic Property Associates of St. Augustine.

nolia Drive in 1925 from which to manage its development. The town council and the chamber of commerce arranged with the company to expand their construction office into an information center for the town. The company and the town shared the costs of a clerk for that dual role, an arrangement undoubtedly facilitated by the fact that Maltbie was both president of the firm and mayor of the town.[143]

Sanlando, The Suburb Beautiful

Sanlando was developed by the Altamonte Homes Company whose chief operating officer was Frank Haithcox, a prominent Orlando business man and amusement promoter. The new suburb was planned for a huge tract lying generally north of Lake Adelaide and encompassing lakes Florida, Marion, and Frances. Acquired from J. E. Bartlett in l924, it included most of the unsold property originally platted by the Altamonte Land, Hotel and Navigation Company. Additional land was added a little later.[144]

Haithcox had grand plans for his development which was marked by an entrance and park at the intersection of Hermits Trail and Altamonte Avenue. He planned eventually to connect the chain of lakes by canals for boating along the lines of the Winter Park system. More immediately, however, he wanted to sell lots, eight hundred of which were ostensibly purchased by Orlando people within thirty days after his first offering. By the fall of 1924, Haithcox was building five miles of streets and electric lines. Construction was shortly under way on homes around Lake Florida.

One of the more active builders there was W. O. Cluff, several of whose structures are still standing. Haithcox built his own home, however, on the northwest corner of Altamonte and North Altamonte avenues, across the street from Fuller's store.[145]

At the request of the Altamonte Homes Company, the Sanlando suburb was annexed by the town in March 1925.[146]

Palm Springs

Palm Springs had undergone a renewal in the early 1920s when Lester Beeman, of the chewing gum manufacturing family, spent a considerable sum in refurbishing it. Managed by Larry Stedman it was attracting groups from Longwood and Sanford as well as Altamonte Springs by 1923. Beeman and several others built cottages there. [147]

Sanlando Springs

It was Hoosier Springs, however, which became the center of attention. Renamed Sanlando Springs in keeping with the spirit of his new suburb, the spring had a central role in Haithcox's plans. A new dam was built to raise the water level in the spring itself, the surrounding area was landscaped with tropical plantings, and a swimming pool and bathhouse were constructed. Proclaimed the first to be built in the area, the Sanlando swimming pool was opened in April 1926. Frank Haithcox invited a large crowd from Orlando and Altamonte Springs for the first swim. At the same time, ground was broken for a fifty-room hotel. Sanlando Springs soon gained a reputation as the playground of Central Florida.[148]

The Sanlando Golf and Country Club

Operating through his Sanlando Springs Corporation, Haithcox had purchased a large tract of land ranging from Hoosier Springs southeasterly toward his Altamonte Springs suburb. Most of it was bought from the Overstreet Investment Company, which held a mortgage of $120,000 on it, dating from April 5, 1925. Although the price was high, it was boom time in Florida and expectations were equally high.[149]

Desiring to add a golf course and clubhouse to his development, Haithcox contracted with Calvin O. Black, an experienced "golf man" from Cleveland to build it. In return for four hundred lots in the development, Black agreed to build an eighteen-hole golf course, a watering system, and a clubhouse with foyer, dining room, golf shop, and men's

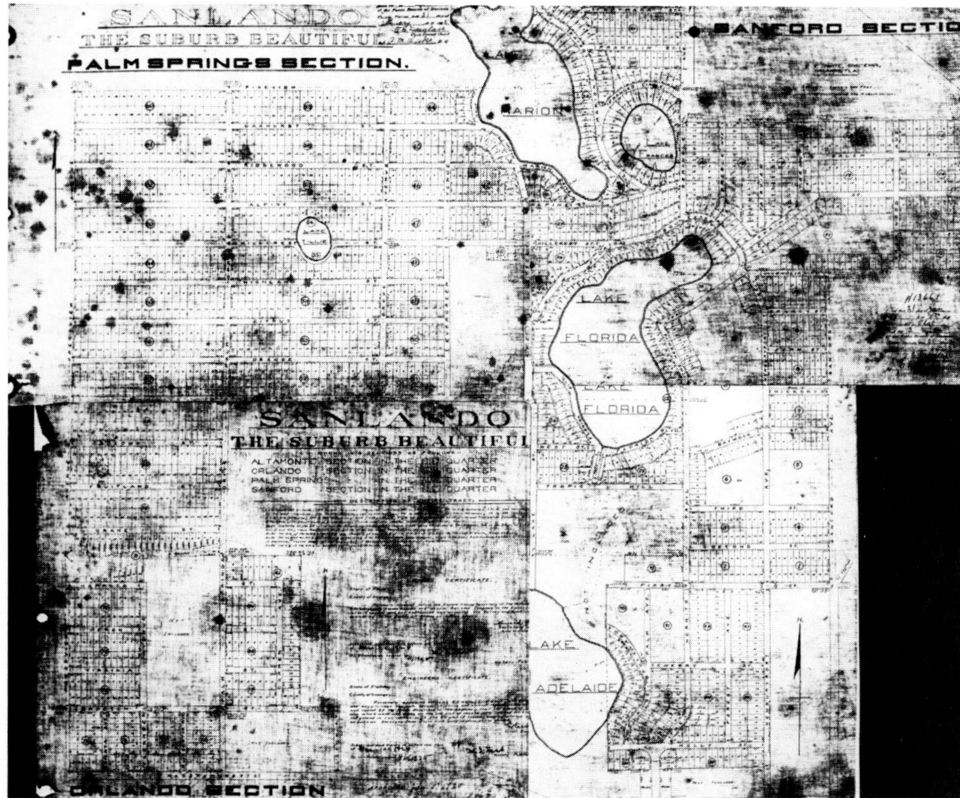

The four combined plats of Frank Haithcox's Sanlando, the Suburb Beautiful.

The Hermit of Altamonte Springs—Hermits Trail, which winds northward from S. R. 436 under an umbrella of beautiful oaks on the east side of Lakes Adelaide and Florida, is presently one of the city's most attractive residential streets. Named by Frank Haithcox, who made it the entrance to his Sanlando subdivision in 1925, it was once the property of a man named Dawson, who for many years, was the town's hermit. Dawson lived in a "barn-like" structure near what is now the intersection of Hermits Trail and Holly Street and discouraged visitors with a "tightly nailed gate," according to Frank Haithcox, Jr. He ran a herd of cattle whose company he apparently preferred to that of human beings. His reclusiveness naturally gave rise to mystery which surrounded him although he seemed quite harmless to the few people who had occasion to converse with him from time to time. Having lived for many years with his cattle behind the protective gate—only a short distance from Altamonte Avenue—he died in the early 1920s. Stories still circulate about the circumstances of his death, but he was then a very old man and apparently died of pneumonia. Reclusive, mysterious, and enigmatic in life, he is honored in death by the naming of a handsome park and beautiful residential street in his honor. (Lisanne Renner, *The Little Sentinel*, October 30, 1981.)

A Sunday School picnic on Lake Florida behind Dr. Atterbury's home in 1927. Atterbury was a retired missionary who had spent most of his life in the Orient. His family was quite active in Altamonte Springs in the 1920s. Marguerite Atterbury was the local correspondent to the Winter Park Herald *and Daisy Atterbury was active in the chamber of commerce, until she followed her father's example and became a missionary.*

This house at 319 Hermits Trail is one of the several built in the booming 1920s by W. O. Cluff. A 1991 photograph by Historic Property Associates of St. Augustine.

This photograph of Palm Springs was taken after completion of the road from Longwood (see Chapter 6).

George Everett Bates at Palm Springs about 1924.

and ladies' locker rooms. Black moved to Altamonte Springs, rented a home in Pinecrest, and went to work. Before the end of April 1926, life memberships in the proposed club had been purchased by Mrs. E. T. Haines, Mr. and Mrs. Walter Ballard, and Mr. and Mrs. C. B. Bowers. As work progressed other memberships were sold. Considerable interest was raised in 1928 when President Hamilton Holt and Dean Anderson of Rollins College joined the club. By that time students from Rollins were playing the Sanlando course.[150]

The course was opened in early 1927, but dances were already being scheduled every Wednesday evening at the club. The Sanlando Golf Club was soon competing with the Altamonte Hotel and the town's Community House as a social center. Especially noteworthy was the celebration of "Ladies Night" by the Sanford Rotarians on March l. Dinner and speeches were followed by a program featuring Mrs. Barnum's troupe and then dancing to the music of Norton's Orchestra from the Altamonte Hotel. While the club was experiencing its first social activities, construction was being completed on the first homes there. Calvin Black and J. H. Kenney both moved their families into new homes, "thus making the

A crowd enjoying the new pool at Sanlando Springs. According to Frank Haithcox, this was the first such pool built in Central Florida.

beginning of a most attractive little community," according to the *Winter Park Herald*.[151]

Like the Altamonte Hotel and much of the town itself, the golf club was largely a seasonal institution. A professional was in residence during the winter but he spent his summers at another country club in New England. The full dining room was also closed during the summer. The course did remain open to players all year and sandwiches and drinks were available at a snack bar.[152]

The Battle of the Mayors

Enthusiasm for golf was sweeping Central Florida even before the Sanlando course was opened. There was golf competition at the Altamonte Hotel links almost every day during the season. Competition between neighboring towns created excitement as well as opportunity for social gatherings. "Civic pride, municipal spirit, and interurban rivalry" were stimulated by "the battle of the mayors" on the Sanford Municipal Golf Course in February 1925. Mayor Forrest Lake led a team of twenty Sanford Rotarians against an Altamonte Springs team lead by Mayor B. L. Maltbie. While the women from Altamonte Springs were entertained at bridge, the Sanford team defeated the visitors. The Altamonte Springs team redeemed itself in a return match the following week.[153]

Golf Equipment Manufacturing in Longwood

Longwood was also experiencing a building boom in the mid-1920s. Joe Tinker, the baseball player, having launched several enterprises in Orlando, expanded to Longwood in 1925. He built a business block and a cement block factory in town and opened a development where lots were being sold by December of that year. Deciding in early 1926 to capitalize on the golf enthusiasm of the area, he recruited Walter Hagen, the famed golfer, to become president of a golf equipment manufacturing company. By April 1926, their plant was in operation making golf bags and they were planning to add other articles for a full line of golf equipment. Joe Tinker managed the operation, but Hagen was an active president. During his frequent visits to the plant, he stayed at the Altamonte Hotel.[154]

The Seminole Jockey Club

In early 1925, the Seminole Jockey Club was organized by a group of Sanford citizens and promoters from Canton, Ohio. Despite opposition from the Seminole County Chamber of Commerce which declared the enterprise "not a wholesome development," the club proceeded with

THE MAITLAND NEWS

and purposes set forth

ıd and the seal of the
ıe Seventeenth Judicial
ɔ, in Orange County,
ay of February, A. D.,

ı. M. ROBINSON,
:uit Court, Orange
Judicial Circuit of

. HOWARD, D. C.

IDA
ŁANGE

given that the under-
:r, intends to apply to
ircuit Court of Orange
th Judicial Circuit of
ense to manage, take
ıtrol her property, and
ealer in every respect.
d this 1st day of Feb-
7.

ANNIE MEER.

ORANGE TEA SHOP

Altamonte Springs

Wishes to announce that
until further notice a

Dinner will be Served

from 6:00 to 7:00 p.m.

for 75 cents

Parties up to fifty can be
be accommodated.

More than twelve in party,
reservations made by
appointment.

Telephone 1208-J

MRS. EARL MURRAY

Mrs. Earl Murray spent her summers in North Carolina and her winters at Altamonte Springs where she lived in one of the large "cottages" built in the 1880s by H. H. Westinghouse. During the winters she operated the Orange Tea Shop, an advertisement for which is shown here. It was taken from the Maitland News *of 1927.*

This is the Trovillion building which was completed in the 1920s. It first housed a pharmacy, a barber shop, and a grocery. This photograph was taken in 1991 after the building was extensively altered from its original appearance. Photograph by Historic Property Associates of St. Augustine.

plans to develop Seminola Race Track. Located between Altamonte Springs and Longwood near the recently built Lyman School, the track was opened on March 20, 1926.[155]

Racing was apparently becoming as popular as golf. Three Orlando men—Graves, Laws, and Cullender—organized the Midway Kennel Club in early1926 with plans for a greyhound race track which they planned to build on Pennsylvania Avenue in the southern part of Altamonte Springs. With the stipulation that it be located no nearer to the center of town than the proposed site, the town council approved the project. The building inspector was authorized to issue "special permits" for construction of a race track, a grandstand, and twenty small houses. Unlike the Seminola Race Track, this one was apparently never built.[156]

The Commercial Center

The commercial zone was experiencing growth almost by the time it was created. The Altamonte Garage had already opened in 1921. Herbert Fuller's store was still handling general merchandise as well as gasoline and oil. G. A. Bryant also operated a store for a while in the early 1920s. B. D. McIntosh's Fargo Lumber Company was cutting and shipping lumber from its mill near the railroad depot. The post office was upgraded to second class status in early 1925 and a new $100,000 ACL depot was announced by station master W. T. Whitehead.[157]

Accompanying news of the new railroad station was Frank Haithcox's announcement of plans for a two-story business block with

George and Virginia Bates on a slide next to the Altamonte Hotel in 1927. The slide was built by Mr. McMahon, the hotel carpenter.

three stores below and apartments above. The proposed builder was A. B. Bell of Nashville, Tennessee. Bell apparently never followed through, but Ray Trovillion of Winter Park stepped in. The Trovillion Investment Company constructed a business block which still stands on Altamonte Avenue. By early 1927 it housed three businesses. The first was the Altamonte Pharmacy operated by C. A. Benson from Chicago. The next was a barber shop which was welcomed as a "great boon to those who feel the need of a trim, yet cannot spare the time to run down to Winter Park." The third business was the Howell and Williams grocery store and meat market.[158]

Other businesses in town at the time included the Orange Tea Shop, Earl Murray's tea shop, and Harry Roberts' Canteen. Bertram O. Smith, a winter resident from Orleans, Vermont, had an antique store and fruit stand. In the commercial area along South Altamonte Avenue, William H. Hardwick had a store and "filling" station.[159]

The Ford family had owned and managed a store in Winwood for many years. It was being managed by Banks Ford in the 1920s. In 1927, he obtained a permit to build a brick and block store at the corner of East Street and North Altamonte Avenue. Two years earlier, Walter Tucker was authorized to build an Odd Fellows Hall on East Street near the railroad to replace an older building which had been used for that purpose.[160]

The Hotel

While it shared some of the social activities with the Community House and the Sanlando Country Club, the Altamonte Hotel remained the center of social life. As the Altamonte Springs correspondent for the *Winter Park Herald* wrote in 1927, "the functions at the hotel contribute so much to Altamonte Springs social life that all residents are looking forward to the opening of the hotel." It also contributed significantly to the community's economic life. As George Bates had announced in 1915, a large annex was added to the hotel property after the end of World War I. The annex itself was enlarged in 1928. Through good times and bad, the people who wintered at the hotel or in their own nearby homes played a large role in all phases of life in Altamonte Springs.[161]

Lake Adelaide as seen from the Altamonte Hotel Springhouse in the 1920s.

George and Everett Bates employed an orchestra which played both classical and popular music for Saturday evening dances and Sunday concerts. There was an annual masquerade ball and a Washington's Birthday ball. There were Christmas parties, and the "watch nights" on New Year's Eve were always popular. There were special events such as the one on a Saturday morning when Mrs. George A. Lewis read some of her own poetry before an appreciative audience. Beginning in the early 1920s, moving pictures were shown on Monday evenings. And there was

This photograph was taken from the sidewalk on the ninth green of the hotel course southward toward the lake.

The Altamonte Hotel dock in the mid-1920s as seen from the seventh fairway.

A wide-angle shot of the Altamonte Hotel golf course. It is easy to see why it was referred to by many of the guests as the "Damned Trees Course."

Guests of the Altamonte Hotel preparing for a golf tournament on the hotel links about 1925. The guests frequently divided into teams with extravagant names. One of the competitions was between the "Puritans" and the "Buffaloes."

A view to the east toward Maitland Avenue across the golf course south of the Altamonte Hotel.

This view is from the Altamonte Hotel golf course, looking west from the eighth and ninth holes. When a "substantial addition" was made to the hotel in 1928, the eighth hole was moved closer to the lake to protect occupants of the new facility from errant golf balls.

Three-year-old George Everett Bates in 1922 leaning on the "win" on the Altamonte Hotel golf course. The R. E. Hoffman house and its water tank are visible across the lake.

View of Lake Orienta from the back of the Briggs-Hoffman house on Boston Avenue about 1925.

Lucia Patch in costume before a show at the Altamonte Hotel in 1922.

Bates family assembled on hotel grounds in 1928. Seated from left are E. C. Bates, Lillian Bates, Virginia Bates Wyman, Violet and Vernon Wilkins. Standing from left: Lillian Wilkins and Harold and Violet Bates. The man standing in back is unidentified.

Tennis on the Altamonte Hotel courts on the southeast corner of Altamonte and Maitland avenues. About 1928.

Nina and Everett Bates at first tee of the Altamonte Hotel golf course.

always golf. Sometimes the hotel guests chose sides and played tournaments. At other times they played in men's tournaments, women's tournaments, or two-ball foursomes. But, whatever the game at a particular time, there was always an enthusiastic audience. And, the hotel dining room was enjoyed, not only by the guests, but by many Central Floridians who drove out for the excellent fare.[162]

The Chamber of Commerce

The Altamonte Springs Chamber of Commerce began about 1921 with the dual goals of improving the appearance of the community and advertising its attractive features to stimulate growth. With Walter B. Ballard as its executive secretary during most of the period, it was active throughout the1920s and then declined during the depression. Most of the residents of the town—including those who spent only the winters there—were members of the chamber. In addition to joining the Seminole County Chamber in advertising through the newspapers, one of its first accomplishments was removing the trolley line through the center of town and replacing it with a cement sidewalk. It also participated in motorcades through the county such as the one in 1927 when Frank Kay Anderson of Orlando was president of the local chamber. With Mayor Maltbie in charge of the motorcade committee, the chamber put sixteen Altamonte Springs cars in a procession of fifty. The chamber worked with Charles Haines to secure the National Newspapermen's Home. Eighty members attended a meeting in early1925 at which it was decided to bring the state press convention to town. They succeeded in bringing the convention to Altamonte Springs, but the larger mission failed.[163]

The chamber's business meetings were also social events. Meetings at the Community House twice each month were always well-attended. The business meeting usually involved discussions of current project and reports from the various committees. They were always followed by suppers and picnics and programs of entertainment which probably helped to keep up attendance.[164]

The Ladies Auxiliary

The Ladies Auxiliary to the Altamonte Springs Chamber of Commerce was organized in late1924. Among its original members were Mrs. B. L. Maltbie, Mrs. Elmer T. Haines, Mrs. A. E. Cline, Mrs. Emma Lyman, Mrs. H. H. Bundy, and Mrs. George Babcock. Its original committees were music—chaired by Emma Lyman, entertainment, Mrs. H. H. Bundy, and supper, Mrs. E. T. Haines. In these roles, the auxiliary members contributed largely to the success of the chamber meetings. But, the group also undertook other important projects.

Benefit bridge parties were held to raise funds. The proceeds—together with appropriations from the town council—were used to beautify the grounds of the Community House and to improve the building itself. The organization also had sewing bees and other fund raisers to aid a "colored" orphanage in Jacksonville. The Lyman PTA also noted its gratitude to the Ladies Auxiliary for the book sales it held on behalf of the school library.[165]

The Christmas Tree

The annual Christmas tree sponsored by the chamber of commerce and the Ladies Auxiliary had become a tradition by 1926. Each year the organizations raised funds to assure that every child in Altamonte Springs received a gift. The programs were held at the Community House until 1926 when they were moved to Sanlando Park. Social customs of the day were rigidly observed. White children were entertained one evening and the "colored" children on another.[166]

An Occasional Lack of Attendance

Genuine civic interest, the suppers, and the entertainment kept attendance high at the chamber meetings. But, they sometimes succumbed to the competition. President Anderson explained that the sparse attendance at the February 23, 1927 meeting was due to the arrival of the Sears, Roebuck Catalogue.[167]

Like other activities in the town, chamber meetings were seasonal. The last meeting of the 1926–27 season was on May 11, but "the program of suppers and meetings will be resumed . . . in the fall." And, they did continue for a while. Chamber officers for 1928–29 were W. O. Cluff, president; James Kenney, vice-president; A. H. Fuller, treasurer; and Daisy Atterbury, secretary. Mrs. W. B. Ballard was president of the auxiliary that year. Both organizations apparently became dormant as the depression deepened after 1929.[168]

Better Music Week

"Altamonte people are doing their bit for Better Music Week," wrote the *Winter Park Herald* in1926. During the week, Theresa Hoffman had performed in two concerts at Memorial High School in Orlando. Mrs. Stanley Bennett sang several selections for the Orlando Kiwanis Club, and Mrs. Emma Lyman sang on WDBO. But that was not unusual for Altamonte Springs. In addition to those mentioned, a number of other residents—for example, Mrs. W. R. Bailey and A. L. Norton—were talented musicians. They played and sang at most of the social gatherings in town.

Relocated from Lake Brantley to Altamonte Avenue in 1908, the Altamonte Chapel was refurbished both inside and out in 1927. This photograph was taken shortly after the work was completed.

Mrs. Lyman was the best known and most active of them. After her husband died in 1924, she devoted much of her time to her music and to public affairs. She was elected chairman of the board of alderman in 1925, frequently acting as mayor when B. L. Maltbie was away on business. She was also active with the Ladies Auxiliary. But, it was as a singer and pianist that she made her greatest contribution to her community. She had a regular program on WDBO, Orlando's first radio station. She sang regularly at the Winter Park Methodist Church. She taught music at the Lyman School. And she sang and played everywhere, at the chamber meetings, at The Jasmine Theater, at the Altamonte Hotel, and at the Sanlando Country Club. When she was injured in an automobile accident in 1927, the *Winter Park Herald* expressed relief that she was recovering because "Mrs. Lyman gives so much pleasure through her broadcasting and singing . . . that any threatened disability causes her friends especial concern." It was ironic that Mrs. Lyman died in an automobile accident sixteen years later.[169]

The Altamonte Chapel

Religious services at the chapel were well-attended during the winter seasons. By the time Dr. B. K. Tapper conducted Easter services in April 1926, residents were planning a major renovation of the building and grounds, but work did not get under way until early 1927. While repairs were being made, services were conducted regularly in the Community House. At that time, Dr. Yarnell of Winter Park and Rev. Hart S. Fuller of Fern Park were holding services on alternate Sundays.[170]

Services resumed in the chapel on March 20, 1927 with Dr. Yarnell in the pulpit. The congregation was pleased with the "bright and shiny new finish of the woodwork" and the flower decorations furnished by

Emma Abbot Lyman, a talented entertainer and staunch community supporter. This photograph, taken about 1905 when she was in show business, was loaned by Mr. and Mrs. Herbert S. Lyman.

E. O. Marshall. In addition to the interior improvements, a well had been dug and the Ladies Auxiliary was landscaping the grounds.[171]

Dr. Yarnell and Rev. Fuller continued to alternate as ministers until early 1928. Dr. Charles A. Campbell of Rollins College then succeeded them. Many people from Winter Park and Orlando joined the Altamonte Springs residents for Dr. Campbell's services, leading some to conclude that "only considerable enlargement of the chapel will serve to accommodate the congregation."[172]

Schools

A consolidated school to serve the students of Altamonte Springs, Longwood, and Forest City was built in 1924. It was named in honor of Howard Lyman, a school board member who died that year. J. W. Osteen and W. B. Ballard of Altamonte Springs and C. W. Entzminger of

Howard Charles Lyman, a Seminole County school board member. Lyman School was named in his honor. This photograph was taken about 1905, when Mr. Lyman was in show business, and was loaned by Mr. & Mrs. Herbert S. Lyman.

Longwood were among those who guided the school in its early years. Its 1926 faculty was Herbert J. Shaffer, principal, and Mrs. Theresa von Herbulis, Miss Vida K. Smith, Mrs. J. T. Jacobs, and Mrs. S. H. Buchanan. George W. Bunnell was one of the first drivers who contracted to transport the children of the district.[173]

With Carl Harding in charge of athletics, the students were soon busily clearing the grounds for soccer, volleyball, and football, each of which was played for the first time in 1925. The Lyman Glee Club made its first presentation in early 1927 under the direction of Mrs. Winifred Kelly. An early school play was *How the Story Grew*, performed for the public under the direction of Mrs. W. McDowell and sponsored by the Parent Teachers Association. There were also musicals, such as *Mary's Garden* and *Toy Shop Symphony* directed by Emma Lyman. Ruth Ballard had the lead in *Mary's Garden*.[174]

Lyman School became yet another social center as well as an educational institution. Dramatic performances, athletic events, and PTA functions drew full houses. In addition, many public meetings of general interest were held there. By 1928 the school had nearly one hundred fifty students and nine teachers. As might have been expected, Mrs. Emma Lyman was teaching music two days a week.[175]

The Altamonte Springs Town Council took an active role in obtaining a Negro school for the community. W. B. Ballard headed a committee which located a site in the Winwood addition. Mayor Maltbie spoke with the county school board about ways of securing the building. The school board apparently obtained some financial assistance from the Rosenwald Fund, which had been established in the early twentieth century to help build Negro schools. The Rosenwald School opened in 1931 to students from Altamonte Springs, Woodbridge, and Forest City.[176]

From Good Times to Hard Times

The1920s had been a busy time for Altamonte Springs, for Florida, and for the nation, but the boom was ended in the state by the disastrous hurricane of 1926. Altamonte Springs had been spending about $11,000 annually since 1926, but even that modest amount was becoming difficult to raise as the decade ended. Even so, the town was less adversely affected than some of its neighbors. A "Hard Times" party was held in December 1928, but it was at the Sanlando Country Club. It was declared "the most successful [party] given this season." Everyone "enjoyed the chance to wear their old clothes." And, there was still some construction. W. O. Cluff had recently sold several new homes in the Sanlando subdivision and he started another one in Pinecrest. Fifty people walked through it during an open house in February 1929. More than forty people arrived at the Altamonte Hotel the same month. Bates and Son made yet another addition to the hotel annex in 1930.[177]

But the worst was yet to come. As the nation sank into economic depression following the stock market crash of October 1929, Altamonte Springs joined the rest of the state and the nation in the economic adversity of the 1930s.

EIGHT

The Depression and the Second World War: 1931-1945

Altamonte Springs was better off than many of Florida's local governments. Like many others, it had welcomed accelerated growth, expanded its boundaries, and provided municipal services. . . . But, unlike many of them, it had issued no bonds to finance its growth.

The state of Florida had been mired in depression since the hurricane of 1926 ended the great land boom. The 1929 stock market crash signalled an even more devastating end to the "Coolidge prosperity" which the nation had enjoyed during the 1920s. By 1931 the bills were coming due in both state and nation. Governor Doyle Carlton called for reductions in the state budget to offset the tremendous decline in tax collections. The national depression continued through most of the 1930s and was not fully resolved until the nation went to war in the 1940s. In the meantime, both governments and individuals struggled to maintain themselves during a deep national depression.

Taking Account

Altamonte Springs was better off than many of Florida's local governments. Like many others, it had welcomed accelerated growth, expanded its boundaries, and provided municipal services—especially the popular "White Way." But, unlike many of them it had issued no bonds to finance its growth. Nevertheless, the town of fewer than three hundred permanent inhabitants was facing a serious situation by 1931. It owed nearly $30,000 in unsecured debt—nearly $5,000 in overdue electric bills and the rest to B. L. Maltbie for street paving loans—and its fixed annual costs were greater than revenue beginning in 1930. There was some consolation in news that R. M. Williams, who had operated a grocery store in the Trovillion building since 1926, was building his own concrete structure on North Altamonte Avenue that year. Two bungalows were being added by the Altamonte Hotel at about the same time. B. L. Maltbie's Altamonte Development Company was also current with the taxes on dozens of unimproved lots in the R. L. Betts addition. But, it was not good news that the lots were remaining unimproved and that Maltbie's company was inactive.[178]

The Altamonte Homes Company was defunct and Frank Haithcox had apparently lost most of his interest in Sanlando, the Suburb Beautiful.

The Overstreet Investment Company had foreclosed on all of his Sanlando Springs development and was operating both the park and the golf course.[179]

Although the town's annual budget had remained quite modest—never exceeding $11,500—during the heady 1920s, declining revenue was causing a mismatch between income and fixed costs. A 1931 budget of $7,465 was accomplished only by a major renegotiation of the lighting contract with the Florida Public Service Company and an agreement that past obligations would be liquidated at the rate of $750 per year. This meant that the White Way and much of the rest of the town lighting was reduced, but there would be even greater reductions later.[180]

The town officials in 1931 were Mayor B. O. Smith and aldermen E. T. Haines (chairman), A. E. Cline, A. H. Fuller, O. W. Locke, and Emma Lyman. They adjusted to the reduced budget, but the problem of mounting tax delinquencies needed attention and the state's new foreclosure law had just been declared unconstitutional. It would be some time before a method of handling delinquent taxes could be worked out.[181]

The Atlantic Coast Line Railroad Company was trying to obtain approval from the Public Service Commission to close the Altamonte Springs depot. The board launched strong protests, but the ACL ultimately prevailed. The express office remained with R. R. Butler as agent, to be succeeded later by L. R. Brookings. Scheduled service ended, but the trains still stopped for prominent individuals arriving to spend the winters at the Altamonte Hotel or at their own residences.[182]

A continuing decline of the economy accompanied by calls from Governor Carlton to reduce the costs of government caused further stringencies. In September 1931, the council authorized the tax assessor to reduce by 50 percent the assessed valuation on acreage in the Olmstead and Miller subdivision, the Stewart subdivision, South Altamonte Heights, and Sanlando. Reduction of 25 percent were authorized for the Fogg addition, the Robert L. Betts addition, the Altamonte Land, Hotel and Navigation subdivision, the Altamonte Commercial Center, and the Frost addition south of Williams Street. Personal property assessments were also reduced by 25 percent. On the other hand, assessments on all property in Winwood Park were doubled.[183]

To Abolish the Town of Altamonte Springs

The tax reductions were not enough to satisfy everyone. There had long been complaints that the town boundaries were too extensive. After Sanlando was incorporated—at the specific request of Frank Haithcox—the town encompassed about 2,760 acres. A considerable portion of that was agricultural and some was "wild land." Dr. Phillips had complained since 1925 about paying town taxes on his grove, although only twelve acres of it was inside the town. Charles Haines had also protested paying taxes on his fernery and groves. Both had lobbied for legislation to exclude their land from the town, but only Haines—in 1927—had tried to have the legislature abolish the entire town.[184]

When Charles Haines died in 1929, Benjamin F. Haines became sole owner of all of his stepfather's property—located on the northwest side of Lake Orienta. A former mayor of Medford, Massachusetts, and an experienced politician, the younger Haines apparently persuaded the local delegation to sponsor legislation to abolish the town. Becoming law in May 1931, "An Act to Abolish the Municipality of the Town of Altamonte Springs, . . ." was to be effective only upon approval of two-thirds of the qualified voters at an election on November 17, 1931. An election board—B. F. Haines, Edward N. Mitchell, E. T. Haines, and James E. Roosa—was appointed to handled the election. Inspectors were to be W. B. Ballard, A. E. Cline, B. L. Maltbie and H. E. Fuller. Webber Haines was clerk.[185]

A companion enactment ended the unique feature of Altamonte Springs' election ordinance which had provided voting rights to anyone who spent at least four months there. Henceforth, requirements were to be the same as those provided in the general election laws. Individuals had to have resided in the town for six months immediately preceding the time of registration. Poll taxes also had to be paid.[186]

A New Mayor and Council

No records of the election have been found, but it seems safe to assume that the voters rejected the proposal to abolish the town. Haines had taken precautions, however. The new town officials for 1932 were Mayor B. F. Haines and aldermen E. T. Haines, Webber B. Haines, E. N. Mitchell, R. E. Hoffman, J. W. Osteen, and A. W. Mullen. W. B. Ballard was town clerk, which made him *ex officio* assessor, treasurer and tax collector.[187]

The new council enacted a list of resolutions aimed at further reducing the budget. Attorneys were dismissed and Webber Haines became *ex officio* town attorney. It was agreed not to hire a marshal, but rather to have the county sheriff appoint someone who lived in Altamonte Springs to serve as a deputy without salary. Despite the recently arranged contract with the power company, lighting was reduced so as not to exceed $1,200 per year.[188]

Reducing the Size of the Town

When he became mayor, B. F. Haines and several other landowners had already filed suit to have their property excluded from the town. The collapse of the Florida land boom had left property titles and the tax structures of the state, the counties, and the municipalities in shambles. One of the several measures enacted to deal with the problem provided that property owners could withdraw their property from small towns—defined as those with fewer than one hundred fifty registered voters—if they could prove that they received no municipal services. The mayor was seeking to have the Royal Fernery and his groves excluded on those grounds. His son, Webber, recently graduated from law school, a member of the board of aldermen, and *ex officio* town attorney, had also filed a suit and was representing Harold Frost of the Southland Fruit Company in another one.[189]

In November 1931, Ed Mitchell had won a suit excluding the Associated Florist Ferneries land from the town. Judge Millard B. Smith had ruled that Altamonte Springs was a town with fewer than one hundred fifty qualified voters and that it provided no municipal services for Mitchell's property. The property was "forever released from all debts, duties and liabilities of said Town of Altamonte Springs," according to Judge Smith. At a council meeting on June 24, 1932, eleven days after he had filed his suit and one day after filing the Southland Fruit Company suit, Alderman Haines advised his colleagues that defense against these suits would be useless since the judge would rule as he had in the Mitchell case.[190]

The *Sanford Herald* of July 22, 1932, reported that factional disturbances that are often characteristic of life at Altamonte Springs flared into prominence again when two opposing groups met at the court house offices of Judge Millard B. Smith to argue against the exclusion of certain properties from the town limits. . . .

According to the paper, one group was headed by Webber B. Haines and Harold Frost of the Southland Fruit Company. The other group was made up of "members of the town council and other citizens" who offered vigorous arguments against removal of the land. After several hours of debate the judge ordered the matter referred to an examiner who would gather information to aid him in rendering his decisions. A little more than two weeks later, Webber Haines resigned from the council.[191]

Judge Smith ruled against the town in the Southland Fruit Company case on March 24, 1933, after which other suits were decided quite rapidly. Similar decisions were rendered in cases involving Webber Haines, B. F. Haines, Chester Fosgate, Mable and Rudolph Haas, R. U. Tracy, and the Orienta Investment Company (of which B. F. Haines was part owner). The suits removed most of the land west of Lake Orienta and south of Western Avenue from the town.[192]

The Fuller Store in the early 1930s. Herbert Fuller is in the center. The others are unidentified.

Mr. and Mrs. A. H. Fuller admiring some gladioli at the corner of their porch in early 1931.

Herbert and Ruth Fuller with their son, Graham, at the corner of the Fuller Store in 1929.

The Red Top "filling station" on the northwest corner of Maitland Avenue and Oranole was the first service station in Altamonte Springs. Built by William H. Hardwick in the late 1920s, it was acquired in 1934 by B. D. McIntosh, Jr., who operated it until he left for service in the U. S. Navy during World War II. This photograph was taken about 1930.

Herbert Graham Fuller in his customized roadster in front of Bide-a-wee cottage in 1939.

View of Lake Orienta with the Fuller home, Bide-a-wee, visible on the right.

An especially difficult case for the town involved a portion of Sanlando, in which Nellie A. Bartlett and fifty-eight other owners brought suit for exclusion. During the good times of 1925 Frank Haithcox had requested that his development be annexed by the town. But times had changed and Bartlett was suing for separation on grounds that the town had no authority to annex the subdivision in the first place. The judge agreed in a 1934 decision and a portion of the Sanlando subdivision was separated.[193]

Putting a Smaller House in Order

Herbert Graham Fuller and his friend, "Had," on Lake Orienta in the early 1930s, apparently with fishing on their minds.

B.O. Smith returned as mayor in 1933 and held that position until 1947. Elected as aldermen at the same were W. D. Holdsworth, James E. Roosa, B. D. McIntosh, Sr., Emma Lyman, Lewis D. Haines, H. E. Fuller, and E. T. Haines. W. B. Ballard pointed out that the Sanlando decision required changes in town records. Sanlando had never been divided into individual lots. It was shown simply as ninety-three blocks on the tax records. There were about two hundred owners of 1,500 lots in those blocks, some of which remained in the town and some of which had been excluded. When the changes were made, the council decided that each lot fronting on Lake Florida or Lake Adelaide would be assessed at one hundred dollars and all back lots would be assessed at fifty dollars.[194]

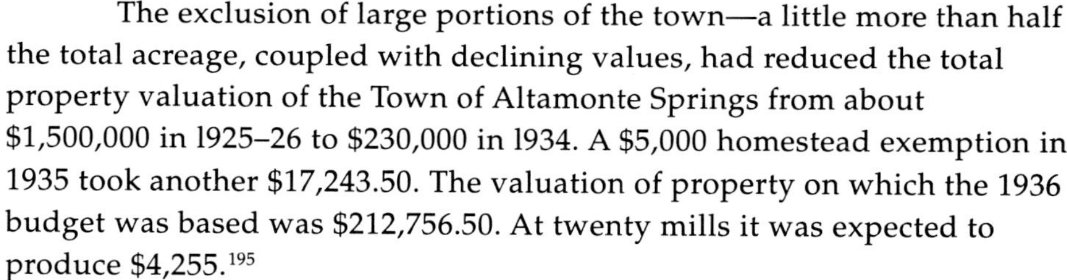

The exclusion of large portions of the town—a little more than half the total acreage, coupled with declining values, had reduced the total property valuation of the Town of Altamonte Springs from about $1,500,000 in 1925–26 to $230,000 in 1934. A $5,000 homestead exemption in 1935 took another $17,243.50. The valuation of property on which the 1936 budget was based was $212,756.50. At twenty mills it was expected to produce $4,255.[195]

Despite the new residency requirements for voting and office holding, Mayor Smith continued to spend his summers in Vermont and the board reduced the frequency of its meetings during that time. When special meetings were held the chairman of the board acted as mayor. As a continuing effort to hold down costs, the street lights were turned off from about May through October. Altamonte Springs was a quieter place in the mid-1930s than it had been a decade earlier.

Mayor B. L. Maltbie (standing on left) as his friend, Dr. James H. Beal, shows some of his shell collection at Cocoa in 1933. President of the Maltbie Chemical Company of East Orange, New Jersey, Mayor of the Town of Altamonte Springs, and president of the Altamonte Development Company, Maltbie was a generous man with many interests. His donation of the Altamonte Springs Community House is well known in his adopted city. But Maltbie had broad interests. Because of his friendship with Dr. Beal and his interest in Rollins College, the mayor donated the Maltbie-Beal Shell Museum which was completed in 1940 and still stands on the Rollins campus.

B. L. Maltbie (right) with Dr. James H. Beal about 1933.

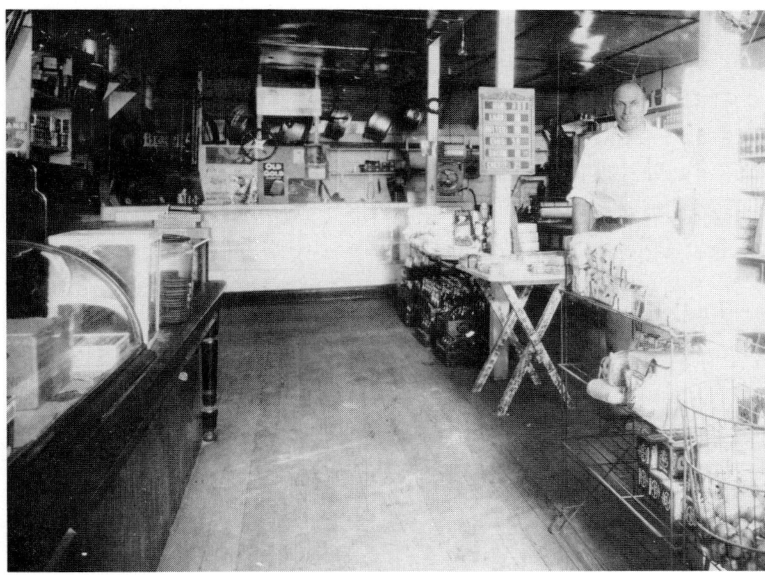

The inside of Fuller's Store as it looked in 1934. Arthur Fuller stands at the side.

The Maltbie Debt

One other financial matter required attention. During the expansive 1920s when he was mayor and president of the Altamonte Development Company, B. L. Maltbie advanced sizable sums to the town for street paving. The debt was unsecured, but Maltbie held receipts for about $25,000. In friendly discussions, he and the council agreed that the loan should be repaid, but the council wanted the amount reduced in the same way that it was accepting reduced payments for back taxes. Maltbie eventually filed suit in September 1933 and obtained a judgment for $10,000. The debt was to run at 4 percent interest and be liquidated as funds became available. Over the next ten years, payments ranging from $500 to $1,000 were made to Maltbie. A small sum was still outstanding when he died in 1942, but the final payment was made to his estate in 1944. A jubilant council noted that the town was "out of debt for the first time in more than a decade." It planned a street celebration complete with barbecue, music, and dancing.[196]

The inside of the post office which was operated by Mr. Fuller for many years.

The Human Side of the Depression

The numbers of people without jobs and in actual need were much greater in the 1930s than ever before and governments at all levels took measures to deal with the problem. Seminole County created a Welfare Board composed of Emma Lyman, Charles Searcy, and B. J. Overstreet. Mrs. Lyman supervised the planting of several acres of cow peas and sweet potatoes at both the Lyman and Rosenwald schools. She was also in charge of distributing surplus government flour to needy recipients. She also brought the matter of needy people before the council. D. B. Kiegan and Alderman H. E. Fuller reported that thirty-three people were in serious need of work to provide basic necessities for their families. Council members did their best to place those in greatest need, although there was little work to be had. Individual employers tried to apportion their jobs so as to do the most good. For example, as manager of a large fernery, L. G. Hattaway assigned his tasks to workers according to the sizes of their family. Men with larger families might get two days per week while others were limited to only one.[197]

The problem of human need was greater than local resources. When Franklin D. Roosevelt was inaugurated in 1933, he launched a vigorous program to relieve those in abject want and to help the nation put its economic system back in order. Under the Federal Emergency Relief Administration, a greater quantity and variety of surplus food was made available to the county for distribution. The Civil Works Administration invited proposals for projects to put people to work quickly. E. T. Haines and W. B. Ballard were dispatched to consult with CWA officials at Sanford about cleanup work in Lake Adelaide and at the entrance to Sanlando Park as well as reopening the road leading eastward from the ACL depot to S.R.3 According to another FERA program, the town council sought assistance to repair Western Avenue, Hermits Trail, Florida Boulevard, Tropic Hill and First Street. The town would provide clay and limerock while the FERA paid for the labor.[198]

A. B. Dodge of Altamonte Springs was in charge of the National Re-Employment Services Office for Seminole County and was responsible for matching unemployed people with both government and private jobs as they became available.[199] After 1935, the Works Progress Administration (WPA) completed several projects around Altamonte Springs. One of them was a county-wide program aimed at eliminating the cattle tick which had plagued the Florida cattle industry for years. In cooperation with the Florida Livestock Sanitary Board, it built dipping vats in which cattle were dipped after they had been found to be infected. One of those vats was located near a pasture where Charles E. Bradshaw was grazing a herd of cattle and where the Renaissance Center is located today.[200]

The WPA also provided labor for construction, resurfacing, and repair of roads. An important one for Altamonte Springs was the grading, clearing, and hard-surfacing of the road from town to Palm Springs.[201]

Even more important was the new S.R. 288. When S.R. 3 was completed in the late 1920s, leaving Altamonte Springs about a mile west of the major route between Sanford and Orlando, the town's leaders realized that a connecting road was essential. There was also need for a road westward through Forest City. The town council urged construction of a road which would run eastward from the Orange County line through Forest City and Altamonte Springs and connect with a road to Oviedo. Everyone agreed to the project, but much coordination was required before work began. While the right-of-way was being obtained, some Altamonte Springs residents protested the possible sacrifice of trees along Altamonte Avenue. That there be no doubt of its intentions, the town council resolved that it "strongly" desired the paving of S.R. 288 and did not wish "to interfere with the relocation of said highway even though it might result in the removal of the trees now growing in approximately the center of said highway." The road was finally begun and was completed in the early 1940s.[202]

Civic Organizations

The local chamber of commerce continued to meet regularly at the Community House in the early 1930s. Webber Haines was president in 1933 and was succeeded that year by Emma Lyman. It hosted a picnic and political rally at Sanlando Springs in 1934 which was attended by more than one hundred people from Altamonte Springs, Forest City, Longwood, Lake Mary, and Fern Park. One of the several speakers was Gordon Barnett, a Fern Park fern grower, who was running for the state legislature.[203]

The chamber became inactive during the depths of the depression, however. In 1938 "the old chamber of commerce fund" of $37.65 was used for painting the chapel.[204]

Several local residents were active in the Seminole County Chamber of Commerce. In 1934, Altamonte Springs members of the board of directors were A. E. Cline, B. L. Maltbie, and B. O. Smith. They were succeeded by B. F. Haines, Mrs. B. F. Haines, and Webber Haines. Walter B. Ballard, who was then chairman of the Seminole County Board of Commissioners, was also active with the organization. One of its major goals during that period was completion of S.R. 288.[205]

An active organization was the Altamonte-Forest City Home Demonstration Club in which Mrs. W. B. Ballard and Emma Lyman were prominently involved. It promoted annual fairs and home demonstration clubs in the county high schools.[206]

Altamonte Hotel dock and southwesterly view of Lake Orienta with the Briggs-Hoffman house and Fuller Bide-a-wee cottage in the background.

This is a view of the Altamonte Hotel from Lake Orienta in the mid-1930s.

Pathway from Altamonte Hotel to the dock on Lake Orienta.

A view across Lake Orienta, of the Altamonte Hotel bungalows, some of which were added in the early 1930s.

Since the Community House was used by civic and religious groups as well as the local government, its maintenance was a matter of continuing concern. During the early 1930s, H. E. Fuller, Emma Lyman and Mrs. Ruth Fuller were the custodians with power to manage the facility. In 1939, a committee of the Altamonte Springs Woman's Club—Emma Lyman, Nora Gilbert, and Mrs. W. B. Ballard—asked that the building be turned over to that organization for maintenance. The town council wasted no time in agreeing to the request. The new custodians gave permission in early 1941 to a Mr. Yates to show moving pictures there.[207]

The Altamonte Springs Garden Club was also active by the late 1930. In 1939 it was authorized by the council to "beautify Hermits Trail Park."[208]

The Jasmine Theater

The Jasmine theater was no longer available for entertainment. The newspaper association sold the property and it was eventually acquired by Rudolph and Mable Haas who made it their home in the early 1930s. They lived there several years during which time the property was acquired by Chester Fosgate. When Fosgate hired Robert Bradford as his packing plant manager in the late 1930s, Bradford and his wife, Grace, moved into the converted theater, made additional improvements, and lived there for many years.[209]

The Altamonte Hotel

After George Bates died in 1931, Everett Bates continued to operate the hotel. The depression had some adverse effect on its clientele, but that was a relative one. Everett Bates' daughter, Virginia Wyman, recalls

Sanlando Springs about 1940. Photograph from the Florida State Archives.

Aerial view of the Altamonte Hotel golf course and northern portion of Lake Orienta. Originally known as Park Lake, the sinkhole in the center was the course water hazard, but it was also hazardous in other ways. When the Capistrano Apartments were later built on this site, the sinkhole was filled in. In time it collapsed and caused difficulties with some of the buildings.

An evening of dancing at the Sanlando Springs pavilion in 1946.

Nina Landman Bates at work on the Altamonte Hotel grounds about 1930.

Swimmers with the "elephant barrel" at Sanlando Springs in 1946.

the case of one longtime winter resident who wrote a long letter lamenting that economic adversity would prevent him from making his customary trek to Florida one year. But, the reluctant guest apparently changed his mind and drove up one day in a shiny new Deusenberg touring sedan.[210]

Bates advertised his hotel in 1934 as a complex of five buildings. The main house was connected to a three-story annex by a piazza. The annex was in turn connected to a lodge of two stories. Two long bungalow buildings of sixteen rooms were nearby. The dining table still offered fine fare. Golf, hunting, and fishing were still available. In addition, the Sanford-Orlando Kennel Club featured dog racing only two miles away and there was a horse track only four miles distant. Opening about December 15 each year, the hotel featured rates on the American plan. A room with bath for one person was available at rates of thirty-eight to

Lillian Grey (Mrs. George E.) Bates in front of the Altamonte Hotel about 1940.

sixty dollars per week. For two persons comparable facilities were fifty-five to eighty-five dollars per week.[211]

A. L. Norton, who had conducted the hotel orchestra during the 1920s, returned as assistant manager during the years of the second world war.[212]

Sanlando Springs

Sanlando Springs Tropical Park remained open after it was repossessed by Moses Overstreet and visitors came from all over Central Florida. About 10,000 azaleas were added in 1935. Special aquatic programs featuring prominent personalities were also added. A popular show was the one by the Marchand family in 1941. Professional log rollers, Frank Marchand and his two daughters, dazzled crowds with a variety of acts twice a day for more than a week. Swimming classes for the public were also offered at the Sanlando pool.[213]

Palm Springs was reopened in 1935 under new management. The waters of the spring had been channeled through a "chute" which was popular among adults and children alike.[214]

In 1944, Moses Overstreet purchased Palm Springs, planning to add it to Sanlando Springs Tropical Park. He declared that this "most complete facility" would be his contribution to the postwar development of Florida.[215]

Schools

Both Lyman and Rosenwald schools remained open for full terms during the depression, although it was sometimes difficult to find funds for salaries. Some work was done on the schools by the Civil Works Administration in 1933–34. E. T. Haines continued as a member of the county school board from his election in the 1920s until his death in 1942. Emma Lyman was still a member of the special tax district through the early 1930s.[216]

Lyman offered all grades for white children, but Rosenwald students were transported by bus to Crooms High School in Sanford. Rosenwald students had a special treat in 1938 when Zora Neale Hurston entertained them with several selections from her books. Hurston, a famous black author who had been born in Eatonville, was brought to Seminole County through the efforts of Jeanette Glover, the county supervisor of the Jeanes Fund. Both schools received funds from the National Youth Administration in 1940 to provide aid to needy students. A different kind of public program was initiated at Lyman in late 1940 when Superintendent W. J. Wells began conducting military drills as part of a countywide defense preparedness program.[217]

Aerial view of Sanlando Springs Tropical Park about 1950.

The Ferneries

The several ferneries in and around Altamonte Springs and Fern Park provided a major source of employment during the period. Employment fluctuated seasonally—there was little work in the late summer—and because of market conditions, but that was characteristic of agricultural work. Charles Haines' Royal Fernery was still the largest single enterprise, although it had changed hands. Benjamin Haines retained the largest portion of the acreage, but R. C. Livingston and W. L. Story had purchased other parts. L. G. Hattaway moved to Altamonte Springs in 1929 as Story's manager. Hibbard Casselberry, who came to Winter Park from Chicago in 1926, bought the entire fifty-five acres from the three owners and Hattaway became his manager. Meanwhile, Casselberry purchased additional land near Lake Concord in Fern Park.[218]

Although some of them—Associated Florist Ferneries and Peerless, for example—had gone out of business, there were still a number of ferneries in Altamonte Springs. In 1934, Frank Vaughan arrived from Kansas and purchased a small one near what is now the Eastmonte recreation complex. After expanding it to about ten acres, he purchased an existing fernery near Lake Concord where Casselberry and Gordon Barnett were also in business. Vaughan expanded and built a large greenhouse complex further north on what is now Highway 17-92. His son, Earl, continued the business there and the land was only recently sold to a developer who built a large shopping center on it. The Vaughan company

These are some of the dwellings which made up the company town at the Royal Fernery. There were about forty of them along with a school and a church.

Some of the lands of the Royal Fernery slatted for protection of the tender plants. It was the expanse of this covering which led one exuberant newspaper reporter in the 1920s to call the Royal Fernery "the largest industry in the nation under one roof."

The front entrance of the Fosgate packing plant which stood near the intersection of today's S. R. 436 and S. R. 434. The company seal (FOZZ) is visible on the sides of the trucks. Photograph from the Seminole County History Museum.

The east side of the Fosgate packing house. Note the water tower at back which was comparable in size to that used by many small towns in the 1930s.

This machinery inside the Fosgate plant was used for sorting and packing the fruit. Photograph from the Seminole County History Museum.

Employees of the Fosgate Company posing during packing season. Most of them are seasonal workers, some of whom came from other states to work during the busy season.

has since relocated to a site on S.R. 46 west of Sanford. L. G. Hattaway acquired Casselberry's fernery near Lake Orienta and he and his family operated it for many more years. By the late 1950s it was known as Hattaway Fernery and Greenhouses and was being managed by L. G.'s grandson, Robert Hattaway.[219]

Casselberry continued in the fern industry for several more years, but he also became interested in town building. In 1940, he founded the "tax-free" town which he named for himself. Centered near Lake Concord it meandered around the Triplett chain of lakes. One effect of the founding of Casselberry was to push Fern Park southward about half a mile.[220]

Citrus

By the 1930s there were more than two thousand acres of orange, tangerine, and grapefruit groves in the Altamonte Springs area. Many residents had small groves, but there were several large ones.

Dr. Phillips still had a sizable one south of town. Harold Frost's Southland Fruit Company was a substantial producer and B. F. Haines had groves in the same area. Long active with the Seminole County Chamber of Commerce, Haines also became a leader in citrus affairs. Heading up the Seminole County Citrus Growers Association, he frequently lobbied in Tallahassee in the interests of citrus growers.[221]

Chester Fosgate owned or controlled about six hundred acres in the area and his packing house at Forest City handled much of the area's fruit and provided employment for a number of people. Stanley Crittenden handled fruit purchases, Albert Connelly took care of sales, and Robert Bradford managed the plant. By the early 1940s the packing house was shipping more than a million boxes of fruit annually. Shipments were facilitated by a railroad siding adjacent to the plant. The plant was reorganized as a growers' cooperative in 1943, but it continued in business for many more years.[222]

Charles E. Bradshaw, a successful insurance executive, moved to the Spring Lake area about 1934 and took an active interest in Altamonte Springs, Seminole County, and Central Florida. He handled insurance for several local businesses, and ran large herds of cattle, a small number of which grazed on land which is now occupied by the Altamonte Mall. He also eventually acquired about 10,000 acres of citrus in Central Florida, some 600 acres of which was near Altamonte Springs. Bradshaw obtained approval of the town council in 1934 to build a packing house on land north of Fuller's store, but he never acted on it. He apparently marketed his fruit through the Fosgate facility and eventually joined the group which reorganized it as a cooperative. Bradshaw was also the founder of Hi-Acres Concentrates, Inc. which was still in production until the 1980s.[223]

Ollie Braddock, an employee of B. D. McIntosh's Fargo Lumber Company, with a team of oxen and an empty log cart. He is heading west on Altamonte Avenue in front of the Altamonte Chapel.

Signs of Economic Recovery

With only sixty ballots cast in December 1937, B. O. Smith was reelected mayor without opposition. Aldermen L. R. Brookings, A. H. Fuller, H. E. Fuller, E. T. Haines, and Homer Sewell, Sr., were also re-elected. New aldermen were R. J. Bundy and B. D. McIntosh, Sr. W. B. Ballard, treasurer, reported a sound financial situation. The annual budget of $4,255 included $700 toward the Maltbie debt and still left a balance in the treasury.

The town had bid in a number of tax delinquent properties and several subdivisions were still inactive, but it was looking for improvement in this regard before long. The tourist season looked promising with every house in town taken and the hotel doing a fine business. Fuller's store was still the place where people met to exchange news. The mail was handled by Ed Mitchell who had been postmaster since 1936. B. D. McIntosh, Jr., was operating the Red Top service station south of town at the corner of South Altamonte Avenue and Oranole.[224]

The Transition to Wartime

Improvements in the local economy were accompanied by mounting concerns about foreign affairs. Even while the WPA was still at work on S.R. 288, the nation's leaders decided it was time to prepare for the possibility of war. The first peace time draft in the nation's history called for young men to be drafted for one year of military service beginning in 1940. Several local youths—among them George Bates and Clifton

This team of oxen is pulling a loaded log cart eastward along Altamonte Avenue in front of the Bradlee-McIntyre house, heading toward the McIntosh mill.

Hattaway—were conscripted for a year of training. Before their year was up the nation was at war. Their terms were extended and others were being called for "the duration and six months." Many did not wait to be drafted. Tolar Bryan had already joined the U.S. Marines. Howard Lyman joined the Coast Guard. Hat Hattaway enlisted and began training in gliders. Among the other local men who went into the service were B. D. McIntosh, Jr., Graham Fuller, Herbert Lyman, Allen Forward, William Gilbert, Jesse Howell, Leon Roux, and Benjamin F. McKinney. W. J. Wells, Jr., principal of Lyman High School, was also drafted in 1942.[225]

On the home front, citizens produced agricultural products for defense and home use. Some may have worked in the bomb parachute factory operated by Hibbard Casselberry. When Skill Gorham and Albert Balzar conducted registration for civil defense, 427 people signed up—the 1940 population of the town was 553. They participated in blackout drills and manned lookouts for possible enemy aircraft. Charles E. Bradshaw was district supervisor for civil defense. Skill Gorham became chairman of the local USO. Joe Bennett was vice chairman and W. B. Ballard was secretary. Ten others volunteered to staff the organization.[226]

Altamonte Springs residents contributed to the Red Cross and met their quotas in each of the bond drives, which were usually managed by Mrs. Ruth Fuller and Mrs. W. B. Ballard. They endured the rationing of gasoline, sugar, tires, and other scarce commodities. They mourned the losses of E. T. Haines, B. L. Maltbie, and Emma Lyman, each of whom had

Members of the congregation leaving the Altamonte Chapel after services in 1944.

made major contributions to local government and society. They applauded when the Orlando Bus Company extended service connecting Longwood, Casselberry, Altamonte Springs, and Sanlando Tropical Park. They endured inadequate telephone service when the Winter Park Telephone Company explained that it could make no improvements to civilian systems until after the war. They supported their men in service, and they applauded when the war finally ended in 1945.[227]

NINE

A Rural Community in Transition: 1945-1960

The population grew to 866 by 1950, by which time real estate valuations exceeded a million dollars. . . . Although quite modest in comparison to what was in store, the growth was accompanied by the need for expanded municipal services.

With fewer than six hundred inhabitants in 1945, the Town of Altamonte Springs was still dealing with depression-related matters when the war ended in 1945. Mayor B. O. Smith and the council—composed of aldermen Leslie T. Bryan, J. B. Douglass, Clifford Gilbert, R. E. Hoffman, Clyde Whitehead, Mrs. B. D. McIntosh, Jr., and H. E. Fuller—were operating on a budget of about seven thousand dollars, derived from property, license, and utilities taxes. Auctions were still being held to dispose of property which had earlier been acquired in lieu of taxes. There were signs of change, however. Sales were brisk at the tax-sale auctions. Housing was in short supply, leading the council to ease the stringent building restrictions which had been imposed in 1925. About ninety new homes were built in the town limits by 1950, and there was additional construction in the surrounding area.[228]

Incorporation of a new chamber of commerce in 1947 suggested renewed enthusiasm. Subscribers were J. E. Matthews, H. E. Fuller, Leslie T. Bryan, Dr. B. F. Sedman, and Clifford Gilbert. Both Matthews, a retired army colonel, and Sedman, a retired physician, were newcomers, but they were permanent residents.[229]

The death of B. O. Smith in 1947 emphasized a subtle but significant change. Having been mayor for nearly two-thirds of the twenty-seven years since the town's incorporation, Smith was the last of the part-time residents to hold office. Winter residents continued to frequent the town and play an important part in its economy, but Altamonte Springs was no longer a "Florida Boston Town."[230]

The population grew to 866 by 1950 by which time real estate valuations exceeded a million dollars. At $11,515, the 1951 budget approximated those of the mid-1920s for the first time in a quarter century. The population was 1,212 in 1960 and the budget that year was about $53,000. Further growth of the town was accompanied by a number of developments outside its limits. Among them were Orienta Gardens, Dol-

Ray Manor, Oakland Shores, Druid Hills, and the Sanlando Subdivision "with its golf and Country Club." The latter, a revival of the defunct Sanlando Golf Properties, Inc., would shortly become known as Rolling Hills.[231]

Although quite modest in comparison to what was in store, the growth was accompanied by the need for expanded municipal services. That expansion would prove turbulent and contentious at times. The death of Mayor Smith, coinciding with the death of L. R. Brookings, the town clerk, was such a case. They were succeeded by J. E. Matthews as mayor and John C. Goddard as clerk, but the special election caused a furor. Matthews had won in an election in which more blacks than whites had voted. Of a total of 204 votes, 117 were cast by black voters. Matthews was accused of violating racial customs by campaigning for black votes. Whether or not he had done so, the town was badly divided for several weeks. Some whites, realizing that black voters outnumbered whites in the town, demanded that the boundaries be redrawn to exclude the black section. The council quickly rejected that proposal and excitement gradually abated. Matthews served only briefly before poor health forced him to resign. The affair emphasized changes which were coming to post-war America and it soon became clear that whites were not alone in desiring boundary changes.[232]

In the Town, But Not of It

Like many small Florida towns, Altamonte Springs, by law, was strictly segregated at the time. Almost a third of the people who had founded Altamonte Springs were black. Blacks and whites lived harmoniously in the same town, dependent upon each other in many ways, but in separate residential sections clearly delineated by law. A new zoning ordinance was adopted in 1945 making the junction of Leonard Street and Longwood Avenue the dividing line between the "white and colored" sections. That change was made after the council learned that Willie Grant (a black man) was building a home near Prairie Lake. Grant was allowed to complete construction but was required to "sell same to white parties only."[233]

By that time a viable black community had evolved in the northeast section of Altamonte Springs. There were four churches. St. Johns Baptist on Longwood Avenue dated from the 1920s. Williams Chapel (also Baptist) had first been located near the original railroad track in 1933, but was relocated to the corner of Williams and Marker (formerly Market) streets. Williams Street was named for the Rev. B. T. Williams who was minister at the chapel. New Bethel African Methodist Episcopal Church was also located on Marker Street. Free Will Primitive Baptist Church on Longwood Avenue was the fourth of the early churches. Since its inception in 1931, Rosenwald School had become a central part of the black community.[234]

The business district of the black community was located at the intersection of East Street (now Merritt) and Longwood Avenue, extending east on East Street and along Longwood Avenue in both directions. Banks Ford had a two-story building which housed his drug store and confectionery. There were tables and chairs out front for his confectionery customers. A beauty parlor occupied the second floor. Irving Bolden's grocery store was adjacent to the drug store. Next, there was Bush's cafe, complete with living quarters in back. Clayton Thomas operated a bar and cafe nearby. Conder Merritt also had a bar as well as a popular movie theater. There was another cafe which included a pool room. A Masonic Lodge not only housed the fraternal order, but is remembered by some older residents as their first school. Completing the business district was a hotel known as the Big House.[235]

On S.R. 436, east of the town limits, Banks Ford operated the Club 436. Morris Foster also had a bar and package store in the area. Almost directly behind the 436 Club on Prairie Lake was a beautiful beach which was frequented by black people from all over Central Florida. In the northwest portion of the black section was a baseball field where black and white teams met in friendly competition for many years.[236]

The Progressive Voters League

Some blacks had always voted in the non-partisan town elections, but they had never been numerous. After the national and state courts outlawed the "white primary" by which blacks had been excluded from the Democratic primaries which had long decided state elections, blacks throughout Florida began voter registration drives. Conder Merritt and his associates had followed the statewide movement in Altamonte Springs. Soon, Merritt was spokesman for a majority of the voters in the town. While he disavowed any desire to elect a black mayor, he made it clear that black residents wanted a more sympathetic hearing from the town council than had been customary. The turnout for the August 1947 election was a result.[237]

The black voters league remained active in local affairs during the next three years, but eventually resolved to withdraw from the town. Conder Merritt and eighty others sued for exclusion of their property from the town limits on the grounds that they were receiving no municipal services in return for their taxes. Since there was no opposition from the council, the case of *State of Florida, et al, v. Town of Altamonte Springs* was decided in November 1951 in favor of the complainants. Eighty acres of the northeast section, housing a majority of the town's black residents were excluded from Altamonte Springs.[238]

The Seminole Grill, Inc.

Just outside the southern town limits, the Seminole Bar and Grill was being operated by Arthur E. Harper of Winter Park and K. T. Rockwell of Pahokee. It included a gambling hall complete with a loft where an armed guard could watch the door. Widespread gambling in Florida came under public scrutiny in the late 1940s. When Orange County began trying to shut down gambling within its boundaries, the Seminole Club—just inside the Seminole County line—became quite active. Whether true or not, it was widely believed that Harper and Rockwell enjoyed the protection of Seminole County Sheriff Percy Mero.[239]

There was excitement in June 1949 when three men attempted to rob the gambling hall of the Seminole Club. Willard Brown, the guard, shot and killed Peter Fantasia and wounded Mike Salvi. A third man escaped, but both he and Salvi were apprehended. The place was closed for a time, but later reopened. Under pressure from public opinion, stimulated by the sensational televised revelations of the Estes Kefauver committee, Governor Fuller Warren investigated gambling in Seminole County and the Seminole Club was permanently closed in 1951. The building and twenty acres of land (Maitland Avenue and Spring Lake Drive) were subsequently purchased by the Catholic Church.[240]

Who Appoints the Marshal?

J. D. Morrison, who had replaced L. R. Brookings as express agent in 1947, succeeded Matthews as mayor in 1949. The board of aldermen then included C. A. Benson, B. O. Burnette, Maury Crews, Sally Faulhaber, R. E. Hoffman, H. E. Fuller, and W. H. Young. Much of Morrison's term was consumed by the question of a town marshal. H. O. Swofford's lengthy tenure had been a stormy one, but he had many supporters. When the mayor dismissed him in early 1950, the town government erupted. In response to petitions signed by eighty-three white and ninety-four black voters—representing a large majority of the town electorate—Swofford was reappointed. The controversial marshal was in and out of office several times after that, but he was still in office in 1954. During the next several years, a number of people were appointed as marshal—or police chief—but there was no continuity. Grady Hall, who had served briefly in the 1930s, was named to the position of chief of police in 1957, with John Wolf as his assistant. He was succeeded in 1960 by Tracy Sullivan who also had an assistant.[241]

This fully equipped fire truck was purchased by the volunteer fire department in 1953 with funds which came primarily from contributions, fund raisers, and a large note signed by some of the volunteers. The city later acquired the truck and responsibility for the borrowed money.

During the controversy over the marshal's position in 1951, Morrison resigned to be replaced by John C. Goddard in a special election. After the regular election in the fall, Roy Randall was inaugurated as mayor in 1952. Aldermen were then Howard Arnold, Brian Kimble, Austel Largent, Raymond Rock, Frank Seaman, Lawrence Swofford, and Graham Fuller. Goddard returned to the position of clerk.[242]

The Volunteer Fire Department

A new volunteer fire department was incorporated in 1952 and soon had forty-five volunteers. With Earl Riley as president, Cliff Sands as engineer, and B. D. McIntosh, Jr., as fire chief, the volunteers undertook a major fund-raising campaign for the purchase of modern equipment and a place in which to house it. Kristian Juthe and Claude Roosevelt were among the most enthusiastic supporters of the new unit. The town provided a site on Altamonte Avenue near Blackford's store for a municipal building. The volunteers raised funds for the new building as well as a new pumper. As members of the department, several individuals signed a note for purchase of the pumper. The new unit was operating in time to fight the great Altamonte Hotel fire in July 1953. It was not long, however, before disagreements arose over the new department's budget and the town's contribution to it.[243]

Altamonte fire station and city hall on Longwood Avenue in 1955. The fire station was constructed through a joint effort of the Volunteer Fire Department and the Town of Altamonte Springs.

The differences between the volunteers and the town council, led by Mayor Richard Sodero and Alderman Lawrence Swofford, mounted until the town filed a lawsuit against the fire department in 1954. The suit was resolved short of adjudication, and the town agreed to assume the debt owed for the pumper and take over responsibility for fire protection. Most of the volunteers resigned.[244]

A new volunteer fire department was organized in early 1955 with Don Van Daley as chief. With about twenty-five members, the new department offered fire protection to all who paid a small membership fee and agreed to pay fifty dollars for each call. A number of individuals followed each other in rapid succession as fire chief. Richard Young held that position in 1960, but Altamonte Springs still depended upon a volunteer fire department through the 1960s.[245]

A Mayor and Council Form of Government

The 1953 legislature authorized a mayor and council form of government in which the mayor would have strong powers to manage the town's affairs. The seven aldermen would be replaced by four councilmen. All were to serve two-year terms. The mayor would preside over council meetings, but would vote only in cases of a tie. The council later divided the town into four wards from which the councilmen would be elected.[246]

Volunteer firemen and their truck in 1952. From the left they are Earle W. Riley, B. D. McIntosh, Jr., Clifford Sands, and J. E. Martin.

Graham, G., Kent, Herbert E., and Arthur H. Fuller in 1948.

B. D. McIntosh, Jr., opened the Altamonte Garage after he returned from military service in 1945 and operated it for many years. Offering Texaco products and full-service automobile repairs, he also had the only towing service in South Seminole County for many years. The station is shown here as it was in 1964.

In the meantime, Acting Mayor J. C. Guest called a special election for September 1954 to elect a mayor to replace Richard Sodero who had resigned. In a three-way contest, Lawrence Swofford was elected by a plurality over B. D. McIntosh, Jr., and Homer Sewell, Jr. J. F. Bateman, Lee Gullo, Henry Hansen, and Horace Weltmer were elected to serve with Swofford. At the regular election that year, Swofford defeated C. W. Seymour. The councilmen then were Horace Weltmer, Frank Obrien, Don P. Van Daley, and Hugo Wolf.[247]

The Town Clerk

By the time Leslie T. Bryan succeeded J. C. Goddard as town clerk in 1953, the duties of clerk, assessor, treasurer and collector were becoming quite onerous for one person. Henry Hansen followed Bryan as clerk,

James Cornell opened his Town Garage at 956 East Altamonte Avenue about 1953. This photograph was taken in 1955. The building has since been renovated and now houses Zembower's Garage.

but plans were already in the works to provide some relief. Legislation was obtained in 1957 to make the office appointive instead of elective; and the mayor and council were empowered to fill the position with one, two, three, or four persons as they deemed necessary.[248]

The Commercial Center

The Fuller store in the 1960s, just before it was demolished to make way for new construction.

The Altamonte Springs business district was still centered near the intersection of S.R. 436 (Altamonte Avenue) and C.R. 427 (Longwood Avenue) when the council voted in 1950 to rezone the south side of Altamonte Avenue from residential to commercial. Fuller's Store was still the general store, but it was soon acquired by Henry Hansen. The building still housed the post office as well as the real estate agency of Homer Sewell, Sr. In the early 1950s, L. D. Blackford opened a grocery store across C.R. 427 from the Fuller building. Raymond Rock's hardware store was just west of it. The Altamonte Garage on C.R. 427, owned and operated by B. D. McIntosh, Jr., offered a towing service, automotive repairs and a full line of Texaco products. Dan Kiegan built and opened a grocery store nearby in the 1940s. It was being operated by C. W. Seymour who lived with his family in back of the store. Seymour added a bar and package store. In later years it became the Rendezvous Club and still later the Linc-Inn. About 1953 James Cornell opened the Town Garage on the south side of S.R. 436 where he dealt in Shell products. Businesses in the 1950s also included a gift shop, and an antique store. In the late 1940s, C. R. Lowdermilk was still serving Altamonte Springs with his "rolling store."[249]

Prairie Lake Drive-In Theater

Built by James Partlow and Associates between S.R. 436 and Prairie Lake, the Prairie Lake Drive-In opened in 1949. With a panoramic screen, the latest equipment, first-run movies advertised in the *Orlando Sentinel*, and the advent of the automobile age, the theater was soon an

Aerial view of Prairie Lake Drive-in between Prairie Lake (lower left) and S.R. 436. The drive-in was opened in 1949 and soon became a popular attraction in Central Florida. It was demolished in 1988.

important part of Altamonte Springs in particular and the Central Florida social scene in general.

At the request of Partlow, the town council agreed to annex the theater. Although it took several years, annexation of the property eventually moved the town limits eastward along S.R. 436.[250]

The Railway Express Agency

Following L. R. Brookings' death in 1947, J. D. Morrison became the express agent. With his wife, Zetta, Morrison built up a large express business, shipping large quantities of fresh fruit, ferns, and foliage from Altamonte Springs, Fern Park, Oviedo, Maitland, Apopka, and Plymouth growers. Because the Altamonte Springs station was more accessible to the growers of those communities, its volume of business was greater than that of Orlando during the 1950s and 1960s. Having worked closely with her husband since they arrived, Zetta Morrison took over the agency when he retired in the 1960s. The agency remained active under her management until the early 1970s.[251]

The Post Office

The post office eventually outgrew the space set aside for it in the Fuller building and was moved to a rented office on the north side of Altamonte Avenue. After several years of lobbying by Postmaster Ed Mitchell and his patrons, a new post office building was erected directly across the street from the rented facility in 1960. Mitchell retired in 1962 after twenty-eight years in office. Altamonte Springs eventually outgrew the new facility and yet another building was constructed on Longwood Avenue where it remains.[252]

The post office building at 954 East Altamonte Avenue, which was opened for business in 1960.

The Winter Park Telephone Company

After the war, Joseph Galloway worked to improve the telephone service which had been so severely criticized during the war years. Automatic dialing equipment was installed in the early 1950s. As growth continued, the telephone company responded in the late 1950s with construction of an Altamonte Springs branch office with two thousand lines to serve Altamonte Springs, Casselberry, Longwood, Fern Park, and Forest City.[253]

The Altamonte Hotel

The hotel had survived depression and war and was still filled to capacity during the winter seasons. Many of the guests had been coming to Altamonte Springs for years. As in the past, Everett Bates and his staff opened the hotel in December and closed it in early April. He then spent the summers in Maine while Fred Faulhaber looked after the hotel and grounds. It was Faulhaber who sounded the alarm when fire broke out in the early morning hours of July 1, 1953. Altamonte Springs Fire Chief B. D. McIntosh, Jr., led the town's volunteer fire department which pumped water on the fire from Lake Orienta. Visible for miles around, the blaze brought fire companies from Orlando, Winter Park, Pine Castle,

Altamonte Springs Mayor J. D. Morrison (left) and the mayors of Winter Park (B. R. Coleman), Casselberry (Paul Bates), Longwood (H. S. Arnold), and Maitland (Richard McCanna) switching the Winter Park telephone system to automatic dialing in 1949.

The Bradlee-McIntyre house in the late 1940s. B. D. McIntosh, Sr., purchased the place about 1947, but lived there only briefly before his wife's death about 1949.

Casselberry, Maitland, Longwood, and Sanford. About fifty firemen fought the blaze for twenty-two hours before it was finally extinguished. The main hotel was consumed, but the annex was saved. Although many of Bates' regular guests asked him to rebuild, he chose not to do so. Some guests were housed in the annex for a while, but the fire ended an era. The *Dixie Flyer* had been removed in the 1920s. The ACL stopped its regular passenger service in the 1930s. Then the great fire destroyed the main hotel building in 1953.[254]

A view toward the west along Altamonte Avenue in 1950.

Civic Organizations

Citizens groups had been instrumental in maintaining the buildings and grounds of the town since the Ladies Auxiliary to the Chamber of Commerce in the 1920s. The Garden Club and the Women's Club were both active in the late 1930s and throughout the war in maintaining the Community House as well as the park, tennis courts, streets, and the Community Chapel. Recognizing that the number of women in the town was small and that the same people were supporting both organizations, the Garden Club and the Women's Club decided to merge. The result was the 1946 formation of the Altamonte Springs Civic Club. Officers were Mrs. Donald Harris, president; Mrs. Robert Bradford, vice-president; Mrs. B. F. Haines and Mrs. L. M. Anders, secretaries; and Miss Anne Cline, treasurer. Most of the women of the town were active in the Civic Club over the years.[255]

Aerial view across Altamonte Springs in 1950. Lake Adelaide is in the upper center. The open space between that lake and Palm Springs Drive was known as Bryan's Meadows where Leslie T. Bryan grazed cattle and horses. Just beyond Palm Springs Drive is Cranes Roost.

The Altamonte Hotel as seen from Maitland Avenue in the late 1940s.

OLDERING HOTEL RUINS—The smoking remains of Altamonte Hotel, 70-year-old Altamonte Springs landmark, are shown yesterday after fire razed the three-story frame structure. [Sentinel-Star Foto].

Altamonte Fire Ruins Guarded

Ruins of the Altamonte Hotel after the great fire in July 1953.

MEMBERS OF THE ALTAMONTE SPRINGS CIVIC CLUB
1952-1953

Mrs. George B. Arnold	Mrs. Henry Hansen
Mrs. W. B. Ballard	Mrs. Don Harris
Mrs. W. M. Beaumont	Mrs. H. J. High
Mrs. C. A. Benson	Mrs. H. T. Jackman
Mrs. C. A. Bigelow	Mrs. K. A. Juthe
Mrs. Dorothy Bowker	Mrs. C. O. Knox
Mrs. Robert Bradford	Mrs. J. E. Martin
Mrs. A. L. Bridgers	Mrs. B. D. McIntosh, Jr.
Mrs. L. T. Bryan	Mrs. B. F. McKinney
Mrs. H. S. Briggs	Mrs. Raymond Morey
Mrs. Inez Briggs	Mrs. J. D. Morrison
Mrs. W. H. Brown	Mrs. H. V. Nelson
Mrs. B. O. Burnette	Mrs. A. P. Phillips
Mrs. Warren Carpenter	Mrs. T. D. Putnam
Mrs. E. O. Choice	Mrs. Fred Rassman
Mrs. N. B. Choice	Mrs. Earle Riley
Miss Anne Cline	Mrs. Raymond Rock
Mrs. M. H. Davidson	Mrs. Clifford Sands
Mrs. Eli Day	Mrs. P. O. Schallert
Mrs. A. B. Evans	Mrs. P. O. Schallert, Jr.
Mrs. W. A. Forward	Mrs. B. F. Seaman
Mrs. H. G. Fuller	Mrs. H. K. Seaman
Mrs. C. H. Gilbert	Mrs. B. O. Smith
Mrs. C. H. Gilbert, Jr.	Mrs. Richard Sodero
Mrs. J. C. Goddard	Mrs. W. L. Swofford
Mrs. W. M. Gordon	Mrs. H. C. Voss
Mrs. T. L. Gorham	Mrs. T. F. Wood
Mrs. Leo Gullo	
Mrs. B. F. Haines	Honorary Member:
Mrs. Webber Haines	Mrs. George Kingsley

Members of the Altamonte Springs Civic Club, 1952-53.

Altamonte Springs Civic Club officials at work. They are from the left: Mrs. J. D. Morrison (Zetta), president; Mrs. B. D. McIntosh, Jr., vice-president; Mrs. H. K. Seaman, secretary; and Mrs. J. D. Voss, treasurer.

Supported by a committee of the town council, the Civic Club was in charge of maintaining the Community House and scheduling the events which were held there. Although the town council employed Herbert Wooten as street supervisor in 1947, the club continued to assist in keeping up the streets and public grounds. Street maintenance and landscaping was done by a garden committee of the club.[256]

The corner of Maitland Avenue and Altamonte Avenue looking east in 1952.

The garden committee apparently evolved into a new Garden Club in 1954. Both men and women comprised the revived club's membership of about one hundred. The two civic organizations continued to do important work with the Community House, the chapel, the streets and the parks. They also took an active role in developing and maintaining the playground and recreation center, a function which undoubtedly found acceptance by yet a third organization.[257]

The Community Club was composed mostly of parents of the town's young people. It sponsored youth baseball, teen-age dances, and general youth recreation. The baseball games were played on a field which was part of the town park and recreation center. Complete with parking facilities, the recreation center was located directly behind the municipal building on Longwood Avenue and extended to Newburyport Avenue.[258]

Churches

Since its relocation from Lake Brantley in 1908, the Altamonte Chapel had been open for religious services only during the winter months when the town's population was augmented by seasonal resi-

Kristian Juthe and H. E. Fuller at the shuffleboard court during the dedication service for the Altamonte Springs playground in August 1955.

The Altamonte Springs Little League team in 1958.

dents. By the 1950s, the permanent population had increased to the point that a Community Church was organized in 1955. John William Claudy was the first pastor. The congregation eventually outgrew the little church, but it remains a beautiful landmark—the oldest building in the city—on busy Altamonte Avenue. It is a popular place for weddings. Regular services are conducted in a new brick building nearby.[259]

The First Baptist Church had its origins in the late 1930s when the Rev. Lewis Haines served as supply minister. When the congregation was organized, Rev. Haines became the first minister. Leslie T. Bryan and Robert Bradford led a building fund drive and the first church building was completed in 1958. In the meantime, services were conducted in rented facilities and, for a time, in the Community House.[260]

Saint Mary Magdalene Catholic Church was started on April 5, 1959, when Father Hubert J. Reason celebrated mass for ninety-five families in the old building which originally housed the Seminole Club. Ground was broken for a new church and school in early 1961. The parish grew so that a new building was erected in 1975 and the older edifice became a social hall. As the population grew on the west side of I-4, a satellite church was established on Montgomery Road. It became the Church of the Annunciation with its own pastor in 1980.[261]

As the town grew, other churches were established. The Altamonte Springs Seventh-day Adventist Church began holding services in a small chapel at 455 S. Maitland Avenue in 1962. Both the congregation and the buildings to house it have grown consistently since then. The Temple Baptist Church of Azalea Park received permission in 1963 to begin holding services in the Community House with a view to starting a new church in Altamonte Springs. A new congregation was organized and the Palm Springs Drive Baptist Church was built and opened in 1967. The church and its Christian School have provided significantly to the community since that time.[262]

The Moravian Church now located on S.R. 434 in Longwood began with services in the Community House before raising its own sanctuary in the late 1960s. St. Marks Presbyterian Church (USA) held its first services in 1970 in the Altamonte Springs Elementary School on S.R. 436.[263] St. Marks was organized in January 1971 with about ninety members. Rev. Harvey Walters was the first pastor. The church building was completed at the corner of Palm Springs Drive and North Street in January 1973.[264]

The Town in 1960

During the last months of World War II, shortly after S.R. 288 was redesignated as S.R. 436, Hat and Tally Hattaway and three other men drove a hundred head of Charles Bradshaw's cattle from a pasture—which is now the Altamonte Mall—eastward to greener pastures not far from the present intersection of Red Bug Lake Road. They met a few cars along the way, but there was no significant interruption of traffic. Such a cattle drive along that route would have been quite unlikely by 1960 and unimaginable within a short time afterward.[265]

There was already noticeable change by 1955 when the new mayor and council form of government was implemented. In addition to matters of police and fire protection, there were serious discussions of a community water system. The town boundaries were extended by legislation in 1957. Plans for new developments were being presented with increasing frequency. An addition was made to the municipal building to provide an office for the mayor and a growing number of town employees. The planning and zoning commission was dealing with plans for the widening of Maitland Avenue. A committee composed of William R. Wigley, Luther Hart, and N. B. Choice was working on a system of street names and numbers.[266]

Mayor Swofford had defeated E. Martin Law to retain his office in 1957 and seemed apparently destined to win another election in 1959, but the idea of a strong mayor with a propensity to promote growth, con-

Robert H. Newell in front of his Elk Station on S.R. 436. The station opened in 1960 and closed in 1988.

cerned many citizens who preferred the town as it was. Only a week before the election, a citizens group began campaigning for the "virtually unknown" Wilbur Hawkins for mayor. With only 271 of the town's 478 registered voters going to the polls, Hawkins defeated Swofford by 142 to 125 votes. A surprised Lawrence Swofford conceded the election and offered his support for the new mayor, but he was destined to return for a long tenure.[267]

Despite the opposition of those who preferred a small, sedentary town, Altamonte Springs was destined for immense growth in the immediate future with or without a growth-oriented mayor.

Robert Newell's Lawn Mower and Hurricane Donna

The normal course of events was interrupted in 1960 by Hurricane Donna which did extensive damage and it was several days before electricity was restored to a large area of Central Florida. Robert Newell had moved to Altamonte Springs from Massachusetts earlier that year and opened an independent service station on S. R. 436 just east of town. Newell had been unhappy with himself for bringing all the way to Florida a reel-type lawn mower which was unsuited to his Florida lawn. But, with the power outage following the September hurricane, he remembered that the mower had a top-mounted engine. Turning his mistake into opportunity, he connected the lawn mower engine to his gasoline pump, making fuel available to desperate area drivers. Word of the ingenious system was picked up by the local radio stations and Newell was busy supplying gasoline to long lines of motorists until electricity was restored. Newell's station remained a landmark in Altamonte Springs until it was closed in 1988.

TEN

The Suburbanization of Altamonte Springs: The 1960s

By the mid-1960s, the question of growth of Altamonte Springs was no longer just a local matter. The Orlando metropolitan area was expanding rapidly in all directions and Altamonte Springs was directly in its path.

Depending upon who was making the assessment, Lawrence Swofford was either a visionary political leader who wisely guided his home town from its sedentary past into its bustling future; or, he was a controversial and ruthless politician who used his position arbitrarily, treated opposing views with contempt, and regarded criticism as simply misinformed. While there is considerable evidence that both these assessments had validity, there is no question that Mayor Swofford was the dominant figure in Altamonte Springs during the 1960s and early 1970s. He had a vision of the kind of town he would like Altamonte Springs to become and the stamina and political sagacity to make it a reality. In the process, he incurred vigorous opposition and criticism. In the long run, however, some of his most severe critics concede that Swofford always tried to do what he believed to be best for Altamonte Springs.

The Midnight Meeting

Swofford's loss of the 1959 mayor's race by seventeen votes surprised many and rankled the mayor. When he won reelection in 1961, he lost no time in announcing his return. Having himself sworn in shortly after midnight on January 2, 1962, he then administered oaths of office to the two new councilmen, Keith Nixon and Frank Gerhardt. When the three met with holdovers Jeff Hodges and John Wolf the next day, Swofford went immediately to work.

He first vetoed a zoning ordinance adopted by the outgoing administration and rescinded its order regarding a bank depository for town funds. But his most dramatic move was the announcement that both Fire Chief Dick Young and Police Chief Tracy Sullivan had resigned. Both men expressed surprise to hear of their resignations. Ignoring their protests, the mayor asked the council to accept the resignations. He then swore in Grady Hall as the new police chief. Harry Brown was named fire chief a few weeks later. The dramatic meeting set the tone for the Swofford era, a period of frequent confrontation and controversy in local government and enormous growth of the town.[268]

The Water System

The proposed water system had been a matter of serious disagreement in the late 1950s and Swofford's vigorous support of it had had much to do with his narrow defeat in 1959. But the town council continued to work on it during the Hawkins administration and a municipal water system was approved in 1961. Revenue bonds were issued for construction.[269]

With Swofford avidly promoting the system after his return to office, it became the focus of continuing debate over growth. Bob Widdis was employed as supervisor of public works in June 1962, later to be succeeded by Don Bundy. Marcella Hanson, a longtime volunteer at the town hall, was employed in 1963 to handle utility billings. Meanwhile, people were sent door-to-door seeking subscribers to the system. Resistance was strong at first, but there were many who desired the convenience. Designed to serve some three hundred homes, the facility was at full capacity when it was completed in early 1964. By that time demand was growing as requests for service came from Glen Arden, Glen Arden Heights, Snead Homes, Oakland Estates and others. There were also requests from developers of apartment complexes who were concomitantly seeking zoning changes to accommodate their multi-family buildings.[270]

By 1965 additional storage tanks and increased pumping capacity were being sought. Mayor Swofford became quite adept at obtaining both loans and grants from the United States government for much-needed public facilities.[271]

Opposition remained strong. The Citizens of Altamonte Springs for Better Government, Inc., demanded an audit of the town's books, with special attention to those of the water department. The mayor welcomed the proposed audit so that it would "clear the town of the false charges."[272]

Opponents of growth might well point to the water system as the culprit. The system and development fed on each other. Developers needed water to obtain approval for their projects and Altamonte Springs had the water. As capacity was reached, the system was expanded. More developers applied for water, and the system was further expanded.

Proponents, on the other hand, regarded the water system as the town's greatest accomplishment to date. It should also be remembered that it was at Mayor Swofford's suggestion in 1967 that Altamonte Springs became one of the first cities to require developers to build roads along with their developments instead of having taxpayers pay for them after the fact. The city was also one of the first to adopt a comprehensive zoning plan, albeit one which permitted more housing units per acre than would subsequently be considered desirable.[273]

By the mid-1960s, the question of growth of Altamonte Springs was no longer just a local matter. The Orlando metropolitan area was expanding rapidly in all directions and Altamonte Springs was directly in its path.

The Action Center of Florida

Continuing military preparedness because of the so-called "cold war" after World War II had kept two air bases in Orlando fully manned. Their personnel created demands for housing construction, their payrolls infused millions of dollars into the local economy, and, perhaps most important of all, new companies were established to provide supplies and services to them. The United States Missile Center at Cape Canaveral, augmented after 1958 by the enormous National Aeronautics and Space Agency (NASA) on Merritt Island, contributed significantly to the evolving economic and population boom which was gathering in Central Florida. Personnel working on the space coast shopped, and often lived, in Orlando. More firms moved in to provide supplies and services to the space program.

One of those firms was the Martin Company (now Martin-Marietta) which opened a large plant in southwest Orange County in 1957. It soon had more than eight thousand, well-paid employees buying homes and spending money in Orlando. The Martin plant also brought in many subsidiary firms (seventy-two in 1958 alone).

By the early 1960s, Orlando promoters were calling their city the "Action Center of Florida."

A Transportation Hub

Aggressive city leaders such as Carl Langford, Martin Andersen, and William H. "Billy" Dial saw even greater opportunity for their city in all the growth. They worked to assure that the Sunshine Parkway (now the Florida Turnpike) was routed through Orange County. By the time it was completed in 1963, they were working to secure a favorable routing of the new interstate highway (I-4) between Tampa and Daytona Beach. The new road not only crossed the turnpike near the Martin-Marietta plant as it wound through Orlando and Winter Park, but it also passed just west of Altamonte Springs. It was completed in 1965.

The McCoy Jetport

An unusual arrangement was made between Orlando and the United States Air Force in 1961 allowing civilian jet aircraft to use McCoy AFB while military planes were still stationed there. The city gained full control of civilian air traffic at McCoy in 1968. Thus began the growth of the jetport south of Orlando which now ranks as one of the sixteen largest in the nation. The Martin Andersen Beeline highway was built between the airport and S.R. 520 in eastern Orange County to make McCoy the airport for the space coast.

Walt Disney World

The convergence of several major highways near a promising airport where large tracts of undeveloped land were available, was probably what prompted a "mystery industry" to begin quietly buying up large acreages in 1965. In November of that year, Walt Disney came to Orlando to announce plans for Walt Disney World, a "bigger and better" version of Disneyland in California. The announcement was hailed by an ecstatic local populace. The theme park would not open until 1971, but in the meantime some four thousand people would be employed to build the facility. Construction of Disney World quickly escalated land values as well as the volume of sales as people rushed to build facilities to house and feed the crowds which were expected to visit the new attraction. Land sales and new construction were not limited to southwest Orange County, but spread northward along Interstate-4 for more than thirty miles.

Northward view along Longwood Avenue in 1964.

A State University and the Naval Training Center

With much less fanfare, plans were also announced in 1965 for Florida Technological University (now the University of Central Florida). To be built several miles east of Winter Park, the new school was expected to accept its first students in 1968. At about the same time the Air Force turned over its Orlando AFB to the United States Navy which opened a large recruit training center there.

The Extension and Widening of S.R. 436

The extension of S.R. 436 and its connection with I-4 completed the final link between the burgeoning Orlando metropolitan area and Altamonte Springs. Orange County authorities first proposed the extension of the road from its eastern terminus near Altamonte Springs to McCoy AFB in the 1950s. Seminole County commissioners agreed in 1959 to cooperate. The two counties began acquiring right-of-way in 1960 and the state road department began planning a four-lane highway. Although many of the trees which had long separated the lanes of the highway through the town had been destroyed by Hurricane Donna, there was a popular outcry when it was learned that the State Road Department planned to eliminate the median and the remaining trees. Despite the protests, the trees were removed in 1964 and the road was widened to four lanes. The intersection with I-4 was completed in 1967.[274]

View of Altamonte Springs Fire Department and City Hall in 1964. Altamonte Garage is directly across the street.

Longwood Avenue toward the south from the Altamonte Garage in 1964. The house on the left is the residence of B. D. McIntosh, Jr. The signs on the right side of the street are DOT warnings of construction on S.R. 436 which was then being widened.

View toward the south along Maitland Avenue when it was being widened in 1961.

This is Maitland Avenue toward the north after the 1961 construction was completed.

The City of Altamonte Springs

Altamonte Springs approved a city charter in 1967 which called for a five member council similar to the old one. Four members were to be elected as councilmen and the fifth member was to be elected as mayor-councilman. The charter authorized the appointment of a city manager, although such an action was unlikely at the time. Swofford had occasionally spoken of employing a city manager, but he seemed to prefer a strong mayor and council form of government, at least as long as he was the mayor. The new charter empowered him to make appointments for approval by the full council.[275]

The Altamonte Chapel in the 1960s when services were still being conducted there.

The new city had about three thousand inhabitants in 1967, an increase of about 250 percent in seven years. It had only eighteen paid employees, but the acceleration of growth was about to change that. Building permits amounting to $2,08,000 were issued in 1967. The Valley Forge Golf Club was in full operation on land leased from Webber Haines on the south side of S.R. 436 near the intersection of Palm Springs Drive. The city was working toward annexation of that property as well as another six hundred acres on the west and south sides of town. A tentative budget of $152,619,000 was approved for 1968.[276]

The water system was being expanded and the council was considering development of a sewage system. There were discussions of a city hall and civic center complex as well as other public services.

The Municipal Court

The mayor's court had already been succeeded by a municipal court with its own judge. Gene R. Stephenson, a former councilman, became the first judge of that court in 1965.[277]

The Police Department

Grady Hall served as police chief until October 1963 when he was succeeded briefly by Russ Milne. During Hall's tenure a ten-man auxiliary police force was organized. These volunteers served for a dollar a year. C. B. Allen assumed the position of chief in 1964 and the town hall kitchen was remodeled for his office. He resigned in 1967 to take a job in the water department. Steve Pulliam served with Allen as a full-time patrolman after 1965. Frederick Folsom succeeded Allen as chief in 1967. He was followed briefly by Frank Papia. Justus East began his lengthy tenure in that position in 1970. By that date he was being assisted by two full-time patrolmen and a radio dispatcher.

The Fire Department

When Harry Brown became fire chief in early 1962, James Cornell was named as his assistant. At that time eight volunteers were appointed as "permanent firemen" at salaries of five dollars per month. The reason for the token salaries was to make them eligible for insurance coverage while on the job. Many of these men dropped out and the fire department was in need of rejuvenation when Councilman Robert Newell was made fire marshal in 1963. Two developments followed which marked the beginning of a professional fire department for the town.[278]

First, Newell induced Howard "Tubby" Willoughby, operator of an Amoco Service Station in Fern Park, to become fire chief and reorganize the department. Then, the town council agreed to provide fire protection

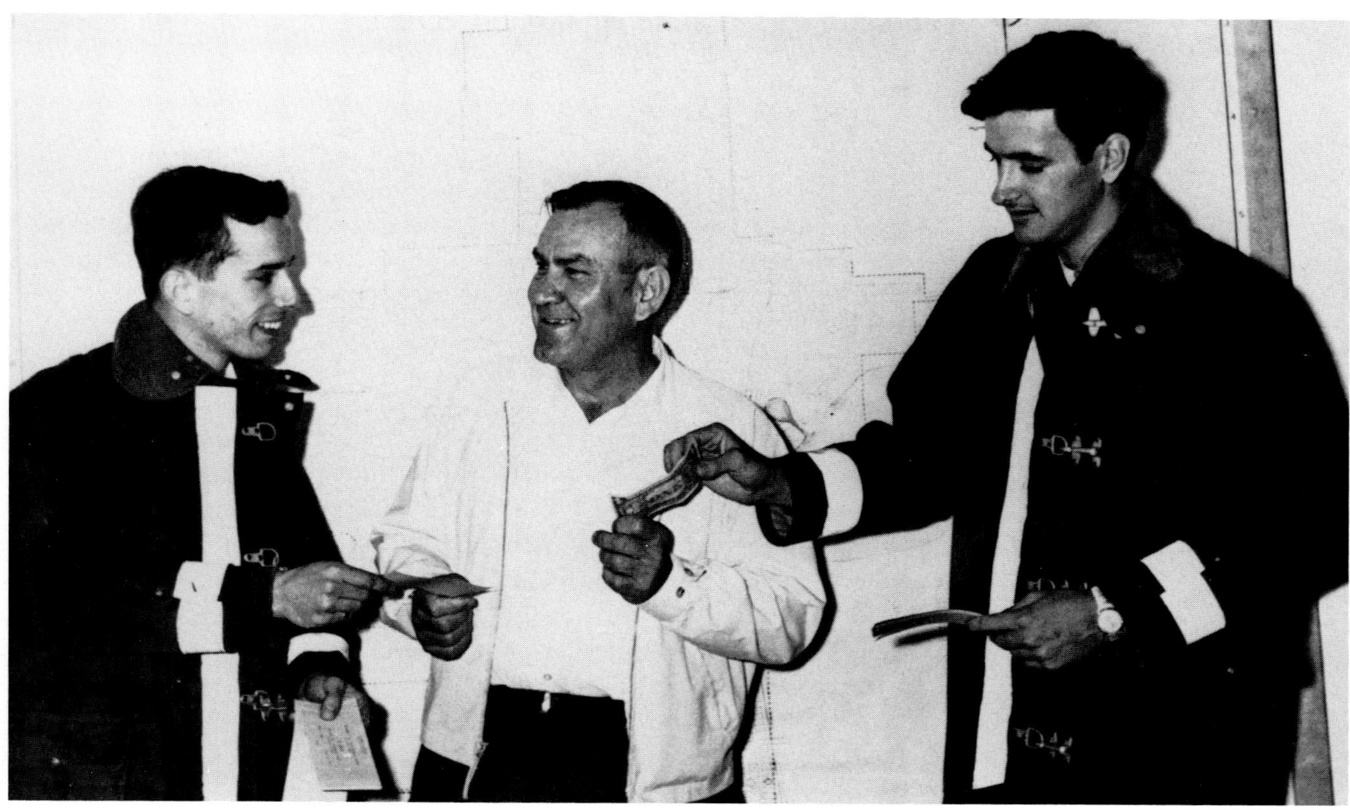

Captain Gary Kaiser (left) and Forest Butler (right) with Mayor Lawrence Swofford (center) in October 1967. The money passing between them is to symbolize their employment as Altamonte Springs's first paid, full-time firemen.

to a suburban fire district which included Rolling Hills, Druid Hills, Hidden Estates, Oakland Shores, Florida Haven, and Fern Park. Willoughby convinced the town council that he would require more personnel and equipment if he were to handle the increased responsibility.[279]

In October 1967, Gary Kaiser and Forest Butler became the first full-time firemen at salaries of seventy dollars each for seventy-two-hour work weeks. A relief man was employed for the Sunday shift. In April 1969, Kaiser was appointed as the city's first full-time fire chief. During his tenure, the department continued to rely heavily on volunteers, but an improved radio alerting system accelerated response times after 1970. Kaiser was also responsible for a 1970 ordinance requiring sprinklers to be installed in new commercial construction. He resigned the office in late 1971 after Mayor Swofford refused to permit the department to provide emergency medical service to the suburban fire district.[280]

The 1967 City Election

The city was growing rapidly by the time the charter was approved and so, apparently, was opposition to Mayor Swofford. His talent for obtaining funds from United States government agencies for expansion of public services was applauded by many, but others still regarded it as a threat to their community. Swofford's methods had also angered many people. The result was a serious challenge to his reelection in 1967.

Backed by several influential business and political leaders of Central Florida, Robert Newell announced his candidacy for mayor. By applying some creative electoral tactics, Swofford defeated Newell and was re-elected along with his close ally, Keith Nixon. But opposition to his leadership was by no means silenced.[281]

The Council Revolt

William Nuckols was elected to the council in 1968. Then, in the following year, incumbents Robert Rogers and Charles Robinson were replaced by Albert Sabbarese and Donald Martin. Nuckols had said little during the first year of his term, but with the apparent support of the two new members he became much more active in 1969. There had been disagreement for some time about the way minutes of council meetings were being recorded. With that as his reason, Nuckols moved to dismiss city clerk Dorothy Bardeen. When she was removed from her office by a three- to-two vote, the city erupted. Keith Nixon resigned in protest and a citizen group circulated a petition calling for Bardeen's reinstatement and Nuckols' resignation.[282]

Amid charges and counter charges, calls for investigations, and threats of lawsuits, the council convened in regular session the following week. Tom Radloff led a protest against Mrs. Bardeen's removal and a petition with eighty signatures was presented demanding Nuckol's resignation. He declined to resign, but declared that he would not seek reelection when his term ended. Upon a motion to reinstate Mrs. Bardeen, the original dismissal was upheld by the same three to two vote. A week later state auditors came to Altamonte Springs and sealed the city records pending an audit which had been requested by Nuckols, Sabbarese and Martin without the knowledge of the full council.[283]

The turmoil continued. Plans had been under way since 1965 to build a city sewage system. To complete arrangements for implementing the first phase of that system, Swofford had scheduled a meeting for June 1969 in Atlanta with officials from the U.S. Department of Housing and Urban Development. When the mayor asked the council to approve expenses for the trip—in the amount of $366—Nuckols objected strenuously. The trip was ultimately canceled, although that seems not to have interrupted progress on the sewage plant. It did, however, continue the breakdown in city government. Citizens criticized Nuckols for the state audit which had been requested without approval of the full council and Swofford's supporters condemned the cancellation of his trip. Swofford wrote Governor Claude Kirk requesting "a complete investigation by the state." In reporting the situation for the *Orlando Sentinel,* Jim Bacchus commented laconically that "the city has boiled with controversy the past several weeks"[284].

Sanlando Springs Tropical Park when the azaleas were in full bloom.

The discord abated after the June upheavals, but it was not fully resolved for several months. Edwin B. Helper was named administrative assistant/city clerk in late 1969. Both Swofford and Nixon were reelected for new terms in 1969 and Helen Keyser replaced Nuckols at that time. Martin and Sabbarese were holdovers, but Martin stopped attending meetings in the spring. The council named Daniel Dorfman to replace him. Sabbarese was succeeded in 1971 by Tom Radloff.[285]

The City at the End of the Decade

Development proceeded unabated by the political upheavals of 1969. Both the water and sewage systems continued to expand.

A landmark was reached in 1970 when Altamonte Springs contracted with Eatonville to provide that community with sewage services at the proposed new plant. Annexations of new land were becoming commonplace at council meetings. Developers were obtaining commitments for water and sewage services for planned developments months and even years in the future.[286]

The Winter Park Telephone Company was moving its entire operation to a new location north of Galloway Drive. An industrial park was being developed north of the telephone company between Newburyport and Sanford avenues. The Florida Power Company had already completed its sub-station at the corner of Sanford and Magnolia avenues. The Florida Hospital had agreed to build a branch facility on S.R. 436. Negotiations were under way to construct what eventually became the Altamonte Mall on S.R. 436 west of Palm Springs Drive.[287]

Sanlando Springs when it was still open to the public.

The 1970 census reflected an Altamonte Springs population of 4,391. Property evaluations had grown to a total of $22,771,000. The budget for 1970 was tentatively set at $375,870 based on a tax rate of five mills.[288]

A Debit Side of Growth

The rampant growth which was sweeping across southwestern Seminole County was not without its costs. Sanlando Springs Tropical Park, which had been a featured attraction of the area for nearly a century, had been improved and expanded by Mr. and Mrs. J. E. Robinson in 1950. For the next twenty years, it was a popular recreational spot for Central Floridians. There was some disappointment, therefore, when it was announced that the park was opening to the public for the last time in 1970. It had been acquired by a developer who was making it part of The Springs, an exclusive residential development west of the Wekiva River. Access to the new development was through a gate opening on S.R. 434 only a short distance from the site of the original Altamont which had disappeared after the freezes of 1894–95.[289]

The Past and the Future

Writing in the *Sanford Herald* in 1969, Gary Taylor perhaps summed it up best, saying "the history of any town is important but to Altamonte Springs, the future is even more important. What has happened to the city since . . . 1920 . . . cannot compare with what will happen . . . in the near future."[290]

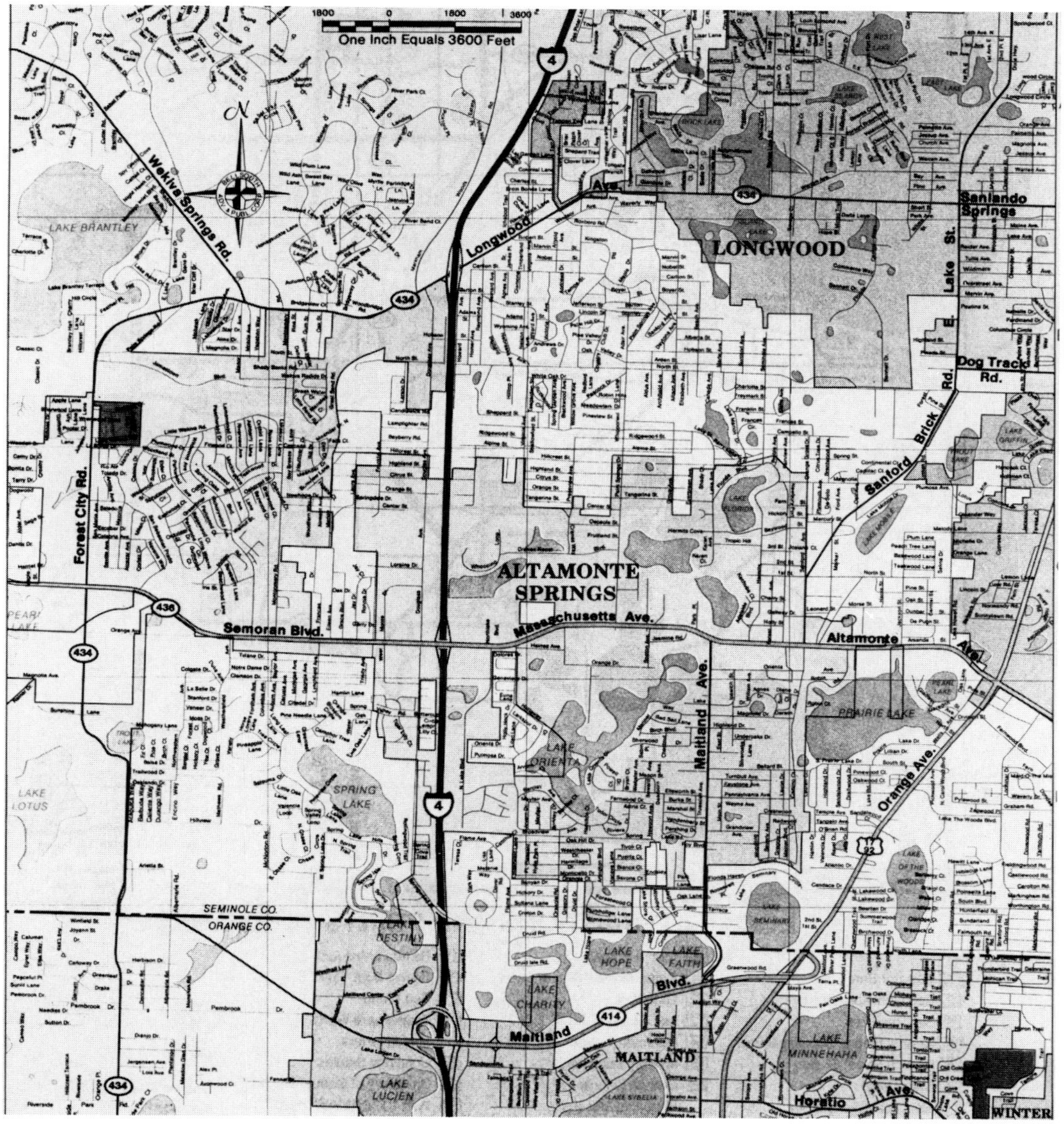

This Bell South Telephone Company map shows modern Altamonte Springs and its relationship to neighboring communities while it also includes some of the old names of the streets and roads. Copyright BellSouth Advertising & Publishing Corporation, 1993. Reprinted with permission of BellSouth Advertising & Publishing Corporation from the 1993 Greater Orlando edition of The Real Yellow Pages® from Southern Bell.

Central Florida residents at Sanlando Springs in the 1960s.

Built in 1971 by the Ben A. Barnwell family at 1049 East Altamonte Avenue and opened for business in the same month that Disney World opened its doors, Barney's Bar-B-Q is believed to be the oldest restaurant still operating in Altamonte Springs.

ELEVEN

The Fastest Growing City in the Nation

New construction soon erased the last vestiges of nineteenth century Altamonte Springs. . . . Hailed as the largest shopping mall in the southeastern United States when it was completed in 1974, the Altamonte Mall was only a part of the building boom of the early 1970s, but it was a very significant one.

By the time Disney World opened to the public in 1971, new residents were literally pouring into Altamonte Springs. The 1970 population of 4,391 increased to more than 13,000 by early 1973. The 1971 tax roll of $18 million grew to more than $80 million in 1973. The pace of growth was exemplified by the 642 building permits issued during the first eight months of that same year. By January 1976, property evaluations stood at $261,758,723, and many construction projects were still under way.[291]

Annexations continued to crowd the agenda of council meetings. The city limits were extended westward to include the Forest City Shopping Center at the intersection of S.R. 436 and S.R. 434. Property was acquired on both sides of S.R. 434 north and eastward toward its intersection with I-4. The new school complex on Sand Lake Road was included in the city limits. The city boundaries eventually reached the Orange County line on the south. Usually requested by developers anxious to obtain utility services, but sometimes initiated by the city wishing to incorporate desirable commercial property, these annexations proceeded so rapidly that they left a number of "enclaves" of county property surrounded entirely by the city. By 1976 there were approximately eight square miles in a city which had been less than two square miles in size in 1960.

Nightmares in a Bedroom Town[292]

Writing in early 1973 about the phenomenal growth of Seminole County, a *St. Petersburg Times* reporter noted "mile-long traffic jams" along S.R. 436 caused by the inadequate interchange at I-4. Mayor Swofford's earlier warnings were coming true. An interchange designed for 60,000 cars a day was jammed with 100,000. Department of Transportation (DOT) officials were estimating that redesigning the interchange would cost at least $10 million for right-of-way alone. The interchange was not the only problem. In 1971, Councilman Keith Nixon had reported "impossible problems on the main thoroughfares of the city." According to him, intersections were hazardous, storage lanes were insufficient, and traffic was "far in excess of what the current roads" could handle. Bud Gemeinhardt of the DOT presented to the council a proposal for alleviating some of the difficulties. He advocated improvements of several arterial roads to include overpasses at I-4. Favorably impressed by the proposal, but realizing its implementation depended on cooperation with other agencies, the council resolved to consult with the DOT, the Seminole County Commission, and CALNO.[293] The county agreed to help with the signal lights and turning lanes. It was also interested in the S.R. 436/I-4 interchange, although that problem would require cooperation by the United States government. It took no action on the suggestion of overpasses at I-4.[294]

Schools

The schools of southwest Seminole County were just as crowded as the roads. A new Lyman High School was built on C.R. 427 in Longwood and the old buildings were left to house Milwee Middle School. Both were on double sessions by the early 1970s. A school complex consisting of Forest City Elementary (1971), Teague Middle School (1971), and Lake Brantley High School (1973) was completed on Sand Lake Road in 1973. It was also soon filled to capacity from the many new subdivisions of Altamonte Springs, Longwood, and Forest City. Lake Orienta Elementary and Spring Lake Elementary were added to alleviate crowding. Altamonte Elementary, built in 1959, soon became unsuitable for use because of adjacent commercial development and the heavy traffic on S.R. 436. A new Altamonte Elementary was opened on Palm Springs Drive and the older school was moved to Paola in 1977. Events were moving so rapidly at the time that DOT crews painted school warning signs on S.R. 436 *after* the building was removed.[295]

Mayor Guides Altamonte[296]

Albeit somewhat grudgingly, the *Orlando Sentinel Star* credited Mayor Swofford for his planning and a "tight hand at the wheel" of Altamonte Springs government. Even while emphasizing the "nightmares" in 1973, the *St. Petersburg Times* applauded Swofford for his foresight in providing water and sewer services before the heavy influx of new residents began. Noting that overcrowded roads and schools were the responsibility of other jurisdictions, the *Times* gave the city and its mayor credit for several important measures for guiding—if not controlling—growth.[297]

Development Pays Its Way in Altamonte

An often embattled Mayor Swofford frequently reminded all who would listen that developers paid for their impact on the city. Although much of his opposition came from those who thought he was too generous with developers, it is unlikely that the latter agreed. With the able assistance of Don Bundy as director of public works and William Palm of Glace and Radcliffe Engineering as consulting engineer, Swofford had continued to expand the city's water and sewage capacities. While it was these facilities which attracted developers, they were also the reasons the city could obtain concessions in exchange. In securing commitments for water and, especially, sewage services, developers were required not only to pay sizable deposits for future services, but also to agree to build roads and utility lines and then deed them back to the city when completed.

Nor were the utilities built with local tax money. Altamonte Springs had been classified as part of the Orlando metropolitan planning area. As such it was qualified for United States governmental assistance in providing public utilities. Mayor Swofford was adept at using this advantage to acquire both grants and loans from the Department of Housing and Urban Development (HUD) and other concerned agencies. The loans were guaranteed by revenue bonds which were amortized with money generated by the utilities themselves.

The Regional Waste Water Treatment Plant

With building in progress all over the city and many more requests for utility reservations coming in daily, Swofford and the council reviewed the situation in early 1972 and decided it was necessary—and perhaps advantageous—to impose a moratorium on building permits for a time. The focus of the moratorium was apparently the numerous apartment and condominium complexes then under construction along S.R. 436 between Maitland Avenue and I-4.

Soliciting the cooperation of several of the builders in that area—some of whom had powerful political acquaintances, Swofford induced the HUD to approve for his city a regional waste water treatment plant, complete with both grants and loans. One of the last such projects to receive both forms of federal aid, the project was shortly underway at a site on Keller Road in what is now southwest Altamonte Springs. With a 7.5 million gallon capacity—about three times the city's existing sewage capability—the plant was intended to serve the region surrounding Altamonte Springs. There was another building moratorium in 1973,

James Singleton, now deputy director of Leisure Services in charge of fleet, facilities maintenance and library, aboard a frontend loader similar to the one with which he solved a problem for the city in 1979. After the police and fire departments relocated to the new safety complex, city officials were concerned with the problem of demolishing the old City Hall with its tall tower. A skilled heavy equipment operator who did not share their concerns, Singleton listened quietly while the matter was discussed. Then, he rose early the following morning and razed the building without difficulty or fanfare. When his supervisor arrived for work the problem had been removed.

although it did not interfere with several large projects such as the Altamonte Mall for which capacity had already been reserved. The Keller Road plant was partially operational by 1976, although it was several years before it was in full service. It provides sewage service for Altamonte Springs, Eatonville, and several other Orange County areas.[298]

I Have Had a Council Which Supports Me[299]

Although Mayor Swofford continued to elicit criticism from time to time and the council meetings were often quite exciting, the council—composed of Swofford, Keith Nixon, Daniel Dorfman, Helen Keyser, and Donald Myers (after he succeeded Tom Radloff)—between1971 and 1973 was generally harmonious. Beginning in 1971, councilmen received salaries of $150 per month. The mayor was paid $300 per month with a small allowance for travel. By 1973, Swofford had become a full-time mayor at an annual salary of $17,500. In the meantime, this small group of "part-time" city officials set the course for an efficient city government which has been able to provide services at reasonable costs for a growing population.[300]

A New City Hall

The old City Hall on C.R. 427 was outgrown by the early 1970s. It was first decided to build a new facility on twenty-three acres of land south of Orienta Avenue, but an agreement was made with the Winter Park Telephone Company to provide enough additional land so that the

Aerial view of the Altamonte Springs Municipal Complex, bounded by S.R. 436 on the south, C.R. 427 on the east, Galloway Drive on the north, and Newburyport Avenue on the west. In the upper right corner is the original water treatment plant which was dedicated in 1964. At the upper left is the City Hall which was dedicated in 1973. The large building across the parking lot from City Hall is the Safety Complex housing the main fire station (Company 11) and the police department. An additional building east of the parking lot between the two existing buildings has since been added.

seat of government could be built on Newburyport Avenue. The recreational facilities there were relocated to the land south of Orienta on what is now South Longwood Avenue (Eastmonte). In 1971 the council approved plans for the new city hall as well as a civic center at the new recreation site. Estimated costs were $340,000 and $220,000 respectively. Youth baseball and adult softball were being played at the new recreational complex by May 1972. Completion of the new site was accelerated by another sizable federal grant. Ground-breaking ceremonies for the new city hall were held on April 18, 1972, and the new edifice was dedicated on May 12, 1973. The old building on C.R. 427 was renovated for use by the police and fire departments until more adequate facilities could be arranged in the government center. The safety complex was completed by 1979.[301]

Florida Hospital Altamonte

The city and Florida Hospital authorities had reached agreement in 1970 for construction of what was then called Florida Hospital North. Water and sewage capacities were reserved for it and the city waived its thirty-five-floor height limit to allow eventual construction of a six-story building. The first patients were admitted on February 19 of that year. After a slow beginning, the hospital was soon adding new facilities and providing medical services for the surrounding area. New buildings for laboratories, doctors offices, and other related services began to line both sides of S.R. 436, eventually extending along Park Place and even Hermits Trail. Now known as Florida Hospital Altamonte, one of its latest improvements was acquisition of the Elmco Building. Renamed the 608 Building, it houses an outpatient physical therapy center.[302]

This photograph was taken for the City Hall dedication program on June 16, 1973.

Completed and opened for patients in 1973 as Florida Hospital North, this facility has been expanded and is now known as Florida Hospital Altamonte.

The 701 Building

One of the first of many office buildings which soon appeared along and near S.R. 436 and Maitland Avenue was the 701 Building, a three-story edifice situated between Lake Adelaide and S.R. 436. Completed in 1973, it was soon occupied by a variety of business and professional entities. The Kirchman Building, housing a computer software firm, was shortly in place on its east side.[303]

Out with the Old

New construction soon erased the last vestiges of nineteenth century Altamonte Springs. The Bradlee-McIntyre House, long occupied by Annie K. McIntyre and then briefly by the B. D. McIntosh family, had been vacant for many years when the Florida Hospital began planning its branch facility. Erroneously known as the "Grant House," the old building was offered to anyone who would move it. Mrs. Robert (Grace) Bradford, a historic preservationist with some personal resources, had already purchased the venerable Longwood Hotel and was refurbishing it. Despite long odds, she undertook the task of moving the old house to a site near the Longwood Hotel. After vigorous fund-raising efforts and much hard work, it now stands in restored splendor in the Longwood Historic District. Mrs. Bradford was also responsible for relocating to that place the Inside-Outside House belonging to the erstwhile sailor, Captain Pierce.[304]

The spring house on Lake Adelaide had succumbed to old age by the time Hurricane Donna left it in shambles in 1960. Its disposition was resolved when the spring, for which the city was named, was capped and covered with paving for a parking lot for the 701 Building.

The Inside-Outside House at its new location in the Longwood Historic District. Brought to Altamonte Springs and assembled by Captain Pierce in the late 1870s, this unusual house was moved to Longwood in 1973 by Grace Bradford and her associates in the Central Florida Society for Historic Preservation. It is now used as an antique shop.

The Bradlee-McIntyre House was moved from its location in Altamonte Springs to make way for the Florida Hospital Altamonte in 1973. It was placed on its new site in the Longwood Historic District and restored by Grace Bradford and her associates in the Central Florida Society for Historic Preservation.

The Altamonte Hotel Springhouse on Lake Adelaide in 1959 after years of neglect and before it was damaged by Hurricane Donna in 1960.

A view across Lake Adelaide toward the site of the Altamonte Hotel Springhouse which was at the edge of the lake behind the center building.

From left to right are the 711 Building, the 701 Building and the 201 Building (which fronts on Park Place). All of them were built and are still owned by Kenneth Kirchman, founder, chairman, and president of the Kirchman Corporation.

Headquartered in the 711 Building, the Kirchman Corporation—which began in 1968 as Florida Software Services, Inc.—is the largest banking software company in the world. With more than 400 employees the company serves over 6,000 financial institutions throughout North and South America, Europe, and the Near East.

Aerial view of Altamonte Springs about 1990, showing the Altamonte Mall at the corner of S.R. 436 and Palm Springs Drive. The Central Parkway at Cranes Roost has not yet been built.

The Galloway Building

There was a strong reaction from the public when Jack Albershardt of Palm Properties applied for a variance which would allow construction of a seven-story building at 850 E. Altamonte Avenue in April 1973. Despite the complaints that such a building would destroy the ambience of the city, the variance was approved. The builder might have wished it had been otherwise when he encountered financial difficulties in 1974. The building stood empty and incomplete until the Winter Park Telephone Company acquired it for an office complex. Renamed the Galloway Building and beautifully maintained it has recently been used as an example of how high-rise buildings can be assets to the city.[305]

The Altamonte Mall

Hailed as the largest shopping mall in the southeastern United States when it was completed in 1974, the Altamonte Mall was only a part of the building boom of the early 1970s, but it was a very significant one. Planned to open with four large department stores and more than one hundred forty smaller ones, its sheer size was remarkable enough. But its impact on the city went beyond size. Its presence at the northwest corner of S.R. 436 and Palm Springs Drive, only a short distance from the I-4 interchange has effectively moved the center of town westward.

Land clearing began in 1970, and despite some delays because of one contracting problem, progress was steady. The city annexed the property in 1972 and reserved adequate utilities for its opening. De Bartolo and Associates held a press conference and party in the fall of 1972 to announce the beginning of construction. Publicity was almost constant after that and when the mall opened in August 1974, great crowds came from throughout Central Florida to see the sight as well as to shop. Traffic jams lengthened on S.R. 436 and it was called "the world's longest parking lot," but people still came—and in increasing numbers. The Altamonte Mall became the second largest tourist attraction in Central Florida.[306]

Another aerial view dated 1990 with a different view from a point southwest of the I-4 interchange toward the northeast. The lakes which attracted the original settlers are clearly visible, but their surroundings have changed immensely.

The Boston Avenue Trees

Land clearing and street realignment were commonplace in the city in the early 1970s. The mayor and council saw little cause for concern when they approved the removal of twenty-four large trees from Boston Avenue. But, several citizens asked for an opportunity to be heard in opposition. The mayor's handling of the matter was not his best moment. Mayor Swofford had never been very tolerant of opposing views and, after three years of uninterrupted successes, he had become even less so. Only three months earlier he had told an *Orlando Sentinel* reporter that he had little regard for public meetings. "I don't think they accomplish much," he said, "They very often bog down progress. . . ." Despite his views, time was set aside at a council meeting for several tree advocates to be heard. City workers removed the trees on the morning before the meeting. Whether or not the trees were cut down was not the major issue for many people, but the denial of citizens' right to petition their government was. People who had little concern for the trees were angered by the mayor's arbitrary action. To an official who had little regard for public meetings it apparently did not mean much, but it aroused a great outcry against the mayor in July and he was facing an election in the fall.[307]

An inside view of the Altamonte Mall which opened for business in 1974 and soon became the second largest tourist attraction (behind Walt Disney World) in Central Florida. The mall has since been renovated extensively. Its twentieth anniversary was observed in August 1994. Photo from a postcard loaned by Ralph Roberts and in the Florida State Archives.

The 1973 City Election

Already embroiled in controversy with the mayor, Police Captain Norman Floyd, launched a strong, well-managed campaign for his office. At the same time, Calvin DeVoney ran for the seat held by Keith Nixon. In the early December election, 1,664 voters came to the polls. Floyd defeated Swofford by a vote of 917 to 747 and DeVoney ousted Nixon by a comparable count. Helen Keyser was reelected without opposition. Daniel Dorfman and Donald Myers were holdovers.[308]

Floyd again defeated Swofford in 1975, thus ending an era—one during which Altamonte Springs had grown dramatically. It was a transfer of power from one strong-willed mayor to another, but Floyd headed a government which largely followed the policies already in place.

The City Clerks

The office of city clerk changed in the years following Dorothy Bardeen's summary dismissal in 1969. The county took over the increasingly voluminous tasks of assessing and evaluating property for tax purposes, leaving the clerk with more time to handle an increasing volume of administrative matters. Connie Hudson served for a time as acting clerk in 1970, to be followed briefly by Rodney Layer. Jane Richards then filled the post from late 1970 until October 1973. At that time Phyllis Jordahl began a tenure which lasted through the 1970s.[309]

The City Attorney

Joseph Davis completed twenty-one years as city attorney in 1979 when he resigned to become a judge. He was followed by James (Skip) Fowler who is still the Altamonte Springs city attorney.

The Revived Chamber of Commerce

Altamonte Springs' third chamber of commerce was the project of Councilwoman Helen Keyser who recruited Betty French in 1973 to help "feel the pulse of the area" about such an organization. Receiving a favorable response, they decided the time was right. The City Council voted in February 1974 to establish a chamber and invited it to use the Community House for its meetings. By the time a March 1974 organizational meeting took place, Casselberry business and government personnel joined the movement so that the new organization became the Altamonte-Casselberry Chamber. The first directors were George Foster, George Brown, Ken Brown, Jim Caltrider, Mark Grayson, Skip Kellog, Helen Keyser, Tom Ross, and Al Sciuto. Officers were George Foster, president; Bob Hattaway, first vice-president; Jim Caltrider, second vice-president; Betty French, secretary; and Helen Keyser, treasurer. A May celebration was attended by 285 people. In 1989, the organization became the Greater Seminole Chamber and moved to Longwood.[310]

Altamonte Springs' First State Representative

With strong commitments to his community, Robert Hattaway was long active in the South Seminole Jaycees while managing his successful Hattaway Fernery and Greenhouses. Then, in 1974, he defeated an incumbent to win a seat in the Florida House of Representatives. After three successful terms in the lower house, he resigned to run for the senate. After losing a close contest, Hattaway returned to his interests in Altamonte Springs, but continued to be active in public affairs. He is currently chairman of the Greater Orlando Aviation Authority.

The City Commission After 1975

A new charter was approved in 1974 providing for a five-member commission, one member of which was to serve as mayor/commissioner. Commissioners were to serve two-year terms while the mayor's term was three years.[311] Floyd continued as mayor. Helen Keyser and Calvin DeVoney were joined as commissioners by Sandra Glenn and George Perkins. Glenn Buschman succeeded Helen Keyser the following year. The next changes came in 1978 when Delores Vickers and Harry Jacobs joined incumbents Perkins, Glenn and Mayor Floyd. The 1979 commission was composed of Floyd, Vickers, Jacobs, Peggy Childress, and Lee Constantine. Glenn had by then moved on to the Seminole County Commission. Twenty-six-year-old Lee Constantine was beginning the first of seven consecutive terms which ended in 1992 when he was elected to the state legislature.[312]

Continued Growth

The national economic recession in the mid-1970s triggered by the Middle East oil embargo and resulting fuel shortages had some impact on the Altamonte Springs building boom. But there was so much building already in progress that the city was still hard-pressed to keep up with demand for utilities. When the Interstate Mall was built it was obliged to install its own sewer system. By and large, the commercialization of S.R. 436 continued apace. A Publix supermarket shopping center was under construction by the late 1970s on what had been the front nine holes of the Valley Forge Golf Course. The back nine was used for another apartment complex. Other stores, restaurants, and businesses were opening along S.R. 436 both east and west of I-4. Annexations continued, especially on the south side of S.R. 436 west of I-4 and on S.R. 434 near the interstate highway.[313]

The City in 1980

The city population reached 18,000 in 1976 and nearly 22,000 by 1980. These figures do not include numerous county residents who lived in the several unincorporated enclaves inside the city boundaries. The total taxable property valuation for 1980 was $500,481,695. There was an additional $136 million worth of tax-exempt property in the city. The operating budget for that year was $8,230,908.[314]

Political Turbulence and the City Manager System

By 1979 Mayor Floyd was encountering opposition which might have reminded him of the situation his predecessor had faced a decade earlier. He had been reelected in 1978 over George Perkins, an erstwhile ally on the commission, who decided to challenge him. Floyd also had opposition within the commission which became more substantial when his ally, Harry Jacobs, was succeeded in 1980 by James Thompson. There was also a bitter assault on the mayor from critics in the general public. Floyd missed several commission meetings, obliging first Harry Jacobs and then Lee Constantine—who had been elected vice-mayor in 1979—to preside during his absences.[315]

These developments caused considerable turmoil on the commission just at the time when the question of a new charter arose. The critical issue was a provision to create a city manager system of government. A strong personality who enjoyed the strong mayor system, Floyd objected strenuously. After a number of long, arduous meetings a compromise was reached. The new charter would include provisions for the city manager, but the new office would not be filled until Floyd completed his full three-year term at the end of 1982. But, when Floyd resigned in 1980 to run for a county commission seat, it was agreed to go ahead immediately with the new system. Applications for the position were solicited and a selection committee was organized to select the best person.[316]

It was one of the ironies of democratic government that out of the turbulence of 1979 and 1980 came a change which has improved the city government, made the commission a true legislative body, and heralded a long period of progress in Altamonte Springs.

Seminole County Commissioners from Altamonte Springs

After two terms as a city commissioner, Sandra Glenn ran successfully for a county commission seat in 1978. The first woman ever elected to that body, she served three four-year terms (1979–1990) during which she was repeatedly elected chairman of the commission.

Three other Altamonte Springs citizens have served on the county commission. In reverse order, they are: Mike Hattaway, 1973–1976; Lawrence Swofford, 1957–1960 and 1963–1966; and Walter Ballard, 1933–1940.

Twelve

The City Government and Its Departments

From a town which was spending about $7,000 annually in 1945 to one where the mayor carried daily collections in a cigar box in the 1960s, Altamonte Springs has become a large city whose budget is a major enterprise. Its financial affairs are managed in a business-like manner by a department which is recognized for its quality.

Since the transition to the city manager form of government in 1981, continuity has characterized the Altamonte Springs city commission. Hugh Harling was elected mayor to serve the single year remaining on Norman Floyd's term. He was followed in 1982 by Raymond M. Ambrose, the second police officer to become mayor. After two terms, he was succeeded in 1988 by J. Dudley Bates who is still incumbent. Lee Constantine, Robert Reis, James Thompson and Delores Vickers served with Mayor Harling. Thompson and Vickers were replaced in 1982 by J. Dudley Bates and Cheney Colardo. The next changes came in 1984 when Eddie Rose and Bruce Furino filled the seats vacated by Reis and Colardo. After a single term, Furino was succeeded by Edward Titen. When Dudley Bates became mayor in 1988, the other commissioners were Constantine, Rose, Titen, and Pat Fernandez. Since then, there have been only two changes on the commission. Russel Hauck replaced Titen in 1990 and Robert Lerner succeeded Lee Constantine in 1992 when the veteran commissioner went to the legislature.[317]

The City Manager

The selection committee concluded its work in 1980 when Jeff Etchberger, a former employee of Seminole County, accepted the position of Altamonte Springs' first city manager. Introduced to the commission in November 1980, Etchberger was shortly at work.

His most impressive contribution was in the budget area. The city was still growing rapidly and the operating departments were trying to keep up with that growth. The new city manager implemented methods of budget planning by which revenues could be better anticipated and matched to needs. In a city where expenditures had only recently risen from the thousands to the millions this was a signal accomplishment. After a little more than two years on the job, Etchberger moved to a position with the Greater Orlando Chamber of Commerce, but his accomplishments during his brief tenure convinced everyone of the value of the city manager system.[318]

Citizens Boards and Committees

The Altamonte Springs municipal government has always depended upon its citizens for advice and assistance through volunteer boards and committees, the number of which has grown over the years. In the mid-1990s there are seven appointive bodies, including:

Personnel Administration Board
Board of Zoning Appeals
Community Redevelopment Agency
Surface Water Quality Advisory Board
Health Facilities Authority
Code Enforcement Board
Planning Board

In May 1983, Phillip D. Penland came from DeLand to succeed Etchberger. Another professional public administrator with experience, talent, and vision, Penland has guided the city government for the past twelve years during which time Altamonte Springs has become one of the most progressive cities in the nation. Its operating departments are constantly implementing innovative programs that other cities often follow.

The City Clerk

Bobbi Floyd succeeded Phyllis Jordahl as city clerk in 1980 to be followed by Penny Conahan in 1983. Then, after two years as Phil Penland's secretary, Patsy Wainright became city clerk in 1985 and has remained in that position.

The city clerk's office was made a department in the 1970s and now is staffed by four people in addition to the clerk. Keeping the records of the commission is still one of its most important functions, but the department also handles about 5,000 occupational licenses for the city's 3,200 businesses. It also published the city newsletter, *Spirit*, and is responsible for administering the recently enacted American's with Disabilities Act. The latter function is largely coordinative since all the city department's cooperate in this matter.[319]

Department of Human Resources

The Department of Human Resources was designated in 1988, but it evolved over a period of about thirteen years before that, beginning with Mayor Floyd's 1975 reorganization of city government. Sam Frazee, the incumbent director, was employed that year in the Department of General Services. In 1981 she became Personnel director, as a staff officer in the city manager's office. She continued as director when the Department of Personnel was formed in 1983. Since 1988 the Department of Human Resources has handled all personnel functions, including recruiting, orientation, training, salaries and benefits, and grievances and appeals for a city staff which presently numbers 488. It also manages special events such as health fairs and holiday celebrations. Like most government departments, it complies with an increasing volume of guidelines laid down by state and national governments.[320]

The Finance Department

The Finance Department also grew out of the 1975 reorganization, but it came into its own when Jeff Etchberger employed Brenda Robinson in February 1981, shortly after he became city manager. Robinson remained director of Finance only a little more than two years before moving to the Orlando city administration. She was then replaced by Mark DeBord who is still the city's director of Finance.

The department now has eighteen employees in a variety of functions. Two of them handle purchasing. Two others handle all of the city's data processing systems. There are seven people in the utility billing section which does everything from reading the meters to collecting payments. Since 1990, one person has been in charge of safety and risk management. Six people work in the accounting section.[321]

The Finance Department is presently managing an annual budget of nearly $42 million, about $21 million of which is for operations. Utility charges now constitute the largest single source of income while property taxes pay for about a third of the operating budget. Other sources of income are franchise fees and utility taxes, impact fees, state shared revenue, fines and forfeitures, recreation fees, and a number of smaller ones.[322]

From a town which was spending about seven thousand dollars annually in 1945 to one where the mayor carried daily collections in a cigar box in the 1960s, Altamonte Springs has become a large city whose budget is a major enterprise. Its financial affairs are managed in a business-like manner by a department which is recognized for its quality. The Government Finance Officers Association recognized this in 1986 with its award for excellence in financial reporting. One of only about a thousand cities in the United States to receive the award, Altamonte Springs is the first in Seminole County to do so.[323]

A squad car ready for patrol in the early 1980s.

The Police Department

Justus East continued as chief of police until 1980 when he was replaced by Barry Cook. Cook served as chief until 1982 when he was succeeded briefly by James Younger. Later that same year, William A. Liquori became police chief and still holds that position.[324]

Chief East had only two paid officers in 1970, but growth was rapid during the next several years. Steven Garver, a twenty-four-year veteran, recalls that he was city employee number 19 and the seventh member of the department when he joined it in 1971. That same year President Richard Nixon recognized the department for outstanding service. The commendation, the first of its kind in the state of Florida, was accepted on behalf of the department by Mayor Lawrence Swofford.[325]

There were forty-five members of the department in 1975 when it was demonstrated that the city's explosive growth carried with it some liabilities. The numerous stores which were ringing up large sales in the

Diana Tilley (left) and Karen Strawbridge in the Police Department Communications and Dispatch Center.

Interstate and Altamonte malls near the easily accessible Interstate-4 became inviting targets for armed thieves with fast cars. Then-Lt. Garver was near I-4 when he received a call that a robbery was in progress at an A&P Supermarket in the nearby Interstate Mall. He sped to the store where Charles Hobbs was at the manager's station emptying the cash drawer while three accomplices acted as lookouts. Hobbs saw Garver enter the store and began shooting. Two shots struck the officer, but he fired back, ending Hobbs' robbery career with one shot. Other officers arrived in the meantime and, while James Perry and others pursued and captured Hobbs' accomplices, Raymond Ambrose—who later became mayor—assisted Lt. Garver and then took him to nearby Florida Hospital North.

In the years since, Altamonte Springs' police officers have responded to many emergency calls. Although few have been as sensational as the 1975 incident, officers have responded with much better protection than Garver had. After that shooting, the city began providing its officers with bullet-proof vests.[326]

The Police Department now has ninety-two sworn officers and thirty-one civilians. The Operations Bureau is headed by Comdr. Jim Perry and consists of four shifts of regular patrolmen and a K-9 unit. Comdr. Garver heads the Special Operations Bureau with a ready response team, the traffic division, and a mobile command vehicle.

The Investigations Bureau is headed by Comdr. Bob Merchant, who is responsible for general investigations, crime scene work, and polygraphs. Comdr. James Murphey has the Management Support Bureau

A squad of officers at briefing before going on patrol. At the left of the picture is Charles Zorbaugh, one of the first policemen to retire from the city.

Chief William A. Liquori addressing a group of police volunteers at a function held to recognize them.

Officer Barry Pruette at work on S.R. 436 near the eastern city limits.

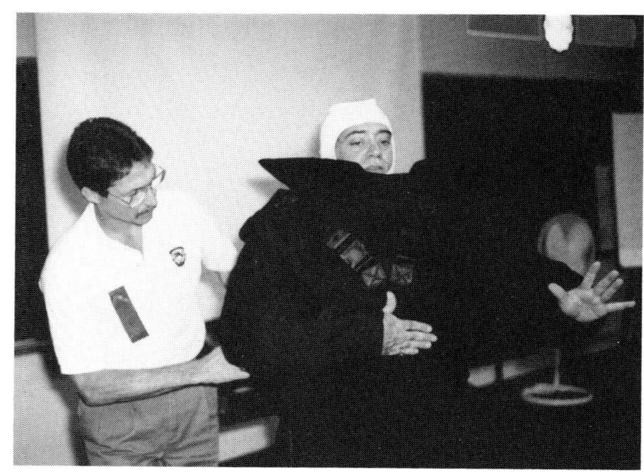

Assisted by Officer Stanley Phipps, Lt. Jack Martin is preparing for an explosive ordinance disposal mission.

Officer Kristen Bates on bicycle patrol at Cranes Roost.

Corporal George Aldrich mounted and about to leave for patrol duty.

K-9 Officer Rick Wisecup and Rambo on patrol at Cranes Roost.

A convivial moment during a ceremony recognizing police volunteers.

Janice Goebel of the City Clerk's office administering the oath of office to Tony Uzzi as he joins the Police Department.

which includes Internal Affairs, Computer Support, Community Relations, and Crime Analysis.

The Services Bureau, headed by Comdr. Dick Laese, handles records, personnel and fiscal matters. He is also responsible for dispatching as well as booking of prisoners.

Altamonte Springs is the only city in the county which still has its own jail. It is used by the bureau for holding prisoners while they are being booked and readied for transport to the county facility.[327]

The department also staffs a sub-station at the Altamonte Mall.

Mutual Aid and Assistance

As the metropolitan area has grown, intergovernmental cooperation has become increasingly necessary. The Altamonte Springs Police Department has often led the way in this regard.

With the support of a federal grant, the department initiated the City-County-State Enforcement Unit which is comprised of all the cities in Seminole County, the county, and nearby Maitland in Orange County. The agreement has only recently been formalized, but it has been honored since 1992. Under the aegis of the county sheriff, officers of all the cities are authorized to work anywhere in the county when and where they are needed.[328]

Under a federal grant, the department purchased and equipped a mobile command vehicle which can be deployed anywhere to deal with hostage situations, DUI sweeps, and comparable field operations.[329]

The K-9 officers also operate on a mutual-aid basis. K-9 units from all the cities and the county train together and act in common whenever necessary. The Investigative Bureau cooperates with other agencies in such matters as narcotics investigations.

The Seminole County Traffic Enforcement and Management Team is also a cooperative effort composed of all the cities plus the highway patrol, the Fire Department, the Seminole County Engineering Department, and the state DOT. Representatives of all these agencies meet regularly to discuss and deal with traffic problems.[330]

Youth Programs

With a school resource officer in every public school in the city, the department hopes to prevent crime by reaching the youngsters while they are still forming their values. The department also became the first in Seminole County to offer a Drug Abuse Resistance Education (DARE) program.

Community-Oriented Policing

Following recent trends in the nation and carrying it a step farther, Altamonte Springs has begun emphasizing community-oriented policing. Beginning in mid-1993, officers were assigned to zones so that they could identify with their specific areas of responsibility and the people there could see the same familiar faces of the patrol officers. Hoping in this way to increase communications with citizens in their zones, officers expect a better opportunity to identify problems and correct them whenever

Shellie Walters, the first school resource officer, with two of her new clients.

possible. As is usually the case in Altamonte Springs, all other departments are cooperating with the police to make the new approach work. Currently, the Public Works Department is helping to improve lighting and remove barriers to vision in critical areas. The city manager and the commission have shown their support by adding five officers to the department to offset the increased work load and to make the new program work.[331]

Recognition

The Police Department has gained recognition for its sound record of maintaining the public safety and its willingness to pursue innovative programs. Chief Liquori is the president of the Florida Police Chiefs Association and president of the Senior Leadership Program, Class II, of the Florida Department of Law Enforcement. He also serves as vice-chair of the Criminal Justice Standards and Training Commission.

The Fire Department

Thomas L. Siegfried was first a volunteer who was then employed by Gary Kaiser as a full-time fireman. When Kaiser resigned in late 1971, twenty-one-year-old Tom Siegfried became the youngest fire chief in the United States. During the ensuing twenty-four years, the department has grown along with the city until it now has fifty-one firemen operating in three platoons from three stations. It has been repeatedly recognized for its innovative leadership in fire protection, emergency life saving, and fire prevention education.

The fire truck which was purchased by the volunteers in 1953 (right) is joined by two more modern vehicles in the bays of the old fire department on Longwood Avenue (C.R. 427) in the mid-1970s.

Warren Brown of the South Seminole Jaycees christening the department's first rescue truck. The Jaycees had purchased an old telephone truck and converted it for rescue service in the early 1970s. Chief Tom Siegfried can be seen watching Brown.

George S. (Steve) Gaston, who is now deputy chief in charge of operations, joined the department as its third paid member in 1972. By the end of that year there were five paid firemen and twenty volunteers. They operated out of the old fire station on Longwood Avenue with three pumpers, a tanker, and a brush truck. Fire fighting and emergency life saving became so technical that extensive education was required for an increasingly professional fire fighting force. As more professional firemen were employed, and cooperation with the county began, the volunteer program was phased out.[332]

When the Public Safety Complex on Newburyport Avenue was completed in 1979, the department moved its main station (Station 11) there. It had opened a second station in 1974 at 150 Montgomery Road to serve the growing areas of Spring Oaks, San Sebastian, and the Wymore-Douglas area. Because of the heavy traffic along S.R. 436 and slow response times in the area south of it, a third station (Station 14) was opened on Hattaway Drive in 1992.

Robert Durham, Building and Life Safety Inspector, testing a residential sprinkler system.

Emergency Medical Service

Beginning in 1973, all firemen were required to be certified Emergency Medical Technicians. That same year the department purchased its first ambulance transport vehicle.

A Rescue Division was established in 1974, and in 1977 Altamonte Springs became the first city in the area to provide advanced life support service.

As the department increased its capabilities in the areas of victim extrication and advanced life support, it placed a new Rescue Unit on line in 1983. That unit was then replaced in 1993 by Heavy Rescue 12, a specialized unit which combines several emergency functions. According

A truck with crew outfitted and ready for duty in front of the old fire station in the mid-1970s.

This is the Fire Department Family, representing all its functions and responsibilities including: Fire Suppression, Rope Rescue, Honor Guard, Medical Services, Command Staff, Building/Life Safety, Hazardous Materials Control, Boy Scout Explorers, Administrative Support, and Public Education.

to Capt. Stan Human, manager of the Emergency Medical Service, it consolidates advanced and basic life support, fire/rescue, patient extrication, hazardous materials first response, and air and lighting support services in a single unit. It is housed at Fire Station 12 on Douglas Avenue.[333]

The Building and Life Support Division

Headed by Fire Marshal Steve Randall, who has a staff of ten, the building and life support division handles fire safety inspections. To facilitate this service the position of building offical was transferred from Public Works to this division in 1980.

City-County Cooperation

As the city and the county grew in the 1970s, Fire Chiefs Tom Siegfried and Gary Kaiser of Seminole County worked out a cooperative first response and mutual aid agreement whereby the closest station would fight the fire regardless of political boundaries. The county Communication Dispatching Center assumed responsibility for all fire dispatches, thus relieving the Altamonte Springs Police Department of that function. This joint response program has been extended so that six of the counties seven municipalities are now part of it. In 1976, Seminole County was recognized by the National Association of Counties for this cooperative program.[334]

This mutual effort was expanded in 1983 by the fire station realignment plan according to which the Newburyport Avenue station was designated Number 11. A new facility at Douglas Avenue and N. Westmonte Drive became Station 12. This enabled the county to move its North Street station to the Sabal Point area. In 1992 the city added its Hattaway Drive facility which became fire Station 14 in the county system.

Other Innovations

The Mini-Maxi system at Station 12 was instituted as a method of cost control when the department purchased its first aerial truck in 1980 at a cost of $318,000. Because it was so expensive to use, the department also outfitted a small truck to be used in conjunction with the larger one. Both are available for quick response, but in those cases which can be handled by the smaller vehicle, the aerial truck is left at the station.

The Fire Department was the first in the area to develop a high angle rescue team which could reach and remove victims from high-rise buildings. It also has the first award-winning extrication team in the county. The team is one of only twenty-two to be invited to national competition in this category.

This heavy rescue (multi-purpose) vehicle was put on line in 1993.

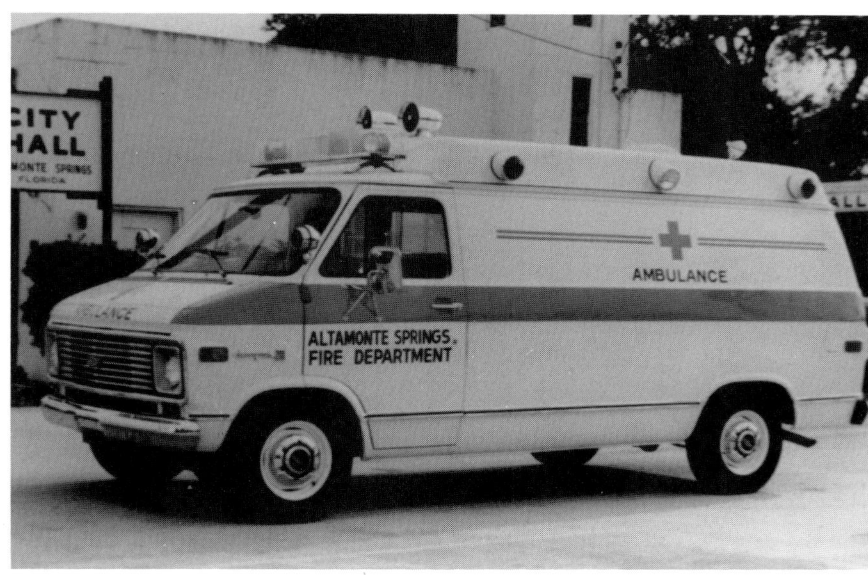

The Altamonte Springs Fire Department acquired the first fire department ambulance in Seminole County in 1973.

Fire Prevention and Public Education

Chief Siegfried and the department were early advocates of installing smoke detectors and sprinkler systems. In 1990, the chief was recognized by the International Association of Fire Chiefs for the department's early advocacy of residential sprinklers. The Orlando Junior League also recognized the department for its smoke detection program. The chief has become well-known throughout Central Florida for public service announcements promoting fire awareness and prevention.

The department also provides a lengthy list of public service programs aimed at educating the public in fire prevention. They range from training in the use of fire extinguishers to "Sparky the Fire Dog" and the Remote Control Fire Truck. One of the more popular programs is the recently introduced "Fire Safety Puppet Show" which is aimed at the younger set. An even more recent offering is the clown show, featuring two fully outfitted clowns, which is available on a first come, first served basis to churches, social groups, and even birthday parties.[335]

Long Range Recruiting

With a total of seventy-six employees, fifty-one of whom are on shifts at the stations, the department is an innovative, capable fire fighting agency. It strives to improve its capabilities and efficiency. Pursuant to that end, it became the first area department to implement a "casual employee" program by which extra personnel are available when they are needed to fill in under special circumstances. In this way qualified individuals work for minimum wages in order to make their availability and qualifications known in the event that permanent positions become available.

Combining education and recruiting is the Fire Explorers Post, a cooperative effort with the Boy Scouts. There are now seventeen youths in the program. Three have matriculated. One has been employed and another is studying fire prevention at the University of Kentucky.[336]

Fire Department EMS crew providing advanced life support to a patient.

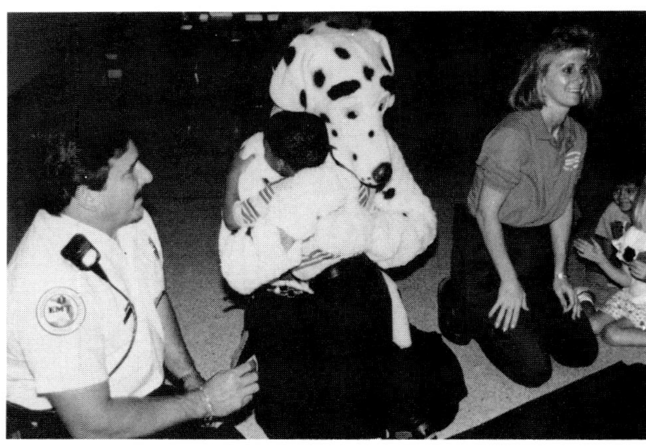

Pete Giglietta and Sandy Bennett and Sparky, the Fire Dog with a group of elementary school children.

When a propane truck was involved in an accident on S.R. 436, a hazardous materials control team responded. The highway was closed for about twelve hours while the team worked to remove the danger.

Fire Department responding to an automobile accident in the early 1980s.

Fire/Rescue high-angle training exercise at the Sheraton Hotel at Maitland Center.

Fighting a fire at the Chatham Harbor Apartments which had been started by a lightening strike.

Results and Recognition

Believing that the best way to fight fires is to avoid them, the department has placed major emphasis on its educational and informational programs. A measure of its success can be seen in the numbers. Of the nearly six thousand calls each year, nearly 70 percent are for emergency medical treatment. More than a third of the latter require advanced life support (paramedics).[337]

The department's overall efforts have attained national recognition. Fire Chief Tom Siegfried was inaugurated as president of the International Association of Fire Chiefs in August 1994.

The Department of Leisure Services

Like the other municipal departments, Leisure Services has evolved from the informality of the early 1970s until it has become a well-defined, multi-purpose agency with several nationally acclaimed programs.

The Department of Parks and Recreation was established in 1975. It was first headed by James Boston, but he was soon replaced by William R. James who has held the position for the past twenty years. With the growth and increasing complexity of the city, Parks and Recreation was reorganized in 1988 as the Department of Leisure Services. By that time the grounds and facilities maintenance division of the Department of Public Works had been transferred to it. Still headed by Bill James, the new department has since consisted of three divisions. Ronald Grasha, is deputy director for active recreation, including all sports activities. Jim Buck is responsible for urban beautification. James Singleton manages fleet and facilities maintenance and such community services as the library and special events.[338]

Parks and Recreation Real Estate

Eastmonte Park and the Civic Center were completed in 1973 as mentioned earlier. Longwood Avenue was then extended southward to provide access to the new facilities. At the urging of Helen Keyser, the civic center was operated separately from the park for several years with Eddie Rose as director. His position was eliminated by Jeff Etchberger's budget reforms in the early 1980s and the civic center gravitated back to the department.

Westmonte was also opened in 1973 but it was first a private club, complete with a large swimming pool. The city purchased it in 1978 for a half million dollars, receiving for that sum a fully developed sports facility as well as a place to house the offices of the department. It was immediately ready for competitive sports, including swimming. The adjacent Merrill Park, a softball complex, was added in 1986.[339]

James Singleton and a crew redesigning the entrance to the Eastmonte Recreation Complex. Singleton is now deputy director of his department and usually wears a white shirt, but this does not keep him out of the field.

The Altamonte Springs Civic Center at Eastmonte.

The city also has eight passive neighborhood parks ranging in size from one-half to two acres. Some have playgrounds for small children and some have picnic tables, but they are mostly lush green areas where the local residents can relax in open space.

Lake Lotus Park in the southwestern corner of the city is a large natural area with extensive wetlands, a variety of plant species, and wildlife. It will be opened this year as a passive park with boardwalks and nature trails.

Cranes Roost Lake Park is still a different kind of park. Not yet fully complete, it is presently a peaceful place near the bustling city center where people can relax during their breaks from busy workdays or shopping sprees. It will eventually be the center of organized special events as well.[340]

Turnbull Avenue in the late 1980s before the property was donated for a park.

An Urban Beautification crew putting the final touches on Turnbull Park (a new neighborhood) in 1992.

Turnbull Park after its completion on donated land.

Altamonte Springs twelve-year-old boys compete for the World Series title at Williamsport, Pennsylvania, in 1984.

Active Recreation

Bill James recently said that "every kid deserves a good childhood." He and Ronald Grasha have worked toward implementing that maxim. Large numbers of youngsters participate in organized and informal sports at the swimming pool and on all the athletic fields at both Eastmonte and Westmonte parks. For almost two decades the opening of the Little League has been the "biggest" day of the year for the department. Chartered in 1974, the Altamonte Springs Little League has placed well in competition. The fifteen-year-olds won the national title in 1984 at Gary, Indiana, by defeating a team from Taiwan. That same year the twelve-year-olds won the United States championship, but lost to Korea at Williamsport, Pennsylvania. The thirteen-year-olds' team went to the finals in 1983 and again in 1989.[341]

Opening day of Little League was always a big day for the Altamonte Springs recreation program.

Merrill Park

Dedicated in 1986, Merrill Park was named in honor of Merrill Schwartz. This amphitheater-styled facility is primarily a softball complex which is not only available to local users, but has also been home to state, regional and national tournaments. It also has the only officially sanctioned inland beach volleyball facility.

The Therapeutic Pool

Brenda Cole came to the department in 1983 to develop a therapeutic program for the disabled. She stimulated an awareness in the

Merrill Park opened in 1986 as a "state of the art" softball complex. An operations center was completed in 1988. In this photograph a softball game is in progress at the complex.

community of how many handicapped citizens there are. Loretta Hobbs and many other volunteers became interested in doing something about it. When the outdoor pool proved inadequate because of the need for controlling the temperature around the pool, the city appropriated $100,000 seed money toward construction of an indoor pool. A lengthy list of individuals and corporations—whose names are engraved on the "wall of fame" near the door of the new building—contributed to the construction of the unusual facility. Ronald Grasha instituted the annual Haunted House program as a continuing fund raising effort for its maintenance. The department also staged "barrier awareness" days to make more people aware of the needs of the handicapped. One result has been to make Altamonte Springs a leader in providing for the handicapped, both in access to facilities and in jobs.[342]

The pool, with its controlled temperature and a lift providing easy egress, is used by about one hundred twenty people a day. In 1990, the department received the National Gold Medal Award for Excellence in Recreation for its work in therapeutics.

The Park Rangers

Because of the special uses anticipated for Lake Lotus and Cranes Roost Lake parks, Altamonte Springs has instituted a park ranger program. The rangers are trained first to be good hosts at the parks and then to handle emergencies, crowd control, and related matters. With the assistance of city manager Phil Penland and police chief William A. Liquori, the seven park rangers will be qualified law enforcement officers, and some of them will have emergency medical training.[343]

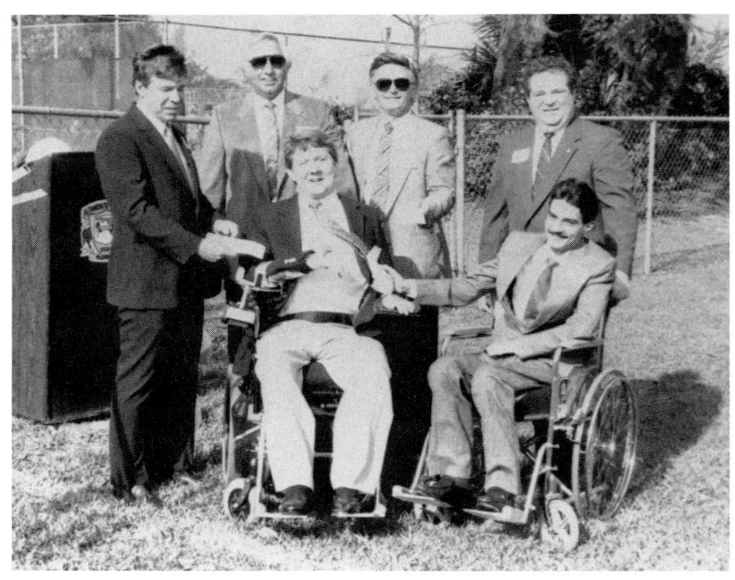

Robert Jones (center), president of the Advisory Board for the Disabled, receiving a check from local businessmen. In the front besides Jones is Dan Green. Back row , from left are Don Boynter, Bob Santulli, Yogi Moore, and Ed Hargraves.

In 1988, the City of Altamonte Springs and the Advisory Board for the Disabled entered into a joint effort with area businesses and service clubs to raise funds for the building of a therapeutic pool. This is the ground breaking ceremony which occurred in August of that year.

Barrier Awareness Day 1992. An annual event to focus awareness on access problems of the disabled. This year, James Brady (third from left), former presidential press secretary, wounded in assassination attempt on President Reagan, addressed the group.

The fully enclosed therapeutic exercise pool at Westmonte Recreation Center. It is the first such public facility in Central Florida.

Urban Beautification

Jim Buck is the deputy director for urban beautification. His division is responsible for the well-maintained streets and public grounds of the city. He has carefully designed the layouts of trees, shrubs, and annual plantings with an eye to beauty as well as the practicality of maintenance. His continuing awareness of the needs of this task include a computerized inventory of the trees on city-owned property. This is required of any Tree City U.S.A., but it also enables the division to provide timely maintenance to keep the trees healthy, safe for the public, and in the right places.[344]

Fleet and Facilities Maintenance and Community Services

Originally employed by Don Bundy in 1976 to develop a heavy equipment capability, James Singleton first worked on the installation of water and sewer lines as well as all public works requiring heavy equipment. In the reorganizations of the 1980s, he was made deputy director of the division of fleet and facilities maintenance. His heavy equipment still provides support for the Department of Public Works.[345]

The Library

The library was supported by the Friends of the Library, until the city assumed responsibility for it in 1977. Its building was expanded jointly with the chamber of commerce in the early 1980s on the site of the old Community House. When the chamber left, the library acquired the entire facility. Several volunteers managed the library until Karen Potter, the first professional librarian, was employed. She was followed recently by Richard Miller who is currently expanding the library services. In 1993, a traveling library Mobile Information Center (MIC) was added with Peggy Gunnell in charge.

Looking north on Maitland Avenue toward its intersection with Altamonte Avenue (S.R. 436) in the 1980s before it was widened and improved.

This is the Altamonte Avenue/Maitland Avenue intersection after it was improved and Jim Buck's urban beautification work was completed. Across the street is the 701 Building and the Kirchman Building. The Jin Ho Restaurant has been removed since this 1992 photograph was taken.

View toward the west along West Altamonte Avenue (S.R. 436) on the west side of I-4 about 1992.

Urban Beautification Supervisor, Mike Insley, conducting a tree-planting ceremony at Spring Lake Elementary School.

Dedication of the City Library in 1980. The participants are from left: Bill James, Bob Reis, Jeff Etchberger, Hugh Harling, and Delores Vickers.

The Mobile Information Center (MIC), the city's rolling library was dedicated in 1993.

Community Services

Singleton's division also manages a variety of community services, perhaps the most visible of which is special events coordinated by Shelly Nooft.

The Lake Brantley Field House

The new Lake Brantley Field House is an example of intergovernmental cooperation. The school needed a larger field house and swimming pool and the city also had need of more facilities. Neither had the necessary funds. Through an agreement between the city, the Department of Education, the Lake Brantley Boosters, and the Tourist Development Council, a $1.5 million field house—with the finest school pool outside of California—was completed at Lake Brantley High School. It is used by the school during its hours of operation and as a city center the rest of the time.[346]

The Department of Public Works

Headed by Don Bundy during the early days when demand for water and sewer capacity kept the city busy, the Department of Public works has been directed by Donald F. Newnham since 1977. The Keller Road Regional Wastewater Treatment Plant was just coming on line at the time. During the next several years, the plant was completed and expanded. It presently has a surplus capacity available for potential users. Correlative to that project was the expansion of a potable water system which could deliver more than ten million gallons a day to users in Altamonte Springs and adjacent areas.

The department then had a city engineer whose duty was to deal with developers. There were also two inspectors whose duties were to evaluate the infrastructures of developments which the city was considering annexing. The two latter positions were transferred to the Department of Growth Management in 1985.

When Newnham took over the department there was almost no staff except for the billing clerks whose duties have since been transferred to the Department of Finance. There were few files and no maps. An administrative system was implemented along with a mapping program. The mapping project is now computerized and is still being developed. The department has capabilities for drafting and engineering and even has its own laboratory. Since the 1985 reorganization, the Department of Public Works has been able to concentrate on potable and reclaimed water, their quality and distribution to users, and the effect of that use on the overall water supply and environmental protection.[347]

Departmental Organization

With a staff of eleven, Newnham concentrates the functions of administration, planning, construction, and engineering in his own office. At West Altamonte, Frank Frost manages streets and environmental services with a staff of four. Korvin Hunter is in charge of water resources and management services with a staff of six. The Keller Road reclamation facility is managed by Rick Hosier and three others. Ray Sharp is in charge of specialized services, including materials and inventory control, customer services, and environmental analysis. He has a staff of six.

Project APRICOT

A Prototype Realistic Innovative Community of Today—understandably dubbed APRICOT—is the most innovative and far-reaching program yet undertaken by an already progressive city. Thinking about an ever-shrinking fresh water supply in Central Florida, a system which was pumping as much as fourteen million gallons a day, and the problems of

Commissioners opening the valve to begin reclaimed water services to the city (Project APRICOT). From the left they are Russel Hauck, Pat Fernandez, Lee Constantine, and Mayor Dudley Bates. The unidentified left arm belongs to Commissioner Eddie Rose. Donald Newnham (on right), director of the Department of Public Works, looks on.

disposing of waste water without damaging the Wekiva River in particular and the water supply in general, Don Newnham conceived the idea of APRICOT. It involved the installation of parallel water lines to every user in Altamonte Springs. Potable water would be pumped through one for household use, and reclaimed water would flow through the other to be used for irrigation, car washing, and similar purposes. It was a huge undertaking which would not only require time, but would also need huge financing before long range savings could be realized.[348]

The city authorities agreed in 1981 when Newnham asked for thirty million dollars to build the system. Even more important, individual water users agreed to have their rates increased dramatically in the hope of seeing them drop later.

The first construction bonds were sold in 1985. The system required seven years to build, with the first water being pumped in 1989. Progress was slow and people began asking the city to accelerate the program. The lines are now in place and all who want to take advantage of the reclaimed water can do so. New construction carries with it the obligation of using the new system. At a cost of about 40 percent of that of potable water, it has pleased consumers. It has also reduced the amount of reclaimed water going directly into the Wekiva River and it also recharges the underground aquifer.

The city has gained considerable recognition for APRICOT as more and more municipalities inquire about it for their own possible applications. Don Newnham has won repeated awards for his work on the system. Initiated by Lee Constantine, the freshman legislator who served on the city commission while the program was being developed, a new law was recently enacted by the Florida legislature encouraging other municipalities to emulate APRICOT. Perhaps most significant of all, the Keller Road plant which treats the water and which was built at the initiative of Mayor Lawrence Swofford was recently renamed in his honor.[349]

The Potable Water System

Implementation of Project APRICOT has reduced the demand for potable water to less than seven million gallons a day. Of the five water plants operating in the1980s, only three are now in service. In case of emergency, any two of them are sufficient to supply daily needs plus fire protection.[350]

Solid Waste Disposal

In the early years of the Town of Altamonte Springs, refuse was deposited at a site which is now part of the governmental complex. It is no longer that simple. The city handles its own residential garbage and

*Public Works Department personnel installing water lines for Project **APRICOT**.*

The City's Regional Waste Water Treatment Plant on Keller Road.

recycling, having found that it is less costly than contracting with private firms. Garbage pick-up is four days a week with newspapers and yard waste being gathered on Wednesdays. The city does its own recycling. Disposition of the sludge from waste water treatment has also become increasingly difficult as environmental regulations have become more stringent.

In this case, the city has contracted with a firm which compacts both sludge and yard waste. It is then taken to a commercial company in Polk County at a cost about half what the county charges for disposal.[351]

Jackie Church of the Public Works Department, laying sidewalk.

The Growth Management Department

The Growth Management Department evolved indirectly from the office of building and zoning which then dealt with both residential and commercial developers. Their authority was limited to oversight of such matters as setback lines, building heights, and use. The result was that during the 1970s, the city evolved with a lengthy commercial strip along S.R. 436, and a traffic problem.[352]

Realizing that planning was essential, city officials assembled a number of committees composed of ordinary citizens, businessmen, and both appointed and elective officials to develop a city planning concept. The result was the 1980 reorganization of the Building and Zoning Department. During the early 1980s the requisite plans and ordinances were developed for implementing the Community Redevelopment Agency in 1986.

A ceremony at which the water treatment plant was named in honor of W. Lawrence Swofford, the man most responsible for its construction in Altamonte Springs. Swofford is standing (left).

Landscaping the Regional Waste Water Treatment Complex.

Wendell Peters was employed in 1981 as the building officer. He was given an additional duty as director of Community Redevelopment when that agency was formed. Peters left in 1986. Tim Wilson, who had only recently been hired by Peters, succeeded him within months after his departure.[353]

The department as it is now constituted was established in 1990 with Wilson as director. The function of the building officer was then transferred to the fire department.

With a staff of about thirteen, Wilson's department does comprehensive planning for the city. Its focus is on land development and redevelopment with special emphasis on transportation. The department works closely with the Environmental Protection Agency, the St. Johns Water Management District, and the county. Although the city has authority to approve new enterprises, it is obliged to keep close contact with the other agencies. Intergovernmental cooperation has become a necessity.

The department's City Plan 2005, adopted in 1991, meets all state requirements and is a guide for the city into the next century. It will be addressed in the following chapter.

A Proximate Conclusion

Orlando Sentinel columnist Don Boyett recently observed that "People are at the heart of a city's success or failure."[354]

The Altamonte Springs city government bears that out. A strong commission and an able city manager have developed a viable government structure, the departments of which are staffed with capable people. Each department first pursues its own mission, but there is also cooperation with each and all of the others. To paraphrase Booker T. Washington's famous 1895 comment, Altamonte Springs' city departments are "as separate as the fingers and as united as the hand."

THIRTEEN

Creating a Downtown for Altamonte Springs

As it celebrates its 75th year as an incorporated municipality, the City of Altamonte Springs bears little resemblance to the rural community beside the Atlantic Coast Line Railroad which was incorporated in 1920 by 43 citizens. It has grown to an area of 9.4 square miles of territory with a population of some 37,000. Within the boundaries of the city—in its urban service area—there are about 10,000 other people living on approximately five square miles of county land.

Antique and classic automobiles assembled for a parade at the opening of Central Parkway in 1992.

By the early 1980s, Altamonte Springs was about to become the largest city in Seminole County, but it had no identifiable center. In less than two decades it had grown from the small community with a few stores at the corner of S.R. 436 and C.R. 427 to a sprawling suburb in the Orlando metropolitan area. The tiny community center of earlier years had been overrun by the strip commercial development which had spread—and was still spreading—along S.R. 436 as well as S.R. 434. This "urban sprawl" was threatening residential areas which were in its path. Altamonte Springs had become known for the Altamonte Mall, the strip commercial development, and the horrendous traffic congestion which accompanied them.

These were the problems which led the city to strengthen its planning capability in the early 1980s. If the city were ever to manage growth rather than merely react to it, then it needed a comprehensive plan and increased authority over land use in order to implement it. Both were accomplished by the mid-1980s.

The plan was based on two major premises. First, the most pressing problem requiring attention was traffic. Something had to be done to reduce congestion on the arterial and major collector roads. That implied both road improvement and reduction of traffic on them. The latter could be addressed by bringing together in a certain place many of the office complexes and commercial establishments which were scattered throughout the city.

The correlative premise was that Altamonte Springs—almost surrounded by other urban areas abutting its boundaries—was about to be "built out." With a minimum of undeveloped land, the rebuilding of the city would have to be based on redevelopment.

City Plan 2000—updated in 1991 by City Plan 2005—established a Regional Business Center focused on the area between Palm Springs Drive and I-4. Its outer boundaries were Montgomery Road on the west, Maitland Avenue on the east, and both sides of I-4 to the northern and southern city limits. The Regional Center was complemented by two

Mayor Dudley Bates addressing an audience at the ceremony dedicating Central Parkway. Assembly is at the intersection of Douglas Avenue and the Parkway.

Aerial view of Cranes Roost Park during the "Arts in April" Festival of 1994.

Dale Ricou, the Police Department clown, filling balloons for the children at Cranes Roost Park during the "Arts in April" Festival, 1994.

smaller, locally oriented ones, the West Town Center near the intersection of S.R. 436 and S.R. 434 and the East Town Center at S.R. 436 and C.R. 427.[355]

The Community Redevelopment Agency

A Community Redevelopment Agency (CRA), with members appointed by the city commission, was empowered to develop the new city center with retail stores, office complexes, hotels, restaurants, commercial entertainment, and public areas. By such a combination of the work place, shopping, dining, recreation, and a quiet place—Cranes Roost Lake Park—to relax, the use of automobiles for local trips would reduced.

The CRA had authority to encourage high-density, high-rise buildings, thereby increasing the value of the land to be redeveloped. The result was to be an esthetically pleasing downtown with the tallest buildings at the center and smaller ones tapering off toward the outer boundaries of the district.[356]

Construction at Cranes Roost Park.

The Tax Increment District

The CRA is financed by revenue from a tax increment district. Recent state legislation permits such districts to freeze property taxes for general use at a certain level. As valuations rise, the additional increment is retained for use within the district. To offset the county's revenue loss, the city assumed responsibility for road maintenance in the area. With the tax increment funds—amounting to $1,860,000 in 1994—the city planned several improvements for the new business center.[357]

Dealing with the Traffic Problem

The agency's first responsibility was to improve traffic conditions. It would encourage mass transit such as the Tri-County bus system and local shuttle vehicles. But road improvements were also planned. Through intergovernmental cooperation, S.R. 436 was widened, and the Central Parkway was completed and opened in 1992. The parkway, extending along the northern edge of the business center from Palm Springs Drive, across I-4, to Montgomery Road has significantly reduced the amount of local traffic which once relied on S.R. 436. Together with the widening of the highway itself, the opening of the parkway has had a beneficial effect on the S.R. 436 traffic flow. There is also longer-range consideration of a station near the business center on a light rail line when one becomes a reality.[358]

City Manager, Phillip Penland, directing tree planting at Cranes Roost Park. The city's tree planting efforts have resulted in its designation as a "Tree City U.S.A."

The beautifully landscaped Central Parkway complements another important project. Cranes Roost has been converted from a blighted area into a beautiful lake surrounded by a city park. Designed eventually to feature special events—including performances on a floating stage—the park offers a quiet place where people can relax during their lunch hours or during breaks from shopping in the nearby Altamonte Mall or the recently completed Renaissance Center. Completion of the Central Parkway and Cranes Roost Lake Park, together with the renovation of the Cranes Roost Executive Center, have transformed what was once a liability into an important asset for the incipient downtown district.[359]

A Development of Regional Impact

The city offers another major incentive for redevelopment. One of the costliest parts of large-scale development is the lengthy approval process. In environmentally-conscious Florida, developments of regional impact (DRIs) must be approved by the East Central Florida Regional Planning Council (ECFRPC) and other agencies. The process often requires as much as two years and costs thousands of dollars. In order to speed up the process and reduce costs for potential developers, Altamonte Springs submitted a request for approval of a DRI for the entire Regional Business Center. With Commissioner Lee Constantine then sitting as chairman of the ECFRPC's project review committee, the DRI was approved in 1986.[360]

Recognition

Altamonte Springs received the ECFRPC's 1988 Grand Award of Excellence "for its bold plan for a new downtown." The award also included recognition of the city's water reclamation project (APRICOT).

Results

Because of some features of the 1986 reforms of the Internal Revenue Code and the economic decline in the late 1980s, construction in the Regional Business Center has not proceeded as rapidly as it might have, but much has been done. The traffic improvements and the beautification of the Cranes Roost area were accompanied by completion of the 250,000-square-foot Renaissance Center and the Embassy Suites Hotel.

Following recent improvements in the general economy, the Redevelopment Agency is seeing signs of activity. Several large developers have reserved land for development in the district. Emerson International, a large English firm with extensive interests in Central Florida, is presently working on plans for a major project there.[361]

In the 75th Year

As it celebrates its 75th year as an incorporated municipality, the City of Altamonte Springs bears little resemblance to the rural community beside the Atlantic Coast Line Railroad which was incorporated in 1920 by forty-three citizens. It has grown to an area of 9.4 square miles of territory with a population of some 37,000. Within the boundaries of the city—in its urban service area—there are about 10,000 other people living on approximately five square miles of county land.

The approximately 6,000 acres of the incorporated city are divided almost equally between residential and commercial zones. The people live in 5,495 single family dwellings and 12,558 multi-family units. There are about 3,200 businesses. The total valuation of both classes of property is about $1.6 billion.[362]

Because it is so nearly "built out," Altamonte Springs is not likely to increase its population much more. But it is entirely likely that its residents will live in stable residential areas in a city with an identifiable downtown.

Endnotes

[1] Roland M. Harper, *Geography of Central Florida* Thirteenth Annual Report of the State Geological Survey, (1921), p. 119.

[2] Rick Dreves, "Archaeological Investigation of 8-OR-17: An Early Aboriginal Campsite on the Shore of Lake Apopka, Florida," *Florida Anthropologist*, 27 (June 1974), pp. 467-76.

[3] John W. Griffin, *The Florida Indian and His Neighbors* (Winter Park, 1949), p. 83.

[4] John R. Swanton, *The Indians of the Southeastern United States* (New York, 1969), pp. 83.

[5] National Archives, Record Group 28, Records of the Post Office Department, Appointments of Postmasters, Microfilm T841-21; and Bureau of Transportation, Domestic Mail Transportation, Volume 297, p. 166; Florida State Archives, Series 914, P. D. Shepherd to Dennis Eagan, September 24, 1875, and George W. Moyers to Eaqan, September 24, December 15, 1875. The original Altamont settlement was spelled both with and without an e. In order to avoid as much confusion of the two places as possible, I have arbitrarily spelled the older Altamont without the e and Altamonte Springs with it.

[6] William F. Blackman, *History of Orange County, Florida* (Chulota, 1973), 26; C. E. Howard, *Early Settlers of Orange County* (Orlando, 1915), p. 26.

[7] Blackman, *Orange County*, p. 26.

[8] *Tallahassee Weekly Floridian*, December 30, 1979.

[9] Blackman, *Orange County*, p. 26; *Tallahassee Weekly Floridian*, January 10, 1882; Sherman Adams, *Orangeland* (Orlando, 1883–84), p. 57.

[10] First Public Time Table of South Florida Railroad, November 11, 1880. Copy in Altamonte Springs Public Library.

[11] Blackman, *Orange County*, p. 26.

[12] *Laws of Florida*, 1885, p. 90.

[13] *Laws of Florida*, 1887, p. 227; *Tallahassee Weekly Floridian*, February 18 and April 8, 1886; *Apopka City Union*, March 17, 1887.

[14] George R. Pettingill, *The Story of Florida Railroads, 1834–1952* (Boston, 1952), p. 85.

[15] *Tallahassee Weekly Floridian*, July 29, 1886; Jerrell H. Shofner, *History of Apopka and Northwest Orange County, Florida* (Apopka, 1982), pp. 74–75; Blackman, *Orange County*, p. 211.

[16] *Laws of Florida*, 1883, p. 106; Orange County, Unidentifiable Miscellaneous Files, Reel 6, *Apopka and Atlantic Railroad v. G. L. Stone and G. W. Farnham; Tallahassee Weekly Floridian*, August 6, 7, 1885, September 9, 1886, quoting *Orlando Sentinel*, and March 26, 1889; National Archives, Record Group 28, M-1126-95.

[17] Pettingill, *Florida Railroads,* p. 124.

[18] *Tallahassee Weekly Floridian,* February 18, 1886.

[19] National Archives, Record Group 28, Records of the Post Office Department, Appointments of Postmasters, M841-21.

[20] Prospectus, Altamonte Land, Hotel, and Navigation Company. (Copy in Altamonte Springs City Library).

[21] *Ibid.*

[22] *Ibid.*, Florida State Archives, Series 186, Corporation Book B, Altamonte Hotel, Land and Navigation Company Charter.

[23] *Ibid.*

[24] Orlando *Orange County Reporter,* May 1, 1884.

[25] The Altamonte, Brochure, 1883; *Orlando Orange County Reporter,* May 1, 1884.

[26] Orange County, Deed Book 28, p. 103; *Jacksonville Florida Times Union*, October 20, 1885.

[27] *Orlando Orange County Reporter,* March 7, 1884.

[28] *Orlando Orange County Reporter,* March 27, December 4, 1884; South Publishing Company, *Florida State Gazetteer and Business Directory*, 1886-1887, p. 58; Original Census Schedules, Population, 1880. The Pierce shown here is apparently the former sea captain who brought the "inside-outside house" to Altamonte Springs, but there is some doubt about his first name. Shown in the Gazetteer as "Charles E.," he has been identified elsewhere as simply "W. Pierce." The 1880 census shows a Robert W. Pierce as an area resident. Whatever his first name, Pierce was a citizen of the community in the late 19th century.

[29] South Publishing Company, *Florida State Gazetteer,* 1885–1886, p. 88, 1886–1887, p. 58; Orange County School Board, Minutes, 1886–1888.

[30] J. C. Rand, *One of a Thousand* (Boston, 1890), pp. 75–76.

[31] South Publishing Company, *Florida State Gazetteer,* 1886–1887, p. 58.

[32] *Tallahassee Weekly Floridian,* January 27, 1880.

[33] *Southern Industry* (New Orleans, Louisiana and Johnstown, Florida, June 18, 1904).

[34] Elliott's *Florida Encyclopedia,* 1889, p. 184; *Tallahassee Weekly Floridian*, September 11, 1888; NA,RG 28, M841-21.

[35] *Orlando Orange County Reporter,* n.d., 1886.

[36] *Apopka South Florida Citizen,* April 9, 1879.

[37] *Ibid.*

[38] George M. Barbour, *Florida, for Tourists, Invalids and Settlers* (New York, 1882), p. 45.

[39] Sherman Adams, *Orangeland* (Orlando, 1883-1884), pp. 67–69.

[40] South Publishing Company, *Florida State Gazetteer,* 1884–1885.

[41] *Orlando Orange County Reporter,* February 2, 1884.

[42] South Publishing Company, *Florida State Gazetteer,* 1886–1887.

[43] *The Altamonte Chapel, A Community Church, 1885–1974* (Copy in Altamonte Springs City Library); South Publishing Company, *Florida State Gazetter,* 1886–1887.

[44] *Elliott's Encyclopedia,* 1889; Orange County School Board, Minutes, 1889–1890.

[45] Orange County Commission, Map of Orange County (circa 1890) in P. K. Yonge Library of Florida History; Elliott's *Florida Encyclopedia,* 1889, p. 184; National Archives, Record Group 28, M841-21.

[46] Orange County School Board, Minutes,1891.

[47] National Archives, Record Group 28, M1126-95; Orange County School Board, Minutes, 1889–1896.

[48] National Archives, Record Group 28, M1126-95.

[49] George T. Belding (compiler), *Florida Railroad Gazetteer and State Business Directory,* 1895; Letter of Herman L. Savage, April 3, 1899, in Ira H. Erickson, *The John Andersons of Sweden, Sanford, Apopka, and Piedmont, Orange County, Florida, 1836–1955* (Blacksburg, Virginia, 1955).

[50] Orange County Deed Books 74, p. 103, 78, p. 460, and 92, p. 140.

[51] Orange County School Board, Minutes, 1895–1896.

[52] National Archives, Record Group 28, M1126.

[53] Mahlon Gore, *Florida, Home, Farm, and Field* (Orlando, 1897).

[54] Orange County, Deed Book 112, p. 103.

[55] Orange County, Deed Book 124, p. 509, and Deed Book 125, p. 12.

[56] Orange County, Deed Book 142, pp. 302 and 307; *Sanford Herald,* October 14, 1909.

[57] *Sanford Herald,* November 28, 1908.

[58] *Orlando Reporter-Star,* January 30, 1912.

[59] *Sanford Herald,* March 5, 1915, quoting the *Orlando Sentinel.* Bates was referring to the First World War which was raging in Europe at that time.

[60] *Ibid.,* August 22, 1913.

[61] Orange County, Deed Book 18, p. 273.

[62] R. L. Polk, *Florida Gazetteer and Business Directory,* 1907–1908, 1911–1912.

[63] *Southern Industry,* (New Orleans and Johnston, Florida, June 18, 1904); *Sanford Herald,* December 19, 1913.

[64] R. L. Polk, *Florida Gazetteer,* 1911–1912; *Sanford Herald,* December 19, 1913.

[65] *Sanford Herald,* August 1, December 19, 1913.

[66] "The Altamonte Chapel, A Community Church, 1885–1974". Copy in Altamonte Springs City Library.

[67] Orange County School Board, Minutes, 1902–1906.

[68] *Ibid.,* Minutes,1912–1914; *Sanford Herald,* August 19, October 2, 1914.

[69] *Sanford Herald,* November 28, 1908, February 13, 20, 1909.

[70] *Ibid.*, February 13, 20, 1909.

[71] *Ibid.,* November 28, 1908, February 20, 1909, August 22, 1913; Orange County, *State Fair Edition,* 1906. Copy in Orange County Historical Museum.

[72] *Sanford Herald,* February 20, 1909.

[73] *Ibid.*, December 10, 1908, November 10, 1911

[74] *Ibid.*, January 23, 1909.

[75] *Ibid.*, February 13, 1909.

[76] *Ibid*.

[77] *Ibid.*, February 20, March 20, 1909.

[78] *Ibid.*, March 20, 1909.

[79] *Ibid.*, July 11, 1913.

[80] *Ibid.*, December 19, 1913.

[81] *Ibid.*, February 26, 1915.

[82] M. F. Robinson, *Florida Orange Groves for Sale* (Sanford, 1911); C. E. Howard, *Early Settlers of Orange County, Florida* (Orlando, 1915), p. 36; Sanford Herald, December 19, 1913; Orlando Reporter-Star, December 18, 1911.

[83] *Sanford Herald*, November 28, 1908; Charles T. Hopkins, *Fifty Years of Citrus: The Florida Citrus Exchange, 1909-1959* (Gainesville, 1960), pp. 4, 5.

[84] *Sanford Herald*, December 19, 1913.

[85] *Ibid.*, November 28, 1908, August 11, 22, 1913.

[86] C. E. Howard, *Early Settlers*, pp. 15, 65; Seminole County, Corporation Book 1, p. 422; Title Abstract, 228 Oakhurst, Altamonte Springs.

[87] *Sanford Herald*, April 29, 1921; Interview with B. D. McIntosh, Jr., June 24, 1993.

[88] *Ibid.*, January 5, 1912.

[89] *Ibid.*, January 23, May 21, 1909.

[90] *Ibid.*, October 2, 1914, September 7, 1915.

[91] *Ibid.*, February 20, 1917.

[92] *Ibid.*, January 21, 1916, September 7, 1917.

[93] Winter Park Telephone Directory, 1913–1914, 1917.

[94] *Orlando Reporter-Star*, December 3, 1912; Orlando Sentinel, February 15, 1913; *Sanford Herald*, December 31, 1912, March 14, 1913.

[95] *Laws of Florida*, Chapter 6511, April 25, 1913; *Sanford Herald*, May 3, 1913.

[96] *Sanford Herald*, April 10, July 24, 1917, July 2, 1918.

[97] *Ibid.*, January 18, March 22, 1918, January 17, August 15, 1919.

[98] *Ibid.*, June 25, 1920.

[99] Proceedings of Meeting, November 11, 1920. Copy in Altamonte Springs Public Library.

[100] *Ibid.* It is not clear how 42 voters cast 45 votes. Perhaps the extra three were cast by late arrivals. In any event, the majority in favor of incorporation was decisive.

[101] *Ibid.*

[102] *Laws of Florida*, Chapter 8913, 1921.

[103] *Ibid.*

[104] *Ibid.* Town of Altamonte Springs Council, Minutes, March 16, 1925.

[105] *Laws of Florida*, Chapter 8913, 1921.

[106] Town of Altamonte Springs, Ordinance No. 5, October 18, 1921.

[107] *Sanford Herald*, November 29, 1924; Orlando *Morning Sentinel*, May 25, 1925.

[108] *Sanford Herald*, July 23, 1920; Town of Altamonte Springs, Ordinance No. 8, February 6, and September 18, 1922; Florida State Archives, LR 21, Altamonte Springs Tax Collector's Office, Tax Records, 1922.

[109] Town of Altamonte Springs, Ordinance No. 6, November 7, 1921; *Sanford Herald*, May 8, 1923; Interview with B. D. McIntosh, Jr., June 24, 1993.

[110] Town Council, Minutes, January 19, April 6, May 4, 1925.

[111] *Winter Park Herald*, May 13, 1926.

[112] *Ibid.*, February 3, 1923.

[113] Town Council, Minutes, January 19, May 4, June 7, 1925; April 19, 1926.

[114] *Ibid.*, November 16, 1925, March 15, 1926, April 4, 1927.

[115] *Sanford Herald*, April 5, 1924, May 6, October 31, 1925, November 1, 1928; Town Council, Minutes, November 7, 1927.

[116] Town Council, Minutes, April 6, 1925; Town of Altamonte Springs, Ordinance No. 3, April 20, 1925.

[117] Town Council, Minutes, April 6, 1925.

[118] *Ibid.*

[119] Town Council, Minutes, March 15, December 20, 1926; Town of Altamonte Springs, Ordinance No. 4, January 6, 1925.

[120] *Sanford Herald*, March 5, 1925; Town Council, Minutes, April 4, August 23, 1927.

[121] *Ibid.*, November 20, 1924, April 29, 1926.

[122] Town Council, Minutes, February 7, 1927, December 3, 1928.

[123] *Winter Park Herald,* August 19, 1927.

[124] Town Council Minutes, March 16, 1925.

[125] *Ibid.*, January 21, 1929.

[126] *Ibid.*, January 7, 1929.

[127] *Ibid.*, November 4, 1929.

[128] *Ibid.*, May 18, November 2, 1925.

[129] *Sanford Herald*, September 19, 1921.

[130] *Sanford Herald*, September 23, 1921.

[131] Seminole County, Incorporation Book 1, p. 300; *Tampa Tribune*, June 10, 1923, p. 12B; *Sanford Herald*, March 21, 1925; Charles Haines to B. F. Haines, April 3, 1921, Haines Family Papers, Altamonte Springs Public Library.

[132] Florida State Archives, LR 21, Altamonte Springs Tax Rolls, 1927; *Sanford Herald*, March 21, 1925.

[133] Seminole County, Corporation Book 1, p. 382; Florida State Archives, LR 21, Altamonte Springs Tax Rolls, 1927; Charles Haines to Whom It May Concern, March 10, 1928, Haines Family Papers.

[134] Seminole Corporation Book 1, pp. 349, 386, 432; *Winter Park Herald*, February 3, 1923.

[135] *Sanford Herald*, January 1, 1922; *Winter Park Herald*, February 25, March 4, 1923.

[136] *Orlando Morning Sentinel*, May 25, 1925; Winter Park Herald, January 14, 1926.

[137] *Winter Park Herald*, February 25, 1926, quoting the *Palm Beach Post*.

[138] *Winter Park Herald*, January 14, March 18, April 1, 8, 1926.

[139] *Sanford Herald*, November 1, 1926.

[140] *Winter Park Herald*, May 20, 1926.

[141] Florida State Archives, LR 21, Altamonte Springs Tax Rolls, 1927; *Sanford Herald*, September 19, 1921; *Winter Park Herald*, November 1, 1928; Eve Bacon, *Orlando: A Centennial History, Volume II* (Chuluota, 1977) p. 120.

[142] Town Council, Minutes, March 6, July 6, 1925; R. L. Polk, *Seminole County Directory*, 1926–27.

[143] Town Council, Minutes, July 6, 1925, April 4, 1927.

[144] Eve Bacon, *Orlando, A Centennial History* (Chuluota, 1977), p. 4, 19.

[145] *Sanford Herald*, October 17, 1924; Interview with B. D. McIntosh, Jr., June 24, 1993.

[146] Town of Altamonte Springs, Ordinance No. 10, March 12, 1925.

[147] *Sanford Herald*, February 10, 1923.

[148] *Winter Park Herald*, April 29, 1926; *Orlando Sentinel*, Orlando Magazine, January 25, 1951.

[149] Seminole County Deed Book 57, p. 116

[150] *Winter Park Herald*, April 22, 1926, November 22, 1928.

[151] *Winter Park Herald*, February 23, March 20, 1927.

[152] *Winter Park Herald*, April 20, 1927.

[153] *Sanford Herald*, February 18, 21, 28, 1925.

[154] *Sanford Herald*, December 10, 1925, March 27, April 26, 1927; *Winter Park Herald*, January 20, 1927.

[155] *Sanford Herald*, January 28, December 11, 1925, March 19, 1926.

[156] Town Council, Minutes, May 3, 1926; *Winter Park Herald*, May 20, 1926.

[157] *Sanford Herald*, September 23, 1921; *Orlando Sentinel*, October 16, 1924; Altamonte Springs Telephone Book, 1924.

[158] *Orlando Sentinel*, October 16, 1924; *Winter Park Herald*, February 23, April 15, 1926, June 3, 1927; Florida State Archives, Altamonte Springs Tax Rolls, 1927.

[159] Town Council, Minutes, April 4, 1927; *Winter Park Herald*, November 8, 1928; Altamonte Springs Telephone Directory, 1926; R. L. Polk, *Seminole County Directory*, 1926–1927.

[160] Town Council, Minutes, November 16, 25, May 16, 1927.

[161] *Winter Park Herald*, October 14, 1927, November 22, 1928.

[162] *Winter Park Herald*, February 23, 25, 1923, February 23, 1926, March 10, 20, 1927, January 6, March 9, November 1, 1928.

[163] *Winter Park Herald*, February 23, 1923, February 3, 1927; *Sanford Herald*, March 26, 1925.

[164] *Winter Park Herald*, April 1, December 16, 1926, April 7, June 3, 1927, March 9, 1928.

[165] *Winter Park Herald*, April 8, 1926, October 7, 14, 1927, September 23, 1928, February 7, 1929.

[166] *Winter Park Herald*, February 23, December 16, 1926, February 3, 1927, December 20, 1928.

[167] *Winter Park Herald*, March 3, 1927.

[168] *Winter Park Herald*, May 20, 1927, December 6, 20, 1928.

[169] *Winter Park Herald*, May 13, April 15, 1926, February 20, October 14, 1927.

[170] *Winter Park Herald*, April 1, 1926, January 3, February 20, March 3, 1927.

[171] *Winter Park Herald*, March 24, 1927.

[172] *Winter Park Herald*, February 16, April 13, December 20, 1928.

[173] Seminole County Chamber of Commerce, *Seminole County, Florida* (1925); *Sanford Herald*, July 9, August 5, 1925, September 18, 1926.

[174] *Sanford Herald*, December 4, 1925; *Winter Park Herald*, April 15, 1926, January 27, 1927, November 22, 1928.

[175] *Winter Park Herald*, October 11, 1928.

[176] Town Council, Minutes, March 7, 1927; *Winter Park Herald*, March 10, 1927; Seminole County School Board, Minutes, 1927–1931.

[177] *Winter Park Herald*, May 20, 1927, November 22, December 20, 1928, February 7, 1929, November 27, 1930.

[178] *Winter Park Herald*, April 23, 1931; Seminole County, Tax Rolls, 1930, 1935.

[179] Seminole County, Tax Rolls, 1930, 1935, 1940.

[180] Town Council, Minutes, November 24, December 1, 1930.

[181] *Ibid.*, January 19, 1931.

[162] *Ibid.*, August 24, 1931; Interview with Zetta Morrison, April 8, 1994.

[183] Town Council, Minutes, September 24, 1931.

[184] *Ibid.*, April 20, 1925, May 3, 1926, April 18, 1927.

[185] *Laws of Florida*, Chapter 15075, 1931.

[186] *Ibid.*, Chapter 15075, 1931.

[187] Town Council, Minutes, January 4, 1932.

[188] *Ibid.*, The marshal's position was restored in 1935 when B. J. Turner was appointed. He was succeeded for a time by Grady Hall. H. O. Swofford began a long tenure in the position in the late 1930s.

[189] Town Council, Minutes, February 16, 1931; Chapter 3049, *Compiled General Laws* of *Florida*, 1940; 18th Circuit Court, Seminole County, Civil Division, Law Case 1963. *Webber B. Haines v. Town of Altamonte Springs*, June 19, 1932, and Law Case 1964, *Southland Fruit Company v. Town*, June 23, 1932.

[190] 18th Circuit Court, Seminole County, Law Case 1926, *Associated Florist Ferneries v. Town of Altamonte Springs*, November 20, 1931; Town Council, Minutes, June 24, August 3, 1932.

[191] *Sanford Herald*, July 22, 1932; Town Council, Minutes, August 8, 1932.

[192] 18th Circuit Court, Seminole County, Civil Division, Law Cases 1927, 1963, 1964, 1975, 2150, 3313, and 3379.

[193] *Ibid.*, Chancery Case 2692, February 16, 1931.

[194] Town Council, Minutes, December 4, 1933.

[195] *Ibid.*, December 3, 7, 1934, December 6, 1935.

[196] 18th Circuit Court, Seminole County, Civil Division, Law Case 2015, *Maltbie v. Town of Altamonte Springs*; *Sanford Herald*, February 6, 1934; Town Council, Minutes, February 7, 1944.

[197] Town Council, Minutes, August 1, 3, October 3, 1932; *Sanford Herald*, August 6, 1932; Interview with Hat Hattaway, April 14, 1994.

[198] *Ibid.*, December 4, 1933, January 2, October 5, 1934.

[199] *Sanford Herald*, January 19, 1935.

[200] National Archives, Record Group 69, WPA Records, Microfilm T-937, Roll 4; Interview with Hat Hattaway, April 18, 1994.

[201] NA, RG 69, WPA Records, Microfilm T-937, Roll 4; *Sanford Herald*, June 7, 1938.

[202] Town Council, Minutes, February 28, 1938; March l6, l936, February 28, 1937, January 2, 1940; *Sanford Herald*, November 1, 1935.

[203] *Sanford Herald*, March 26, June 4, 1932; March 30, April 27, 1934.

[204] Town Council, Minutes, November 21, 1938.

[205] *Sanford Herald*, August 22, 1934, September 9, 1937, January 4, 24, 1939.

[206] *Ibid.*, January 31, 1931, March 26, 1932, July 8, August 29, 1939.

[207] Town Council, Minutes, November 11, 1934, October 2, 1939, February 3, 1941.

[208] *Ibid.*, October 2, 1939.

[209] 18th Circuit Court, Seminole County, Civil Division, Chancery Case 3611, *Chester Fosgate v. J. W. Osteen, et al*; Town Council, Minutes, March 1, 1937.

[210] Interview with Mrs. Richard Wyman, April 8, 1994; *Sanford Herald*, January 7, 1933.

[211] Altamonte Springs Hotel, Brochure, 1934, in Rollins College Library.

[212] Interview with Mrs. Richard Wyman, April 8, 1994.

[213] *Sanford Herald*, April 26, 1935, October 15, 1937, October 28, 1940, February 1, December 13, 1941.

[214] *Ibid.*, July 31, 1944.

[215] *Ibid.*, July 31, 1944.

[216] *Ibid.*, June 11, 1932, September 6, 1936, February 16, 1942.

[217] *Ibid.*, April 26, 1938, September 26, 30, 1940.

[218] Interview with Hat Hattaway, April 18, 1994; *Sanford Herald*, October 28, 1940.

[219] *Ibid.*

[220] Florida State Archives, Record Group 406, Governor's Correspondence, Leonard Button to Spessard Holland, November 5, 1942.

[221] *Sanford Herald*, January 15, 1938, April 21, 1939, October 28, 1940, January 10, 1941.

[222] Interview with Albert Connelly, March 26, 1994.

[223] Town Council, Minutes, March 5, 1934; Eve Bacon, *Orlando: A Centennial History*, Volume II (Chuluota, 1977), p. 86.

[224] Town Council, Minutes, March 18, 1935, December 7, 1937; *Sanford Herald*, December 11, 1937, January 15, 1938.

[225] *Sanford Herald*, March 23, August 7, 1942, October 31, 1945; Interviews with B. D. McIntosh, Jr., January 27, 1994, and Hat Hattaway, April 18, 1994.

[226] Town Council, Minutes, March 16, 1942; *Sanford Herald*, June 9, 16, 1941.

[227] Town Council, Minutes, August 3, September 8, 1942, August 20, November 19, 1945; *Sanford Herald*, August 27, 1943, February 4, June 21, 1944, March 26, 1945.

[228] *Sanford Herald*, April 29, 1946; July 21, 1949; Town of Altamonte Springs, Minutes, December 14, 1945; October 28, 1946; *Orlando Evening Star*, February 25, 1950.

[229] Seminole County, Incorporation Book 3, p. 17, Articles of Incorporation, Altamonte Springs Chamber of Commerce.

[230] Town of Altamonte Springs, Minutes, July 14, 1947.

[231] Article by Rosena McIntosh, *Orlando Evening Star*, November 27, 1958.

[232] *Orlando Evening Star*, July 9, 1947, August 20, 1947; Town of Altamonte Springs, Minutes, August 14, 1947.

[233] Town of Altamonte Springs, Minutes, March 19, May 7, 1945.

[234] Interview with Mrs. Paul Snead, May 29, 1994.

[235] *Ibid.*

[236] *Ibid.*

[237] Town of Altamonte Springs, Minutes, August 14, September 2, 1947.

[238] 18th Circuit Court, Seminole County, Civil Division, Law Case 2566, *State of Florida, et al, v. Town of Altamonte Springs.*

[239] Florida State Archives, Records Group 102, Series 235, Extract from Sheriff P. A. Mero hearing before Governor Fuller Warren, March 29, 1951.

[240] *Ibid., Orlando Evening Star*, June 6, 1949.

[241] Town of Altamonte Springs, Minutes, November 21, 1949, February 11, through April 3, 1950, April 8, 1957, January 12, 1960; *Orlando Evening Star*, November 27, 1958.

[242] Town of Altamonte Springs, Minutes, August 17, September 17, 1951, January 7, 1952.

[243] *Ibid.*, March 17, 1952; Interview with B. D. McIntosh, Jr., May 24, 1993.

[244] 18th Circuit Court, Seminole County, Civil Division, Chancery Case 8486, *Town of Altamonte Springs v. Volunteer Fire Department* April 6, 1954; Town of Altamonte Springs, Minutes, April 1, 6, 1954.

[245] Town of Altamonte Springs, Minutes, May 24, 1954, April 8, 1957, August 8, 1960.

[246] *Laws of Florida*, 1953, p. 28; Town of Altamonte Springs, Minutes, April 1, 1958.

[247] *Orlando Evening Star*, October 23, 1954; Town of Altamonte Springs, Minutes, August 23, September 20, 1954, January 9, 1955.

[248] *Laws of Florida*, 1957, p. 18.

[249] Town of Altamonte Springs, Minutes, January 20, April 2, 1947, February 6, 1950, December 6, 1954, February 13, 1956; *Orlando Sentinel*, "Parade of Progress," p. 11, November 24, 1954. The building which housed the Town Garage is now occupied by Zembowers.

[250] Town of Altamonte Springs, Minutes, September 19, 1949; *Laws of Florida*, 1957, pp. 19-20.

[251] Interview with Zetta Morrison, May 18, 1994.

[252] Town of Altamonte Springs, Minutes, December 6, 1954; *Winter Park Sun Herald*, May 9, 1960.

[253] *Orlando Sentinel*, May 29, 1960.

[254] *Ibid.*, July 1, 1953; Interview with Mrs. Richard Wyman, April 18, 1994.

[255] In addition to the founding officers, some of the others were Mmes. R. J. Bundy, W. B. Ballard, T. L. Gorham, B. D. McIntosh, Jr., Homer Sewell, Jr., Leslie T. Bryan, Kristian Juthe, E. N. Mitchell, Fred Faulhaber, J. D. Morrison, Clifford Gilbert, B. O. Burnette, Henry Hansen, Paul Schallert, H. G. Fuller, W. A. Forward, W. Brown, H. J. High, C. O. Knox, A. L. Bridgers, L. B. Mann, H. K. Seaman, and H. C. Voss.

[256] Town of Altamonte Springs, Minutes, April 2, 1947.

[257] *Orlando Sentinel*, "Parade of Progress," November 25, 1954; Town of Altamonte Springs, Minutes, March 11, 1957, October 13, 1958.

[258] *Orlando Evening Star*, November 27, 1958; Interview with B. D. McIntosh, Jr., May 25, 1993.

[259] The Altamonte Chapel, A Community Church, 1885–1974. Copy in Altamonte Springs Public Library.

[260] Town of Altamonte Springs, Minutes, April 8, 1957; Interview with Tolar Bryan, April 26, 1994.

[261] Saint Mary Magdalene Parish Committee, *History of the Parish* (privately printed, 1992). The stories which circulate about Saint Mary Magdalene's risque antecedents on the original 20-acre tract are exaggerated. There was open gambling at the Seminole Club, and Peter Fantasia was shot to death in a failed robbery attempt. But there is nothing to support stories of any other illicit activities there.

[262] Town of Altamonte Springs, Minutes, February 6, 1963, February 8, 1967.

[263] Built in 1958, the school was subsequently moved to Oakhurst and Palm Springs Drive because of its incompatibility with the growth surrounding the Altamonte Mall.

[264] Interview with Mrs. Walter Wood, June 6, 1994

[265] Interview with Hat Hattaway, April 14, 1994.

[266] Town of Altamonte Springs, Minutes, July 11, 1955, January 27, April 14, 1958, May 18, 1960.

[267] Town of Altamonte Springs, Minutes, December 8, 1959; Article by Betty French, copy in Altamonte Springs Public Library.

[268] Town of Altamonte Springs, Minutes, June 22, 1961.

[269] *Ibid.*, June 20, 1962, April 4, 1963; *Orlando Evening Star*, January 10, 1964.

[270] *Ibid.*, June 20, 1962, April 4, 1963; *Orlando Evening Star*, January 10, 1964.

[271] *Ibid.*, February 5, 1964, July 7, 1965.

[272] *Ibid.*, November 18, 1964.

[273] *Ibid.*, July 5, 1967.

[274] Mayor Swofford vigorously protested the way the interchange was built, arguing that it should have included more lanes to handle anticipated growth. This should have been done, he reasoned, before commercial development at the interchange rendered future improvements extremely expensive. He was ignored at the time, but a costly widening project a few years later proved that the mayor's arguments were well-taken. *Sanford Herald*, April 29, 1951, November 23, 1967; Seminole County Commission, Minutes, March 15, 1960; Town of Altamonte Springs, Minutes, February 21, June 22, 1967; Interview with Robert H. Newell, June 17, 1994.

[275] *Laws of Florida*, Chapter 67-1079, 1967.

[276] *Seminole Sentinel*, October 10, December 26, 29, 1967.

[277] Town of Altamonte Springs, Minutes, April 21, 1965.

[278] *Ibid.*, March 7, 1962.

[279] *Ibid.*, April 1, 1964, July 12, 1967; Altamonte Springs Fire Department, "History and Organizational Development," (Copy in Altamonte Springs Library); Interviews with Sandra Glenn, October 1, 1994, and Gary Kaiser, October 12, 1994.

[280] *Orlando Sentinel*, December 29, 1971; Interview with Gary Kaiser, October 12, 1994. The difference arose because of changing views about the role of fire departments. The mayor represented the older view that fire fighters were supposed to fight fires, no more and no less. The young fire chief represented a new view—still in its infancy—that emergency medical service was an integral part of a fire department's responsibility. He was perhaps more committed than some because only five months earlier he had responded to an emergency call to find his father dying of a heart attack.

[281] Town of Altamonte Springs, Minutes, January 3, 1968.

[282] *Ibid.*, January 8, May 7, 969; *Orlando Sentinel*, May 8, 10, 1969.

[283] Town of Altamonte Springs, Minutes, May 14, 21, 1969; *Orlando Sentinel*, May 18, 1969.

[284] *Orlando Sentinel*, June 5, 1969, p. 1-B, and June 3, July 23, December 22, 1969. In order to obtain the large federal grants with which Altamonte Springs built its sewage system, Mayor Swofford was obliged to travel frequently to the DHUD office in Atlanta. He paid for many of the trips from his own pocket. At the same time, Councilman Nuckols was busily trying to block his efforts to build the system which most people now believe was vital to the future of the city. Interview with Mayor

[285] Town of Altamonte Springs, Minutes, November 12, 1969, January 8, May 10, 1970.

[286] *Ibid.*, January 15, 1969, June 16, December 1970, July 20, 1971.

[287] *Sanford Herald*, March 12, October 27, 1969; City of Altamonte Springs, Minutes, March 12, 1969, January 27, 1970; Interview with Robert H. Newell, June 17, 1994.

[288] City of Altamonte Springs, Minutes, October 1, 1969.

[289] *Orlando Sentinel, Orlando Magazine*, January 25, 1961, and February 20, 1970, 3A:8; Brochure, Sanlando Springs Tropical Park, 63 East Pine Street, Orlando, Florida. Copy in Rollins College Library.

[290] *Sanford Herald*, October 27, 1969.

[291] *Orlando Sentinel*, April 27, 1973; *Sanford Herald*, October 30, 1972; *St. Petersburg Times*, January 7, 1973; Leonard E. Zehnder, *Florida's Disney World: Promises and Problems* (Tallahassee, 1975), *passim*.

[292] Quotation, *St. Petersburg Times*, January 7, 1973.

[293] CALNO was an association of the South Seminole County municipalities of Casselberry, Altamonte Springs, Longwood, and North Orlando (now Winter Springs) which was formed to address some of their common problems.

[294] City Council, Minutes, January 12, November 16, 1971, April 3, May 9, 1973.

[295] Interview with James Singleton, August 9, 1994.

[296] Quotation, *Orlando Sentinel Star*, April 15, 1973.

[297] *Orlando Sentinel Star*, April 15, 1973; *St. Petersburg Times*, January 1, 1973.

[298] City Council, Minutes, February 1, August 1, 1972; January 7, March 4, 1975; *Orlando Sentinel Star*, April 15, 1973; Interviews with Delores Vickers, August 11, 1994, James Singleton, August 9, 1994, and Lawrence Swofford, October 26, 1994.

[299] *Orlando Sentinel Star*, April 15, 1973, quoting Mayor Lawrence Swofford.

[300] Interview with Daniel Dorfman, August 9, 1994; City Council, Minutes, March 9, 1971.

[301] City Council, Minutes, December 21, 1971, April 11, May 16, 1972, April 10, 1973.

[302] Don Bradley, "Florida Hospital Altamonte." Copy in author's possession.

[303] City Council, Minutes, September 3, 1973.

[304] *Orlando Sentinel*, July 15, 1972.

[305] City Council, Minutes, April 17, 1973; Interview with Lee Constantine, August 17, 1994.

[306] City Council, Minutes, May 16, 23, October 17, 1972; Interview with James Singleton, August 9, 1994.

[307] *Orlando Sentinel Star*, April 15, July 29, 1973; City Council, Minutes, July 24, 1973.

[308] City Council, Minutes, December 5, 1973; Interview with Sandra Glenn, October 1, 1994.

[309] *Ibid.*, June 11, 1969, October 18, 1973.

[310] Altamonte Springs, *Citizen News*, October 9, 1974; City Council, Minutes, February 5, April 16, 1974.

[311] City of Altamonte Springs, Ordinance No. 313–74.

[312] City Commission, Minutes, November 12, 1974, January 7, 1975, November 7, 1978, April 29, November 4, 1980; Interview with Delores Vickers, August 7, 1994, and Lee Constantine, August 17, 1994.

[313] City Commission, Minutes, March 4, 11, September 9, 1975, June 15, 1976; Interview with James Singleton, August 9, 1994.

[314] City Commission, Minutes, July 30, 1980; U. S. Census, 1980; City of Altamonte Springs, *Property Value and Tax Rate.*

[315] City Commission, Minutes, November 7, 1978, July 8, `980.

[316] City of Altamonte Springs, Ordinance No. 501–79; City Commission, Minutes, October 22, 1979, March 18, 1980.

[317] City Commission, Minutes, *passim.*

[318] Interview with Sandra Glenn, October 1, 1994.

[319] Interview with Patsy Wainwright, September 9, 1994.

[320] Interview with Sam Frazee, September 8, 1994.

[321] Interview with Jackie Sova, September 1, 1994.

[322] City of Altamonte Springs, *Fiscal Year 1994–95 Annual Budget.*

[323] Interview with Jackie Sova, September 1, 1994.

[324] Interview with Commander Steven Garver, September 1, 1994.

[325] *Ibid.*, City Council, Minutes, August 3, 1971.

[326] Interview with Steven Garver, September 1, 1994.

[327] *Ibid.*

[328] *Ibid.*

[329] *Ibid.*

[330] *Ibid.*

[331] *Orlando Sentinel: Seminole Extra,* September 11, 1994.

[332] Interview with Steve Gaston and Stan Human, September 8, 1994.

[333] Interview with Stan Human, September 8, 1994; City of Altamonte Springs, *Spirit,* May 1994.

[334] Interview with Steve Gaston, September 8, 1994; Interview with Gary Kaiser, October 12, 1994; *Orlando Sentinel: Seminole Sentinel*, June 6, 1976.

[335] City of Altamonte Springs, *Spirit*, May, 1994.

[336] Interview with Steve Gaston and Stan Human, September 8, 1994.

[337] Interview with Stan Human, September 8, 1994.

[338] Interview with Bill James, August 29, 1994.

[339] Interview with Sandra Glenn, October 1, 1994.

[340] Interview with Bill James, August 29, 1994.

[341] *Ibid.*

[342] *Ibid.*

[343] *Ibid.*

[344] *Ibid.*; *Orlando Sentinel: Seminole Extra*, August 24, 1993.

[345] Interview with James Singleton, August 9, 1994, and Don Newnham, September 6, 1994.

[346] Interview with Bill James, August 29, 1994.

[347] Interview with Don Newnham, September 6, 1994.

[348] *Orlando Sentinel*, August 26, 1987.

[349] Interviews with Lee Constantine, August 17,1994, and Don Newnham, September 6, 1994; City of Altamonte Springs, *Project APRICOT: A Reclaimed Water System.*

[350] Interview with Don Newnham, September 6, 1994.

[351] *Ibid.*

[352] Interview with Tim Wilson, September 7, 1994.

[353] *Ibid.*, Interview with James Singleton, August 9, 1994.

[354] *Orlando Sentinel: Seminole Extra*, September 4, 1994.

[355] City of Altamonte Springs, *City Plan 2005*, Volume I, p. 4–64.

[356] *Orlando Sentinel*, February 24, 1985.

[357] Interview with Philip D. Penland, June 23, 1994.

[358] *City Plan 2005*, Volume I, p. 3–74; Interview with Sandra Glenn, October 1, 1994.

[359] *Ibid.*

[360] Interviews with Phil Penland, June 23, 1994, and Lee Constantine, August 17, 1994.

[361] *Orlando Sentinel: Seminole Extra,* August 7, 1994.

[362] City of Altamonte Springs, *Infrastructure Fact Sheet* (January, 1994).

Bibliography

Interviews

L. Tolar Bryan, April 6, 1994.
Mark Butler, September 19–23, 1994.
Albert Connelly, March 26, 1994.
Lee Constantine, August 17, 1994.
Judge S. Joseph Davis, August 8, 1994.
Daniel Dorfman, August 9, 1994.
Sam Frazee, September 8, 1994.
Steven W. Garver, Sr., September 1, 1994.
George S. Gaston, September 8, 1994.
J.R. "Hat" Hattaway, April 14, 1994.
Stan Human, September 8, 1994.
William R. James, August 29, 1994.
Gary E. Kaiser, October 12, 1994.
B. D. McIntosh, Jr., June 24, 1993.
Zetta Morrison, April 8, 1994.
Robert H. Newell, June 17, 1994.
Donald Newnham, September 6, 1994.
Philip D. Penland, June 23, 1994.
Dorothy Whitehead Sanborn, June 24, 1994.
James Singleton, August 9, 1994.
Mrs. Paul Snead, May 29, 1994.
Jacki Sova, September l, 1994.
W. Lawrence Swofford, October 26, 1994.
Delores Vickers, August 11, 1994.
Patsy Wainright, June 15, 1994.
Tim Wilson, September 7, 1994.
Mrs. Walter Wood, June 6, 1994.
Mrs. Richard Wyman, April 8, 1994.

Documents

Altamonte Springs. *City Plan 2005.*

________. Council, Minutes, 1925–1974; Commission, Minutes, 1975–1990.

________. *Fiscal Year 1994–1995, Annual Budget.*

________. *Infrastructure Fact Sheet*. January 1994.

________. Ordinances, 1921–1975.

Eighteenth Circuit Court (Seminole County), Civil Division, 1931–1954.

Florida State Archives, LR 21, Local Records, Altamonte Springs Tax Rolls, 1921–1927.

________. Record Group 102, Governor's Correspondence, 1913–1970.

________. Series 186, Articles of Corporation, Book B.

________. Series 914. Letters to Registrar and Receiver of Public Lands.

Laws of Florida, 1885–1967.

National Archives. Record Group 28. Post Office Department, Appointments of Postmasters, T841, Roll 21.

________. Record Group 28. Post Office Department, Bureau of Transportation Domestic Mail Transportation, Registers for Star Route Contracts, 1814–1960.

________. Record Group 28. Post Office Department, Cartographic and Architectural Branch, Special List of Post-Route Maps. Entry 18.

________. Record Group 28. Post Office Department, Reports of Site Locations, M1126, Rolls 95 and 98.

________. Record Group 69. Works Progress Administration, Index of Official Proposals.

________. Record Group 69. Works Progress Administration, Records, T937, Roll 4.

Orange County Commission. Map of Orange County, 1890.

Orange County. Deed Books, 1885–1913.

Orange County. Unidentified Miscellaneous Files. Microfilm in UCF Library.

________. School Board, Minutes, 1874–1913.

Seminole County. Commission, Minutes, 1934–1961.

________. Corporation Books, 1921–1928.

________. School Board, Minutes, 1925–1931.

________. Tax Rolls, 1930–1960.

Manuscripts

Frost, George, Papers. Boston Public Library.

Haines Family Papers. Altamonte Springs Library.

Whittier, Charles, Papers. Boston Public Library.

Prospectus, Altamonte Land Hotel and Navigation Company. Copy in Altamonte Springs Library.

Newspapers and Newsletters

Altamonte Springs, *Citizen News,* 1974.
Apopka City Union, March 17, 1884.
Apopka South Florida Citizen, 1879.
City of Altamonte Springs, *Spirit,* May 1994.
Jacksonville, the *Florida Times Union,* 1885.
Orlando *Orange County Reporter,* 1890.
Orlando Reporter-Star, 1911–1958 (title varies).
Orlando Sentinel, 1913–1994 (title varies).
Sanford Herald, 1908–1965.
St. Petersburg Times, 1973.
Tallahassee Weekly Floridian, 1878–1888.
Tampa Tribune, 1923.
Winter Park Herald, 1923–1940.

Books, Articles, Pamphlets, and Brochures

Adams, Sherman. *Orangeland.* Orlando: 1883–1884.

Altamonte Chapel: A Community Church, 1885–1985. Altamonte Springs, 1985.

Altamonte Land, Hotel and Navigation Company. *Prospectus.* Printed at Newburyport, Massachusetts: Altamonte Springs Library.

Altamonte of Florida. Brochure. 1887. P. K. Yonge Library.

Bacon, Eve. *Orlando, A Centennial History.* Two volumes. Chuluota, 1977.

Barbour, George M. *Florida for Tourists, Invalids, and Settlers.* New York, 1882.

Bates, E. C. *Altamonte Hotel.* Brochure. 1934. Rollins Library.

Belding, George T. (compiler). *Florida Railroad Gazetteer and State Business Directory.* 1885.

Blackman, William F. *History of Orange County, Florida.* Chuluota, 1973.

Bradley, Don. "Florida Hospital Altamonte."

Cofran, Frank. *The Altamonte of Florida.* Brochure. 1886. P. K. Yonge Library.

Elliott's Florida Encyclopedia. Orange County Library.

Erickson, Ira H. *The John Andersons of Sweden and Sanford, Apopka, and Piedmont, Orange County Florida, 1836–1955.* Blacksburg, Virginia, 1985.

Florida. State Planning Staff. *Land Use Planning Seminole County.* Gainesville, 1940.

Francke, Arthur E., Jr. *Early Days of Seminole County, Florida.* Sanford, 1984.

Gore, Eldon H. *History of Orlando.* Second Edition. Orlando, 1951.

Gore, Mahlon. *Florida, Home, Farm and Field.* Orlando, 1897.

Historic Properties Associates, Inc. *Historic Properties Survey of the City of Altamonte Springs, Florida.* St. Augustine, 1992.

Hopkins, James T. *Fifty Years of Citrus: The Florida Citrus Exchange, 1909–1959*. Gainesville, 1960.

Howard, C. E. *Early Settlers of Orange County, Florida: Reminiscent, Historic, Biographic.* Orlando, 1915..

Rand, J. C. *One of a Thousand*. Boston, 1890.

Richards, John R. *Orange County Gazetteer.* 1887.

R. L. Polk and Co. *Florida Gazetteer and Business Directory.* 1911–1912.

Robinson, M. F. *Florida Orange Groves for Sale.* Sanford, 1911.

Sanlando Tropical Park. Brochure. Rollins College Library.

Southern Directory and Publishing Co. *Florida State Gazetteer.* Volume I. 1886–1887.

Southern Industry. New Orleans and Johnston, Florida. June 18, 1904. Orange County Museum.

St. Margaret Mary Parish Committee. *History of the Parish.* Privately printed, 1992.

Strong, Hope, Jr. *Tales of Winter Park.* Orlando, 1982.

Webb, Wanton S. *Webb's Historical, Industrial and Biographical Florida.* New York, 1885.

Zehnder, Leonard E. *Florida's Disney World: Promises and Problems.* Tallahassee, 1975.

Index

B

C

G

H

M

N

R

S

T

U

Y

Z